DEMOCRACY AND THE ARTS OF SCHOOLING

DEMOCRACY AND THE ARTS OF SCHOOLING

Donald Arnstine

State University of New York Press

Published by
State University of New York Press, Albany

Printed in the United States of America

For information, address State University of New York Press, State University Plaza, Albany, N.Y. 12246

Production by E. Moore
Marketing by Dana E. Yanulavich

Library of Congress Cataloging-in-Publication Data

Arnstine, Donald.
Democracy and the arts of schooling / Donald Arnstine.
p. cm.
Includes bibliographical references and index.
ISBN 0-7914-2721-8 (alk. paper). — ISBN 0-7914-2722-6 (pbk. : alk. paper)
1. Education—United States—Aims and objectives. 2. Education--Social aspects—United States. 3. Educational change—United States. 4. Aesthetics—Study and teaching. 5. Educational tests and measurements—United States. I. Title.
LA217.2.A76 1995
370'.973—dc20 95-4243
CIP

10 9 8 7 6 5 4 3 2 1

To my family.
We all enjoyed helping one another grow up.

Contents

Acknowledgments

The eight years it took to write this book were filled with false starts and blind alleys that would have produced little more than wastepaper had it not been for the encouragement, support, and penetrating criticism of my friends, my colleagues, and my family. There is space to mention only a few of these people, although the list is extensive.

In the first, difficult years of the enterprise, work at times slowed to a crawl. Gerald Phillips helped keep the project going with encouragement, support, and something concrete to work for.

I'm grateful to Harvey Siegel, who managed to make me feel guilty (and stay on task) when I couldn't report to him that I'd finished a chapter. Beyond that, he riddled me with strong arguments and gave me a good example of problem-solving.

In our voluminous correspondence, James McClellan's warm support never kept him from incisive critical comments on material in every chapter of the book. He also directed me to some wonderfully helpful reading materials.

Paul Hirst gave me considerable help in articulating my views about the aesthetic. A writer needs an antagonist who not only believes you're mistaken, but who graciously offers an elegant argument to show you why.

Tom Green raised questions about educational policy, and in particular standardized testing, that prompted me to reexamine and alter some things I'd written on those topics. Carl Spring directed me to some very useful resources, and as a friendly antagonist forced me to think more clearly about cognitive functioning. But I couldn't convince him, either.

Bill Hay suggested in a few well-chosen words that a different final chapter was needed. Despite my protestations, he was right, and the rewritten concluding chapter does not suffer from the same ills (heaven be praised) as the one I threw out.

Finally, my wife and colleague, Barbara Arnstine, didn't complain once about having to stay at home weekends watching the

49ers while I pecked away at the computer. But she supplied much more than the support and sympathy and clean underwear that writers think they have coming to them. As a teacher and a scholar, she offered indispensable criticism and useful suggestions for every chapter in the manuscript. She even helped me understand what Bill Hay was talking about. I don't like to think about what the book (or I) would have been like without her.

I'm grateful to the members of the California Association for the Philosophy of Education, who offered collegial support and constructive criticism when I tried out my ideas on them; to Patricia White, John White, Graham Haydon, and the Institute of Education of the University of London for allowing me to offer pieces of this work for the critical consideration of members of the Research Seminar; and to the University of California, Davis, for the freedom to develop my own ideas in my teaching, and for two quarters of sabbaticals during the period when the book was written. I'm especially grateful to my students, undergraduates and graduates, who were bright and hard-working, who cared, and who never let me get away with anything.

Introduction

> . . . Living has its own intrinsic quality and . . . the business of education is with that quality.
>
> —John Dewey, *Democracy and Education*

Education is not such a difficult or dangerous business that it can't be tried at home. There must be hundreds of parents who've done it, although I'd bet on hundreds of thousands, or hundreds of millions if we're talking in global terms. So why do schools have such a hard time promoting education?

We're all aware of everyday learnings that go on outside of school. A child learns to fly a kite, another learns to take care of her little brother. A boy learns to clean up his room,[1] a girl learns to play the guitar. Children learn to talk, and many of them learn to read, just for the fun of it. All this education happens in homes. Not just in the homes of parents who hold graduate degrees, but in "average" homes. In anybody's home.

The examples just mentioned were picked because they all involve the learning of difficult and complex things, and in some instances take much time. What schools try to teach is usually much simpler; learning to add and subtract ought to be easy compared to the above examples. So why do schools have such a hard time of it?

When we consider the problems of educating, the differences between home and school seem vast. At home we confront just a few of the young, we know them well, and we care about them deeply. A teacher confronts in one room dozens of youngsters whom she barely knows (at the outset). At home, we do what we think is best (whether it is or not). What's done at school is under countless constraints, from state laws and school board policies to outside testing agencies and insurance policies. In schools, what's simple and worthwhile (education) must find its way through an overwhelmingly obfuscating concatenation of laws, policies, rules, standards, expectations, and complaints from janitors who want you to straighten out the rows of desks before you dismiss the kids.

This book will try to explain how education, as a result of all this, has slipped from the agenda of schools and has been replaced by socialization, which simply gets kids used to doing what they're told. I'll try to show why a democratic society can't abide such a system of schooling, for both individual and social reasons. And I'll try to show what teachers and others can do to make the socialization of schooling more defensible, and to foster education as well.

Reform movements in education focus almost exclusively on tightening up academic requirements: more math and science, more homework, higher academic standards, and so on. But we'll look at education not simply as a twelve-year sequence of mandated academic lessons. Rather, we'll consider the conditions needed to help the young acquire dispositions and traits of character that we think of as being grown up: sensitivity to other people and the environment, democratic attitudes, a capacity for sustained effort, developed and refined talents and skills, and the individuality that comes with the development of taste, wit, curiosity, and intelligence.

We'll see that the quality of a learner's experience has much to do with the character of what is learned. Infants don't learn to walk and talk because they get lessons in it, or because they are graded for it. They learn these immensely difficult things because they're felt to be intrinsically worthwhile—simply put, for the fun of it. And because the older people around them tolerate it and don't get in their way, and even encourage it and often participate in it by the way of sharing.

You can always tell when it works. The infant finally pulls herself to her feet and her smile is a mile wide. When you finally solve a tough problem you experience it as a rush. Maslow called it a "peak experience," Csikszentmihalyi called it "flow." I will refer to it as experience that is aesthetic in quality.

I will try to show how the aesthetic is central to an understanding of learning and education, and to the development of a rich and fulfilling personal life. I'll also try to show that there can be no such fulfilling personal life without a social life to sustain it, and that the personal traits we seek for our children cannot flourish apart from a democratic social setting. Those who control an authoritarian society cannot afford to have subjects who are tasteful, witty, curious, humane, and intelligent. A society that aspires to be democratic must have schools that are democratic, too. Only if teachers and children participate in the design of their own teaching and learning will the young be able to participate in a democratic society as responsible citizens.

PART I

Education, Democracy, and the Aesthetic

1 Education, Socialization, and the Aesthetic

We get used to schools. We hardly notice how peculiar they are; how they differ from other social settings and institutions. For example, when people work hard in school and achieve some success, they get letter grades. These are symbolic rewards, not real ones. We shrug and say, it's always been that way. We even think it *has* to be that way in order for education to go on.

Consider the most familiar feature of American public schools, the classroom. Inside are two or three dozen young people listening to an adult who talks most of the time. They all stay in the room most of the day, five days a week. When the children get older, the classroom is emptied every fifty-five minutes, and it is filled with another batch of young people.

No characterization of this setting captures its fundamental absurdity better than Albert Shanker's:

> Imagine that we had no schools, that the United States was a very poor country that for centuries had been sending its kids off to work in the mines or the fields at the age of three. All of a sudden we discover great wealth and are about to design a school system. What if somebody said: Let's build huge buildings and divide them into classrooms that seat thirty-five or forty children apiece. Let's bring those kids in at 8:30 in the morning and make them sit in those seats until 3:00 in the afternoon, and during that time an adult will stand in front of them and talk. Well, someone else might reasonably ask: What makes you think these kids would sit still and keep quiet? And why would any adult in his right mind want to be locked up with them under such conditions?[1]

The only conceivable answer is this: they get used to it. When children are first sent off to school they have no choice about it. Some of them resent it, but at the age of six they are no match for the adults in charge. As the years go by, the misfits either respond to special treatment or they disappear from the school system. From among those who stay in school the longest come the people who will become teachers. After all that schooling, it seems to them quite normal to spend most of their day in a single room, talking in front of two or three dozen children. It doesn't seem absurd at all.

Socialization

If we wanted to *educate* those two or three dozen children, the standard structure of the school classroom does seem absurd. How could that sort of organization promote the cultivation of critical thought? of social skills or moral conscience? of aesthetic taste or the uniqueness that distinguishes individuals from one another? For these ends, the standard school classroom appears to be as absurd as Shanker says it is.

But school classrooms may not seem so absurd if we conceive of them as being arranged for ends other than those just noted. Suppose we gathered all those children into a classroom with a single adult not to educate them, but to socialize them. Suppose what we really wanted to do was not cultivate critical thought, aesthetic taste, or individuality, but get them used to the authority of an adult, to the routines of a bureaucratic institution, and to conforming to the behavior of others in a large group. Then the organization of the classroom wouldn't seem so absurd. It might even be well suited to achieving our goals.

The kind of socialization just described might not appeal to everybody, but that doesn't mean there's something sinister about socialization itself. In fact, no society could do without it:

> If it were necessary for a living being to grope *de novo* for an appropriate response to every stimulus from the environing situation, threats to its integrity from many sources would promptly effect its disorganization. This is why, with respect to that which is most vital, the reaction of an organ is predetermined; certain modes of behaving necessarily recur under similar circumstances. . . . Social life is subject to the same imperatives, and regularity is no less indispensable for it. At each point in time, it is necessary that the functioning of familial, vocational, and civic life be assured; to this end, it is altogether

> necessary that the person be free from an incessant search for appropriate conduct. Norms must be established which determine what proper relationships are, and to which people conform. Deference to established norms is the stuff of our daily duties.[2]

The process of acquiring the norms to which all the members of a society conform is called socialization. Our concern throughout most of this book will be with education. But because children get socialized both in and out of school, and because the conditions of education and of socialization are so different, we must be clear enough about how they differ so we don't mistake socializing practices for educative ones.

Virtually all children get socialized in every society—ancient or modern, primitive or industrial, authoritarian or democratic. Socialization is needed by adults as well as children. On the one hand, children must learn acceptable ways of getting on with others, and they need to learn how to support themselves. On the other hand, adults need the responsible participation of the next generation in order to carry on activities that maintain the social order. To be socialized, then, is to become effectively adapted to the patterns of behavior, the customs, and the values of the social group into which you are born.

Socialization is mandatory; no one is excepted from it. People who are not socialized are (depending on the particular society) ostracized, institutionalized, or put to death. And because it is so universal, it is not reserved for special groups like the gifted, an ethnic elite, or the rich or the poor. But the members of certain groups or subcultures may be socialized in different ways.

Because it is universal, socialization does not depend on specially trained teachers or specialized techniques. After all, children have been socialized for millennia—long before schools were invented, long before teaching became a specialized occupation. Parents and siblings, neighbors and the extended family all participate in socializing children.

As long as adults are in agreement about the value, the scope, and the limits of their major activities—the production of food, shelter, and clothing; the beliefs and practices governing family relations and political and social forms; ceremonial and sacramental occasions, and so forth—socialization can proceed quite unself-consciously. Its procedures will be simple and direct. When the young are not playing, they participate as best they can in adult activities.

Participation is accompanied to a greater or lesser extent by conversation, wherein the young receive instructions, explanations, warnings, corrections, praise, and criticism. And sometimes a hug or a smile, a kick or a scowl.

In most societies, socialization goes on informally—at home, in the neighborhood, at work. Schools are not needed. But the societies that have developed in the twentieth century are different. American society, for example, has a political system that is at once both representative and unrepresentative, democratic and oligarchic. Its culture embraces not only the traditions of many different nationality groups, but traditions within Western culture as disparate as Christian fundamentalism and Enlightenment rationalism. Amid all these incongruities, the pressures created by developing technology and international competition have resulted in constant cultural change—change often accompanied by conflicts of values, attitudes, and practices. Thus it has become difficult for the ordinary, informal mechanisms of socialization to be effective with the young. That may be why schools have taken on so many socializing functions, and why so many school practices seem so absurd *when they are mistaken for educational practices.*

For these reasons, contemporary societies use their schools to socialize the young. This may complicate and even thwart efforts to educate them. But the need for socialization cannot be dismissed. This will become clearer if we look at an example or two of why it is so hard to socialize children *out* of school.

All societies inculcate in their young habits and attitudes toward work. These habits and attitudes will differ, depending on whether the society depends on agriculture or hunting, whether it is stable or nomadic, whether its climate is tropical or temperate, whether its resources are abundant or scarce. But children in contemporary postindustrial societies like the United States find themselves at once members of several different groups, each of which tends to inculcate a different attitude toward work.[3]

By means of its curriculum and its instructional practices, the school socializes children into work that is competitive and almost exclusively utilizes reading, writing, and calculating (this is often indiscriminately called "intellectual" work). But these same children may live in homes that inculcate the value of manual labor, and socialize them into work attitudes that are interpersonal and cooperative. Away from home and school, children's peer groups may socialize their members into attitudes that are contemptuous of ordinary kinds of work.

Traditionally, children are socialized into the values and customs of what we would call the "wider" society. But when values and attitudes and traditions in the wider society differ about various kinds of practices (like work, sex and marriage, drug and alcohol use, abortion and divorce, the right to strike, minority hiring, ad infinitum), the ordinary sort of socialization becomes impossible. The process breaks down as children face multiple and often competing values and traditions. There *is* no simple, unitary "wider" society into which the young can be socialized.

There is another and equally daunting obstacle to the ordinary processes of socialization: the growing separation between the socializers and those who are to be socialized. Throughout most of the history of human civilization, children were raised in a family or an extended family. Plenty of adults, in varying degrees of intimacy, were available to participate in the socialization of the young. But now, adults are becoming a scarce commodity in the world of children.

To begin with, industrial and corporate growth along with rapid modes of transportation have produced a mobile population. For many children this means growing up in a "nuclear" family whose only adult is mom or dad (or sometimes both). Uncles and aunts, older cousins and grandparents, are all back in Pittsburgh. While socialization is a relatively simple process when it takes place in a community, it's a heavy burden when it falls on two adults (heavy enough to divide the adults, split marriages, and break down families). The distances that now separate homes from workplaces often remove one of the adults from the everyday lives of small children, and the economic and social conditions that have sent 40 percent of America's mothers into full-time jobs have even further reduced the contact between children and caring adults.

When children reach the age of five or six they are sent to school. Leaving home further reduces their contact with adults, since a teacher, responsible for two or three dozen or more children, cannot effectively socialize any of them to the world *outside* the school. But if this is so, you may wonder what sort of socialization *is* going on in schools? A single adult in a school classroom cannot socialize a large group of children to the world outside. But with the support of a *system* of time divisions, discipline practices, promotion policies, examinations, and articulated grades and schools, that adult can socialize children *to the school system*. Most children can and do learn to adjust to the customs, values, and regular practices of the school. They learn this uncritically, without giving it much thought.

Thus in addition to the absurdity of running schools that do not educate is another absurdity: they do not socialize, either, except to the very narrow world of the school itself. Since the world of the school is very different in important respects from the world outside it, one may wonder what is to be gained by this narrow form of socialization.

One thing can be said with assurance. If children are not socialized to the school system, they will become alienated and probably be quite unhappy. They will surely not learn anything that adults would like them to, and they will probably drop out of school early. So it can be said that socializing the young to the school system enables them to survive in that system as long as they are in it.

But that would be the ultimate absurdity of the school system: that it operates only to accustom its inmates to itself. Before we can swallow that conclusion, we must ask more seriously whether schools educate children. For unless some significant education is going on, it would appear that schools serve only as holding pens, allowing the authorities twelve years to sift some of them out for further schooling in colleges. But the question of whether education does or can go on in schools depends first on clearly distinguishing education from socialization.

Socialization and Education

There is no need to define so elusive a term as 'education' here. We've seen what socialization is like, and all we need is to be aware of what makes education something other than that. We've already seen that socialization excludes none of the young. By means of it a society inculcates and thereby preserves what is vitally important and agreed on. Whatever 'education' might involve, then, we can expect that it will exclude some children and that it will transmit things that are neither vitally important for everyone to know, nor agreed on by everyone in the society. Still, this only indicates what education *doesn't* do.

Until the middle of the present century, only a minority of people in a society received an education. They usually got it from a tutor or in a school. Males from wealthy families were taught what was needed to maintain what their families possessed (for example, social skills, horsemanship, the skills of combat, and most important, how to manage one's inferiors). What these privileged males learned thus differed markedly from the understandings, values, and beliefs into which *all* the members of their respective societies were socialized. In the middle ages, boys who were to become priests also received an education and, shortly thereafter, so did prospective physicians, lawyers, and teachers. These professional men acquired some skills not usually expected of the sons of the ruling classes: the ability to read and write.

In Western history, then, the expansion of education, the development of schools, and the growth of literacy were all associated. An educated man was a literate man: a man who could read. Reading was a more revolutionary enterprise than you might think. Of course, it enabled people to examine what was agreed on in their society. But it also exposed people to understandings that were unique to different societies, and—what turned out to be an enormous threat to the Church and to the ruling classes—it exposed people to different and sometimes conflicting opinions about what ought to be believed, valued, and done in their own society. Although you might never guess it from the way reading is taught in today's schools, it has been a significant instrument of social change.

But that puts us a little ahead of the story. For now, as we distinguish education from socialization, we can see how the former has come to signify a process whereby the young learn how to read, write, and calculate and, by virtue of such learnings, come into contact with ideas and understandings that will help them to work productively and live well in a world where jobs are specialized, where agreement is not universal, and where beliefs, values, and habits of action are often in conflict.

Of course, the simple ability to decode the written word, and mere exposure to ideas, does not necessarily make a person any wiser. For *that* to happen, one must learn how to *do* things with ideas. But for the moment, we need only distinguish the features of education from those of socialization and then ask, can we find *both* of these processes going on in schools?

First, let's summarize the distinctions made thus far. The socialization that affects all children focuses on everyday but important social agreements. It aims not to cultivate thought, but simply to adjust the young to their world, and it succeeds when the learner effectively acquires values and modes of action that are approved by society.

Education, more selectively dispensed, focuses on things considered important by more specialized groups (e.g., ministers, biologists, literary scholars), even when members of those groups do not always agree with each other. Because it deals with material that is more specialized, that is new, and that is often in dispute, education, unlike socialization, aims at understanding and critical judgment. It succeeds when learners can find their own reasons for what they believe and for what they think is worth doing.

Socialization is characterized by imitation, participation, and obedience to instruction and command. Its outcome is the acquisition of adaptive habits, skills, and attitudes. The processes of education (which will be focal to this book) are far more subtle, adding to the above processes two-way communication, initiative, creativity, and criticism. The outcome of educational processes is the acquisition of attitudes and dispositions, knowledge and skills, that are individualized and critically thoughtful.[4]

The School As Agent of Socialization

We ask again, can education as well as socialization be found in schools? Although the public has been led to believe that schools aim at education, that belief may be mistaken. While socialization is expected of all children, history does not reveal any society that has tried to educate all of its children. More specialized and more demanding than socialization, education calls for aptitudes and abilities in learners that are not universally shared. Nothing in principle prevents a society from *trying* to educate an entire new generation. But doing so would mean that significant differences among children, and significant differences in educational aims and procedures, would have to be acknowledged and acted on. That's because education, unlike socialization, aims not at common beliefs, values, and habits, but at individuality, diversity, and the disposition and the ability to make and act on reasoned choices. Are schools organized to achieve such aims?

Virtually identical physical arrangements are provided for children in schools. Each child has a standard-size chair about a foot away from other such chairs in a standard-size classroom. Everyone is subject to similar organizational and scheduling procedures, to a curriculum that has become increasingly the same for all, and to a testing and evaluation system that is becoming universal for all. These more or less uniform structures and procedures are appropriate for socialization, but not for education.

You may object that the aims and outcomes of schools demonstrate a commitment to education. But we must not mistake rhetoric for reality. Many of us would like to turn children into thoughtful, creative, critical, and unique individuals. But the system of examinations in schools is deliberately and elaborately designed to produce just the opposite. At the end of each semester, in their effort to qualify for college admission, our young people all strive to discover the *same* correct answers to the same or similar questions. When we (or the teachers, or the test publishers) know the right answer beforehand, we can hardly appeal to the creativity of our students, any more than we can appeal to their reasoned judgment about disputed issues.

Classrooms that keep students passive and prompt them to make only the responses their teachers look for are, of course, the rational way to prepare for exams. For those who succeed in school and therefore remain longest in the system, the outcome is a set of habits (especially classroom, study, and test-taking habits) that enable them to conform to the demands of the system. *That* is not an educational outcome. It is a matter of effective socialization. To say that a student is successful usually means that she was effectively socialized to the school system.[5]

The Need for Education

There are good reasons for schools to try to socialize the young. But trying to foster education is not just a romantic ideal, an idle wish. For when social practices and social values are diverse and often at odds with each other, people who have been merely socialized cannot understand or sympathize with viewpoints and practices other than their own. In a simple society, socialization produces people who think and act alike. They constitute a community. But in a complex and changing society like ours, socialization is likely to produce groups that are mistrustful and intolerant of one another.

Socialization requires firsthand experience (you don't get socialized by reading about what other people believe), and because schools are isolated from the rest of society, children are adapted only to the school system itself. Thus most of the young in complex industrial societies are adjusted, more or less, to the school, and their values and attitudes toward the rest of the world are the consequence of the socializing agency (usually parents or peers) that makes the strongest impact on them. As noted above, the result of all this is often the creation of hostile and intolerant groups—peaceful as long as they don't have to interact with one another, but not ready to work together on enterprises for the common good.

More, or more effective socialization cannot make this situation any better. What is required in a society that values diversity is for people to learn how to become thoughtful about their differences, and to learn how to overcome disagreements by recognizing their common concerns. Only education can achieve this, and that's why education is not a romantic ideal, but a practical necessity for a society like ours.[6] The sociologist Durkheim said as much nearly three quarters of a century ago:

> Since social life [in simple societies] is quite self-consistent . . . custom and unreflective tradition are quite adequate. Indeed, custom and tradition have such power and prestige as to leave no place for reasoning and questioning.
>
> On the other hand, the more societies become complex, the more difficult [it is] for morality to operate as a purely automatic mechanism. Circumstances are never the same, and as a result the rules of morality require intelligence in their application. Society is continually evolving . . . [and] this requires that morality not be internalized in such a way as to be beyond criticism or reflection . . . Individuals, while conforming, must take account of what they are doing; and their conformity must not be pushed to the point where it completely captures intelligence.[7]

Socialization occurs naturally in people's everyday interactions. Education does only sometimes. Socialization maintains a society as it is. Education is called for only when the natural processes of socialization are insufficient to maintain social stability. As the twentieth century draws to a close, the stability of the community of nations is seriously threatened. Many nations possess the technology to destroy most living things on earth. Just the unregulated pursuit of profit by multinational corporations has resulted in serious damage to the atmosphere and the water resources, the farmlands and the forests of the earth. The same economic forces that have led to environmental destruction have also resulted in human misery to an unprecedented extent, in terms of hunger, disease, and the loss of freedom. Once typical of the third world, this misery is now common in industrial nations. It is apparent in the streets of every major city in America, and it can be found in many of America's hospitals, asylums, prisons, and schools—although it is hidden in such places from public view.

When such a crisis reaches international proportions it is wise to seek political solutions. But political negotiations are typically undertaken by people whose socialization was predicated on world conditions very different from those that exist today. Older generations grew up adjusting to a world that was. Their children were socialized to that world. To an obsolescent socialization has been added the growing influence of world capitalism, which socializes the young to become competitive consumers. Now there is reason to believe that the resources of the earth can no longer survive this kind of socialization. It produces attitudes that fit this precarious world as well as the rearing of African bushmen prepares for the operation of jet aircraft, automatic weapons, and nuclear power plants. Socialization cannot be depended on to produce people who can successfully negotiate for the survival of life on this planet. Only education will enable future generations to understand themselves and the world in such a way that political solutions will make sense.

Most people think that school is the place to get an education. But because the facts don't support this assumption, we need to discover what changes in schooling would be hospitable to education. Before we consider the institutional setting, however, we must ask, what are the conditions under which education becomes possible? We do not ask what causes education. It cannot be caused at all, because it involves the voluntary participation of the learner. Certain kinds of socialization can be caused, but for education, only certain kinds of conditions can be established. This book is about those conditions.

Education for Individuals and the Quality of Experience

We have seen that socialization produces conformity to the group, while education results in independent judgment. People who are only socialized can be expected to do what others do. Those who are both socialized and educated can be expected to do what others do if they find sufficient reasons for doing so. The educated person, exercising judgment, acts as an individual. This doesn't mean that she necessarily rejects the group. It means that she thoughtfully considers the appropriateness of what the group is up to.[8]

There are two other senses of the term, individual, that are not intended in this discussion. To avoid misunderstanding they will be noted here. In one sense, "individual" refers to the fact that every person is *different* from every other. Differrences in this sense are the result of the combined effects of genetics, chance environmental influences, and whim. In contrast, *"individual" is used in the pre-*

sent discussion to refer to differences which result from choices that people deliberately make.

Individuality, which is the concern of education, must also be distinguished from another sense of "individual": the sense that is implied when we speak of individualism. Individualism is largely an economic term, referring to the capacity of a single person to be self-sufficient. Individualism thus refers to a point of view about the capacities of people. This point of view is not empirically testable. Can people *really* manage for themselves in this complex society? What would it *mean* to be really self-sufficient? And since it underlies a broader point of view about how an economic system ought to work (on the basis of competitive individual entrepreneurship) it is part of an ideology. When the terms "individual" and "individuality" are used in the following discussion, no reference is intended to the ideology of individualism, or individual entrepreneurship. I mean only by "individual" a person whose education has enabled her to develop, on the basis of her own reasoned judgments, a range of unique talents and skills.

Education, then, is concerned with individuals (this is why most events that occur in a lecture hall *may* be informative, but cannot be educative). As we'll see later on, the education of individuals is sometimes best carried on within groups of people. But just as the focus or aim of socialization is on the community or social group, so the focus of education is on the individual. And because individual persons are the main concern of educators, what must be of primary importance to educators is the quality of the experience of learners.

The quality of learners' experience is not ordinarily regarded as a high priority by educators. School personnel are usually focused on the material thought appropriate to teach—that is, on the curriculum. They are also concerned about the psychology of child and adolescent development. All of this is important, because it helps us establish aims for education and it helps us recognize limits on the possibilities of growth. Yet an exclusive concern with the curriculum and child development can blind us to what is most critical for an education to occur at all. That critical element is the character and quality of the learner's experience. To be effective, educators must have a concern for what is happening to learners from *their* point of view, in terms of how they feel, or apprehend their experience. The welfare of the community must never be lost from view, but that is the special concern of socialization. For education, the growth of individuals is primary. And that growth can be fostered only when the experience of those individuals is taken very seriously, understood, and enhanced.

The procedures of socialization are relatively easy to understand. They have been effectively carried on in all human societies, including our own, until at least quite recently. But the procedures of education have been far less easy to understand. That's partly because education has been confused with socialization, and partly because adults have cared more for educational outcomes than they have for the processes on which those outcomes depend. It's also partly because of the growth of a class of professional educators willing to call any enterprise "educational" (including the techniques of animal training) as long as it was regarded by their peers as publishable research. To dispel misunderstanding about the procedures of education, we must attend, first and foremost, to the quality of the experience of the young whom we would educate. But we need to get clear about the meaning of this phrase, "the quality of experience."

The term "quality" suggests value of some sort; we speak of high and low quality. We would like learners to have experiences of high quality, but what *constitutes* a high-quality experience? The phrase will be used here to indicate an experience that is valued for its own sake. Sometimes it's called "intrinsically valuable," or "consummatory" (in contrast to "instrumental"). A lot of people eat popcorn when they go to the movies. Popcorn may have nutritional value, but that's not why most people eat it. They eat it just because they like to. Because it tastes good, or because it gives them something to do. Eating popcorn is thus intrinsically valuable. It is a high-quality experience.

But you may object to this. "Wait a minute," you may say. "Eating *popcorn* a high-quality experience? Let's get serious! Any nitwit can eat popcorn! What's so 'high' about the quality of *that* experience? Now, consider listening to a Mozart piano concerto. *There's* a genuinely high-quality experience."

There is no quarrel with this objection. Listening to the concerto *is* a high-quality experience for many people. But to say that an experience is of high quality implies no comparisons to other experiences. That's why eating popcorn is also a high-quality experience for those who like to do it. If you should ask whether listening to Mozart isn't a *higher*-quality experience than eating popcorn, there's no answer. It depends on who's having the experience.

There is a tendency among many people to arrange the things they value into a hierarchy, from high to low. Then they make judgments about others on the basis of whether they cherish the same hierarchies. For example, there are people who put expensive automobiles high in their scale of values, while others put Mozart on the top of the list. Still others may value an evening at the movies, eating popcorn. Quite often it turns out that the people in each of these groups have a low opinion of those in the other groups, largely because they don't share the same values. This is unfortunate—a form of snobbery, regardless of what occupies the top spot on one's list of values. For there is no good reason why the sorts of things that afford high quality to one person's experience ought to afford high quality to another person's experience. People's biological structures and life experiences are very different. You may denigrate or exalt the values and tastes of other people, but such judgments don't alter the fact that other people may be *having* experiences that for them are high in quality.

Keeping this in mind, we can see that any number of events might contribute to experience that one regards as being high in quality, or intrinsically valuable. Some people write letters to friends, not because they have an important message to convey, but just because they enjoy it. That's an intrinsically valuable experience for them. Some people like to go to the park at the end of a long day and feed the ducks; for them, that's a high-quality experience. Some people find high quality in the experience of running in marathon races, others find it in visiting art museums. Many people find sexual intimacy to be intrinsically valuable; there are others who find high quality in the experience of work, who feel that their jobs are intrinsically valuable.

Later on it will be argued that one important aim for education is to enable young people to find high quality in a greater range of experiences than those that they presently value. And because there are reasons for believing that some things and events in the world are more likely than others to initiate high-quality experiences for people (there are objective factors in taste as well as subjective ones), it will be argued that education should help learners to discover what can function for them as *sources* of high-quality experience. But for now, the aim is only to make clear what it means to say that a person is having an experience of high quality. And to make equally clear why the quality of experience is so important in a person's education.

The Aesthetic

The fine arts afford experiences that are ordinarily regarded as being high in quality. Those experiences are called aesthetic. The term "aesthetic" applies to any intrinsically valued experience of something that has been artistically organized. The phrase, "artistically organized" is what distinguishes an experience that is simply high in quality from one that has aesthetic quality. Eating popcorn and listening to Mozart can both be high-quality experiences. But since there is no artistic organization in the eating of popcorn it cannot, as Mozart can, be experienced aesthetically. A person's experience of visual art is aesthetic when she responds with satisfaction to relationships of color, patterns of light and dark, and so on. The experience of music is aesthetic when one responds emotionally to relationships of rhythm, melody, dynamics, and so forth. To literature, response is aesthetic when a reader is moved by the way in which language creates convincing relationships between plot and character.

But the reference of the term "aesthetic" is not limited to the fine arts. Other kinds of high-quality experiences are referred to as "aesthetic" because they resemble features of experiences of the fine arts. Because they have educational value, it will be helpful to see how experiences unrelated to the arts can be said to have aesthetic quality.

Few people eating lunch at MacDonald's think of their experience as aesthetic. But aesthetic quality may dominate the experience of dining at a gourmet restaurant. Dinner is served by people who may legitimately consider themselves artists. Diners, of course, may not appreciate the labor and the creativity that went into the creation of a recipe, the locating of ingredients, and the cooking itself. Once the meal is prepared, the setting of the table and the presentation of food is done with attention to their visual effect. The flavors and textures of the foods and beverages, and their sequence, are organized to so as to enhance one another. Even the conversation is in part regulated by the meal (it would be "bad taste" to be critical of your companions, boorish to discuss strategies for dealing with a business problem). Under these conditions, artistically organized features of the meal contribute to a consummatory experience—one that is enjoyed for its own sake.

Let's return to some of the everyday instances of high-quality experience mentioned earlier to see how they can be aesthetic in quality. Writing a letter can be very satisfying when we successfully search for a way of articulating what we mean; when we put into words an idea that we never had before; when we imagine what our reader will think when she reads what we've written. *What* we wrote may not qualify as literature, but our experience writing it was similar to the creative experience of a literary artist, and that experience is normally described as aesthetic.[9]

A visit to the park to feed the ducks after a long day can help a person disengage from the problems and routines of the day's work. Relaxation comes as thought is freed from daily concerns. Exhilaration attends the spontaneous entry into a world of hopes and dreams, or perhaps just into a world of hungry, squawking ducks. That's high-quality experience for those who have it, and it is akin to the experience of many artists who must wrench themselves from the everyday and the ordinary in order to cultivate the spontaneity and fresh perspectives that characterize their art. For the artist, this freedom and exhilaration is called aesthetic, and it is no less so when experienced by other people cultivating *their* ideal worlds. For all, the experience is felt to be intrinsically valuable.

Running long distances might be punishing for a lot of people, but there are those who see it as a challenge, who condition their minds and their bodies through practice, and who experience an almost ineffable satisfaction in overcoming the pain of running the distance and achieving the goal they set for themselves. There is a similarity in such an experience to what Michelangelo must have felt as he worked on the ceiling of the Sistine Chapel, lying on his back, reaching upward endlessly for what must have seemed a lifetime. Those who assisted the great painters of ceilings—the Tiepolos and the Tintorettos—may have toiled as laboriously as they did, although they achieved no more fame or glory than most of the people who run marathons. Only the quality of experience can explain their labors. Not its outcome—crossing the finish line or applying paint to the last empty space—but the continuous, extended experience of challenge, thought, effort, hope, satisfaction, followed by the next challenge—the next mile, the next hill, the next color, the next space—and the consequent feelings that are similar for runners and for painters. In both, they are aesthetic in quality.

These examples show how everyday, nonartistic experiences can be regarded as aesthetic when they are high in quality and have features that resemble artistic forms of organization. Later on (in Chapter 4) it will be necessary to formulate in more explicit ways just what an artistic form of organization is, for it is *that* which makes a high-quality experience an aesthetic one. But now we need only note the connection between high-quality experience, artistic forms of organization, and the aesthetic. Earlier it was said that education is dependent on the quality of a student's experience. Yet there is no reason to believe that high quality alone will guarantee education. People may enjoy eating popcorn, but they won't learn much from it. On the other hand, they can learn a lot from listening to Mozart, writing letters, and running marathons. Thus when it was said that education is dependent on the quality of a student's experience, the implication is that *education is dependent on the aesthetic quality of a student's experience.*

One of the main tasks of this book will be to show that only by deliberate attention to the aesthetic quality of the experiences of learners will learning actually occur. That is, to get the kind of learning we want, educators must arrange school conditions in such a way that the experience felt by students is aesthetic in quality. As the above examples suggest, this does not mean that learning must always be like reading a novel or watching a movie. It often entails hard work, practice, and even drill. But it does mean that these usually arduous activities can succeed only in contexts where the students' experience is aesthetic, and that these contexts won't appear unless they are deliberately set up by teachers or other adults. The remainder of this book is organized to show why this is the case, how it can be managed, and what kinds of obstacles to doing it will have to be overcome.

The Argument of the Book

In the next chapter I discuss some practical implications of the idea of democracy. If these implications are not well understood, education will be an aimless undertaking that will actually undermine a democratic way of life. A little more will be said about this at the conclusion of this chapter.

Five chapters make up Part II, Educational Ideals: What's Possible, and How. This part of the book discusses the kinds of conditions that must be created in order to promote learning. It begins, however, with a discussion of traditional educational aims that have never been fulfilled.

For centuries schools have aimed at goals that are impossible to achieve. They still do. That's why it's so common for teachers to feel harassed, children to feel frustrated, and the public to be disappointed. In Chapter 3 we'll see what's involved in learning, why some of our educational goals are unrealistic, and why certain kinds of dispositions are worth aiming at because they are both justifiable and achievable.

Chapter 4 will begin our exploration of how educational goals can be achieved. I'll examine here the nature of the aesthetic and discuss the particular educational conditions that are likely to foster aesthetic quality in students' experience. Chapters 5 and 6 will continue our examination of the conditions that foster learning. We'll see how the aesthetic is related to matters as diverse as the pursuit of curiosity, problem-solving, lectures, creativity, and repetitive drill work.

Chapter 6 will also shift our focus from individual experience to social concerns. We'll see that when high-quality experience is achieved in a social setting, it can advance the legitimate goals of socialization as well as education. We'll also see why schools cannot avoid socializing their members. Schools do it now, but they don't do it well. Chapter 7 will examine how it can be done better, and it will offer some examples of schools that have successfully offered students both education and a democratic kind of socialization.

Three chapters make up Part III, Educational Realities: Confronting the System and Escaping the System. In these chapters the ideal conditions for learning discussed in Part II are contrasted with actual conditions found in schools. An effort will be made to explain why school conditions persist that are so anaesthetic and so inimical to education. Part III will also indicate the kinds of changes that would make it possible for teachers and children to learn together.

Chapter 8 will show how schools are a part of a vast, interconnected school system that includes schools at all levels and a variety of nonschool agencies like textbook and testing companies. It will be shown how the purpose of this school system is incompatible with education, and why education reform movements, aimed at shining up the school system, are irrelevant to education.

The last two chapters focus on just a few features of the school system that must be changed if any serious efforts to educate the young are to succeed. Chapter 9 will show why the system of standardized, machine-scored testing of students must be abolished. It will also discuss the need for greater autonomy for teachers, and it will propose broad changes in the ways that teachers are educated, trained, placed in their jobs, and organized, so that they can do their work more effectively.

Chapter 10 will show why segregated schools cannot be good schools, whether they are located in ghettos or in wealthy suburbs. It will offer reasons for abolishing segregated schools and segregation within schools by ability and by age. The chapter will conclude by suggesting how the young can be educated through selected work experiences as an alternative to full-time academic study. The implications of this for teachers and for teaching will be discussed, and it will be shown how the aesthetic dimension of work can be as effective in fostering learning as activities undertaken in school.

Before we examine education itself, we'll examine in the next chapter the character of the social environment that education requires. If we aim to cultivate reason, judgment, and individuality in our young, we must be aware of the kinds of social conditions that will allow these traits to flourish. These social conditions are democratic ones. Since individuality is prized in a democracy, its public institutions—and most especially its schools—must foster the conditions that will develop and support individuality.

We will not try to define democracy in a logically tight or scientifically rigorous way. Instead, we'll treat it as an ideal, or as a broad mosaic of ideals. Blurred at its conceptual edges and seldom exemplified in our everyday practice, the ideal of democracy can still offer guidance for changes in how we educate the young. As this ideal gets elaborated in the next chapter, we'll see how its practical use stands in sharp contrast to the use of educational "standards" in directing change. This will help us to see the proper, but very different roles of standards and ideals in the conduct of education.

After sorting out the respective roles of standards and ideals, Chapter 2 will show why social ideals are required to give direction to educational practice, and what kinds of social ideals are implicit in the idea of democracy. Then we'll see how democratic social ideals establish the conditions for individual autonomy and freedom. Thus we'll be able to understand how aesthetic quality in the experience of learners—which makes learning possible—is dependent on establishing democratic social conditions.

2 Democracy and Education

Standards, Ideals, and the Schools

Education can succeed only if teachers know what they're teaching *for*. Their immediate aims and objectives are shaped by their values, but their long-range goals are guided by ideals. Their activities are regulated by standards, too. Not just academic standards, but standards of discipline as well. Even standards of decorum.

Because public attitudes toward education tend to be conservative, the public periodically calls for more rigorous standards for schools. This happened in the late 1950s. The Soviets had launched the Sputnik satellite, and the public was convinced that more math and science in the schools would produce more and better scientists and engineers.

A generation later it happened again. The decline of America's global economic dominance was blamed on schools. Bizarre as that sounds, it renewed the demand for rigorous academic standards. School districts and even entire states required more academic courses of everyone. Standards for grades and for promotion were raised, swelling the ranks of students who would be at risk of failure. Minimum competency standards threatened the loss of a diploma for those who failed to meet them.

But in the rush to establish standards, the role of ideals in education is easily forgotten. This is not a trivial role. We need to keep in mind how important the difference is between standards and ideals for the way we run our schools.

Ideals are what people strive for. Standards are what they try to meet. You can fail to achieve an ideal, yet not be a failure. But falling short of a standard is what we *mean* by "failure."

Ideals keep us going when the world seems oppressive and unrewarding. They embody our values, our hopes, our deepest beliefs. Specific enough to aim at, ideals are broad enough to allow some freedom of action. While often personal, ideals can be shared with others because their breadth has room for disagreement about the actions they imply. In this way ideals unite people in common efforts without dictating what their behavior must be. The open-endedness of ideals makes it possible to share them, and thus makes possible distinctively human communities. The U.S. Constitution is an embodiment of shared ideals. It commands broad allegiance while at the same time inspiring heated argument over its implications for action.

Standards, on the other hand, are explicit, precise, and quantifiable. Unlike ideals, they specify exactly what behavior is called for and what results are acceptable. Standards are what we get when authorities agree about performance within an explicitly defined range of activities. There is a standard foot and a standard meter. There is a standard for performance (par) on every golf course. There are standards for automobile emissions controls and for elevator safety.

The initial phases of complex human enterprises are guided by ideals. Standards aren't applied until much later, when the enterprise has become widespread, manageable, and familiar. The Wright brothers were guided by their ideals in the development of their flying machine. Today's commercial airliners are expected to meet the standards of the Federal Aviation Administration.

Human civilizations are inspired and guided by ideals. They are regulated according to standards. But when one is substituted for the other in an activity, there is bound to be some confusion if not conflict. Ideals are too vague to regulate anything with precision. On the other hand, the uniformity and specificity of standards makes them unsuitable for inspiring effort in people. That may be why establishing and raising standards as a means of school reform has produced only harassed test-takers rather than scholars.

If anything lends itself to the inspiration and guidance of ideals, it is the education of the young—"to the limits of their potentials," we say, whatever those potentials might be. "To be President," we hope, or another Shakespeare, another Madame Curie. "To make the world a better place to live in," is another ideal; "to be self-sufficient" is still another. The best efforts of teachers and parents are inspired by ideals. Sometimes, of course, the ideals are too vague to be very useful.

But standards are applied in education, too. They direct our efforts and distinguish success from failure. Just as an automobile that doesn't meet standards goes back to the factory, students who don't meet standards go back to the classrooms from which their classmates just graduated.

But the parallel between industry and education is difficult to maintain. In industry, the uniformity of standards promotes fairness and helps decision-making. If car manufacturers complain that they can't meet uniform safety standards, they can be told to stop production until they can. Applying the standards protects consumers and plays no favorites among carmakers.

In education, matters are not so clear-cut. Suppose some students fail to meet a certain standard of reading proficiency, and suppose their teacher insists that they simply cannot meet the standard this year. What is to be done? There is no production line that can be stopped. But the apparent defects of these children call for treatment considerably more delicate than is likely to be given to the defective welds on a Pontiac chassis. We can require the children to take another year to try to meet the standards they are currently failing, but research evidence shows that retention does little good for students who fail, and may do plenty of harm.[1]

There are times when standards can be applied to people in a precise and fair way. Someone who wants to be a physician or a competitor in the Olympic games has to meet the same standards as any other applicant or contestant. If the applicant can't meet the standards, she can change her goals and pursue another activity or career. But what can students do who fail to meet school standards? They can't pursue another activity or career because school is the only one the law allows: it's compulsory. Even if they fail to meet the standards, they must remain students.

Thus the use of standards in educational settings raises serious problems, and not just for students who are at risk of failure. Many young people in school have talents and interests that don't match up with the standards that are popular at a given time. Since by definition standards are uniform (i.e., they're the same for all), these young people are disadvantaged. For example, eligibility for college is currently dependent on meeting standards of curriculum distribution among academic courses. But the school day is finite, and an increase in the number of required academic courses leaves little room for electing nonacademic courses. As these electives become more scarce, the school loses its capacity to serve its diverse population. Fewer students find opportunities to discover, try out, and develop their talents, their interests, and their abilities.

The application of standards to children in schools raises such serious educational and ethical problems that we may suspect the wrong standards are being used. But the error lies in applying any standards at all. Many important human relationships have no room for the strict application of standards—among friends, for example, or between lovers, or within families. In the wider community, there are very few standards that must be met for a person to be a citizen. Common to all these relationships is their relative permanence. People expect to live with each other for better or for worse, for richer or for poorer, and whether or not they even like each other. That's how parents and children are related, and teachers and students are related in a similar way.

So there is good reason to question the application of uniform standards to all of the children in a school. Not only do we create insoluble problems over what to do with those who fail to meet the standards, but we come to demand the same activities and the same performances from all of our children, despite their great and valuable diversity. If, for example, students must all take the same examination in chemistry, then it's only "fair" that they take the same kinds of chemistry courses and study the same materials. This is obviously hard on those who have no interest in chemistry. But it's even worse for those who *are* interested in the subject, because they must march along in lock-step with their sometimes slower and often apathetic peers. Thus academic (as well as nonacademic) interests are sacrificed on the altar of uniform standards.

Although many people think about education in terms of standards and how they should be raised, little more will be said in this book about standards. Schools are not so much in need of regulation as they are of inspiration. Of uniformity, they have had enough. What's lacking is variety. For inspiration and variety, ideals are needed (but not ideals that are so vague as to permit virtually any sort of school policy and practice).

You can hold people accountable for meeting standards, but standards will not motivate them to excel—especially when the task is difficult and unappealing. Faced with accountability but lacking motivation, teachers and students are in a lot of trouble. Teachers can at least quit. Students can't.

This predicament can be corrected by examining ideals that are deeply embedded in American culture, and seeing what they imply for education. When we join to the results of this inquiry an understanding of the ways learning can be fostered, we'll discover some worthwhile new directions for educational practice. Teachers and students cannot be held accountable for the achievement of ideals, but being unable to achieve them doesn't mean that it's impractical to have them. As long as our ideals are clear enough to inspire and guide effort, they're the most useful things we can have.

No ideals have been closer to the heart of American culture than the ideals of democracy. They will be focal to the remainder of this chapter.

The Need for a Conception of the Democratic

From a purely practical point of view, one major function of schooling is custodial. We send our kids to school so we can get on with our business. But we expect more of schools than that. We expect them to help children acquire some basic academic skills and adjust to our society and maintain our way of life. But America embraces many ways of life—probably more than can be found in any other single nation. If only there *was* a clearly understood way of life in which all Americans engaged, a school program could readily be developed to maintain it. But because of the great diversity of ways in which people live in America, our agreement that schools should preserve our way of life seems to imply no particular educational program, no particular educational instrumentalities.

Into this vacuum step policymakers urging schools to aim at specific national goals that have captured the attention of the public. These goals are often transient. In the middle of the twentieth century the dominant national goal was military security, symbolized by the National Defense Education Act. School funding, the curriculum, educational research, and teacher training were all aimed at defending America from its presumed enemies. Without giving up their other goals, schools tried to emphasize science and math (for the eventual development of weaponry), foreign languages (to enhance diplomacy), and guidance and counseling (to ensure that the brightest students would study science, math, or foreign languages).[2]

In the last quarter of the century, policymakers focused on economic competition as a national goal. This was perhaps best symbolized by the Presidential Commission report, "A Nation at Risk."[3] Schools and educational research were expected to help the United States compete successfully with economically productive countries that we formerly dominated. Curiously enough, science and math maintained their prominence in the schools. These studies were now intended not to destroy other nations but to regain economic dominance over them by building better products, conceiving new ones, and marketing them more effectively than our competitors marketed theirs.

There is a paradox in using schools to promote these kinds of goals. For as long as children are treated as means to the immediate, short-term ends prized by certain groups, schools will be unable to work toward broader and more pervasive social goals and ideals. This can be understood by calling to mind one of the more important of these pervasive social goals: equal opportunity for all.

For a long time the United States has been recognized as the land of opportunity. For some, opportunity was the chance to worship as they chose. For others, it was the chance to make their fortunes. For many, it was the chance simply to choose what to do with their lives: to find a mate, to choose friends, to find a job, select a career, or at least voluntarily accept or reject what might be offered. Opportunity meant that one would not be pressed into the navy, conscripted into the army, or required by church, government, or social custom to follow the calling of his father or the example of her mother. Opportunity meant that the social and economic status of one's family was not to be the sole determinant of one's future.

The ideal of opportunity that attracted our ancestors still attracts waves of immigrants. While it is often violated in our institutional practices, equal opportunity for all remains a dominant theme in American culture. It is one of the first things many Americans would mention if they were asked to name something distinctive about American democracy. It is an ideal of which most Americans are proud.

Schools have traditionally been considered a primary means for making opportunities equally available. While historians differ about the reasons and the motivations for establishing our free, compulsory schools, the rhetoric of the early champions of public schooling was unambiguous. Only schools, they claimed, would keep open the avenues of opportunity for all.[4] To a land of seemingly unlimited resources came people from all around the world. They spoke different languages, held different religious beliefs, maintained different traditions. Only public schools, providing an education common to all, would provide opportunities equal for all.

Respect for equal opportunity and the role of schools in making it a reality come directly into conflict with the narrower school goals that accompany changes in political climate. For example, if the goal of schools is to turn out students who will contribute to national defense or successful economic competition, then students who have an interest in studies compatible with *these* goals will receive favorable treatment. They will get high marks and go on to college, secure in their hopes for a successful career. Students who lack these interests, and who may even lack the relevant abilities, will be pressured by parents, school personnel, and curriculum requirements to pursue studies in these directions anyway. If students have inclinations in other directions, they must pursue them at their own risk.

Look at the matter in terms of individual cases. Marc enjoys mathematics and Carole is interested in chemistry. They get good grades and eventually enter a highly selective university. From there they move smoothly into graduate work or into a high-paying job.

Now consider Jack and Jill. Like most high school students, they haven't identified any academic interests that might lead to a career. Jack lives in a middle-class family that expects him to attend college, so he takes the curriculum required for admission by selective colleges. He struggles with his studies (especially math and science), manages to survive, and is eventually accepted at a state college. But he doesn't know what to choose for a major because he still hasn't developed an interest in anything academic. High school requirements, driven by narrow and transitory national goals, have kept him from discovering interests of his own.

Jill is less fortunate than Jack. Hers is a low-income family. She has no academic interests and she never intended to go to college. The classes she takes are filled with students like herself. She never sees, let alone interacts with college-bound students. No one expects Jill to contribute to national defense or to the nation's economic competitiveness. She'll be in the most crowded classes in her school, and she'll be taught by less experienced teachers. Her books and other materials will be simpler and duller.[5] She'll try some vocational courses, and she'll learn that the jobs available to her will not require those courses. Jill won't finish high school.

Fred and Ginger have abilities and interests as strong as Marc's and Carole's, but they aren't academic ones. Ginger loves music and plays the violin. She and her parents expect her to attend college, so she dutifully confronts a high school program crammed with academic courses. The legislature in her state has lengthened the school day, and her district has mandated more extensive homework assignments. Because the violin calls for several hours of practice a day, Ginger gets frustrated by her slow progress. She's afraid to drop her academic courses, she doesn't want to give up her social life, and playing the violin is the one thing she really loves to do. She'll have to choose, however, and the pressures of narrow school goals guarantee that she'll give up something important to her.

Fred hasn't yet identified anything that could be called a career interest, but he has demonstrated an ability to organize other people in order to get things done. Adults recognize him as a "natural leader." What he leads, however, is a street gang. He doesn't exercise leadership in school because leadership requires interactions among people who have common goals. But the expansion of academic requirements and uniform standards for all has resulted in increased competition among students. Thus the goals of students are not shared, and there is no common enterprise for which a leader would be appropriate. Social intercourse in these competitive classes is called "talking," cooperation is called "cheating," and students are penalized for talking and cheating. Fred feels isolated and alienated in his classes and will probably drop out at the end of the year. He'll exercise his leadership in the streets.

Marc and Carole, Jack and Jill, and Fred and Ginger are representative American adolescents. They illustrate the paradox of a school policy based on narrow, short-term goals that block the realization of broader and more pervasive goals. The ideal of equal opportunity is important and pervasive in American culture. Schools have been expected to maintain that ideal: to transmit it to the young, and to make it a reality in their lives. In our examples, Marc and Carole got the opportunity they wanted because their interests happened to match national goals that were current at the time. The other four (who are far more typical of American high school students) did not get opportunities anywhere near equal to Marc's and Carole's.

When an overriding concern with immediate but temporary national goals is carried into the formation of educational policy, opportunities are radically diminished for many students. But there is another drawback to the focus on immediate goals: it tends to obscure what our long-term goals and ideals *are*. A passion to protect our way of life by economic or military means, and to prepare children to help us in this task, can cause us to forget just what our way of life is. We take it for granted and talk vaguely about freedom and pluralism.

Vagueness about our way of life leaves schools without direction or purpose. Their aims are disordered and lack clear priorities. Teachers are acutely aware of this. We are expected to prepare youngsters for college, they complain, and at the same time curb their delinquent tendencies. We're expected to teach basic skills, offer emotional support, and make them sensitive to the needs of others. We're expected to prepare them for economic competition and cultivate their intellects. We're expected to counsel them and judge them, to reward them and punish them. We're expected to help them overcome physical handicaps, deal with abusive parents, and equalize their chances in a world where opportunities are not equally distributed.

To have a multitude of aims is not in itself a bad thing. But what's frustrating is the fact that these aims are disordered: it isn't clear which ones take precedence over which others. Since they can't all be equally well achieved, teachers could use help in deciding which ones to give up in cases of conflict or insufficient time. Only getting clear about what's worth preserving in our way of life can provide the order, the priorities, and the direction that teachers need. Lacking such priorities, teachers become targets of criticism from every direction, since they *can't* achieve *all* the goals cherished by every parent and every interest group.

This chapter will specify some of the distinctive features of our way of life that can supply guidance for schools. Because schools are intended to educate all children, and because they serve "American culture" in its broadest sense, the features of our way of life that direct these efforts cannot be politically or religiously partisan. I will use the term "democratic" to refer to these features. This term doesn't specify exactly what we all agree on, but it does connote a way of life different from what's found in societies that are not democratic, and it suggests that there are values and beliefs on which we can agree despite our differences.

As we look for characteristics of a democratic way of life to order our priorities for schools, we must avoid a narrowly political use of the term "democracy." Our aim is not to specify how representation is to be managed, how political units are to be governed, or how political change is to be fostered. These are serious concerns, but our explication of the idea of democracy is for the purpose of guiding the development of the young. This will not only help teachers act with commitment, but it will also dispel the mistaken belief that schools can be neutral about the social arrangements for which they are preparing the young.

The belief that schools can be neutral about ways of life (which is to say, about values) is frequently based on theories of child development. Influential researchers have promoted the idea that children grow in "stages," and that these stages follow one another in an invariable sequence. These stages are said to be inherent within persons and, thus, independent of cultural patterns.[6] The purpose of education should (therefore) be to facilitate the passage of the young through these stages. To follow this advice implies that schools can operate similarly in any culture.

The fallacy of this view lies in the assumption that human development occurs independent of a particuar culture's (or subculture's) beliefs, values, and accepted practices. These cultural commitments cannot be withheld from children until they are grown up, or until their education is completed. All the adults in the child's world embody these commitments to a greater or a lesser extent. It's not simply that neutrality toward them would be intensely difficult to achieve. It would be morally irresponsible even to try.

Most of us care about our culture at least in the sense that we appreciate living in it, and we'd probably reject living in another one. We take it for granted that our culture will be transmitted to the young. And because we also realize that not everything characteristic of the culture is worth transmitting (for example, racial prejudice or political bribery), we don't oppose helping the young to become critical of some aspects of the culture. Thus a conception of child development as occurring in stages within a cultural vacuum is incoherent. Children grow up to become members of this culture or that culture, and when we deliberately guide this development, we do it with our own cultural commitments in mind. Neutrality is not even conceivable.[7]

Some people claim that the school's responsibility ends with the teaching of the three *R*'s, or the "basic skills." These people, too, believe that instruction can remain neutral with respect to social and moral values and beliefs.

But supporters of a basic skills approach to education give little consideration to how people learn. The teaching of reading, for example, requires that *something* be read. It makes a big difference whether a first grader reads about Spot digging up bones in a suburban backyard, or about sixth graders extorting lunch money from third graders. And it matters whether a third grader writes about her summer vacation or about why her mother is never at home in the evening. It also matters *to whom* the child writes—teacher, friend, or parent. Many teachers give careful attention to the choices they make in these areas, and to the choices they make available to their pupils. But choices can't be made from a posture of neutrality. Teachers need to ask what's *worth* reading about, or writing about, and to whom is it worth writing? The three *R*'s need not be as bland as they often seem, but when they are, it's because teachers or school districts chose to make them so. Skills taught using materials that are dull are learned only with the greatest difficulty. But whether dull or fascinating, soothing or upsetting, materials have to be chosen. And they have to be chosen on the basis of some values, some grounds. Thus even matters as uncontroversial as the three *R*'s cannot intelligently be taught from a neutral posture.

Without some conception of what our way of life is about, all these choices become confused, tentative, diffuse, and even self-contradictory. Pursuing many different directions at once, schools seem "aimless." But aimlessness may seem only a harsh term for what many of us value as pluralism. Pluralism is normally thought to be a constituent if not one of the chief virtues of a democratic society. Our traditions are, after all, rooted in cultures that developed on several different continents.

If you complain about this diversity of traditions, you might be called a curmudgeon, or worse. Yet if diversity is *all* there is to our way of life, then there really is *no* way of life for the schools to transmit, preserve, or advance. We have seen that even the teaching of skills requires choices. But if there is no way of life to guide those choices, they will be shaped by the pressures of special interests external to the school. Thus even while some teachers will be able to justify the choices they make, schooling on the whole will appear either aimless or driven by particular political and economic interests.

Despite the many ways of life that Americans pursue, there are values and commitments to which most of us agree. Often violated in practice, they are what make Americans distinctive. Like magnets, they still attract multitudes to our shores. Taken together, they provide a meaning for democracy that goes deeper and further than mere reference to political arrangements. It's time now to explicate that meaning in order to set a framework for school policy and practice.

The Import of Democracy for Education

The term, "democracy," is rich in meaning. But this richness has been troublesome for political scientists and sociologists. Physical scientists made rapid progress when they reconstructed the meanings of their key concepts to refer to what could be seen or tested in some visible way. Seeking similar success, social scientists tried to reduce their key concepts in the same way. But when for the purpose of empirical testability you simplify the concept of democracy, you come up with a theory about something that's artificially simple.

This theory will bear little resemblance to the social and political arrangements we're concerned about.

The simplification of the concept of democracy most widely used by social scientists reduces it to a mere political method or to a set of institutional arrangements at the national level. Joseph Schumpeter defined democratic method as "that institutional arrangement for arriving at political decisions in which individuals acquire the power to decide by means of a competitive struggle for the people's vote."[8]

Such a thin conception of democracy offers no insight into social organization and social interaction, and it provides no guidance for schools. Because it reduces democracy to a mere technique that is applied periodically, it has no application to the daily lives of people. Such a conception renders meaningless the idea of education for democracy, since only elites, working within political parties, would engage in the struggle for votes. People vote only once in a while, and schoolchildren don't vote at all.

To conceive of democracy as just a technique frees it of value implications. But for most of us, the idea of democracy *is* value-laden. It's something to be desired and it justifies our policies and practices (including our voting procedures). But if it's taken to be only a political method, then it has no justification of its own. Why use this method of finding leaders rather than some other method?

The procedures of political campaigns and the mechanics of voting can be justified in a nation that calls itself democratic only insofar as they actually maintain democratic values. Here is what this means in practice. In capitalist nations, elections and legislative actions are heavily influenced if not actually determined by the amount of money spent during a campaign.[9] This gives disproportionate political power to wealthy individuals and corporate groups and thus threatens what many people think of as democracy. It would be dangerous (for the preservation of a democratic society) to dismiss this threat by insisting that the struggle for votes, *however* it was carried on, is what democracy *means*. On the contrary, the role of money in the electoral process needs to be examined in the light of democratic values. If those values are threatened by such procedures, then we must ask how those procedures can be changed. Thus however it may actually be carried on, the competitive struggle for the people's vote is not the *meaning* of democracy. Rather, the character of that struggle must itself be justified by an appeal to the very concept—democracy—that some academics use to *label* that competitive struggle.

Thus we need to look beyond political procedures for a sense of democracy that can give guidance to education. When we do this, we find ourselves examining the ways that people are related to each other in their varied social organizations. Democracy is the way we characterize these relations when participation is fullest among the members of groups, especially with respect to the making of decisions. But decisions are not limited to just the formal, political arena. They are made in every area of life: at home, at work, at leisure, and not just in voting booths. Because they are so pervasive, it makes sense to speak of democracy as a "way of life."[10] If, on the other hand, the concept of democracy were limited to its political dimension, it would be of interest to only a few of us, since activity that is specifically political plays very little part in the way of life of most Americans.

But what sort of a way of life is it? Many ways of life exist side by side in America. But to speak of democracy as a way of life is not to refer to some pattern of activities that's common to these diverse lifestyles. Lifestyle is not at issue. Rather, the idea of democracy focuses our attention on a set of ideals on which most Americans agree.

Equality of Opportunity

One of these ideals was discussed earlier: equality of opportunity. Like any ideal, there is some vagueness in it. But its status as an ideal makes apparent the failure of actual conditions to meet it. For example, the daughter of a migrant farm worker and the son of a corporate executive surely don't have equal opportunities with regard to their future education, occupation, income, or social status. It's not even clear what we mean by saying that their opportunities *ought* to be equal, since most of us believe that it's right to work hard for the sake of your children. That includes giving your children whatever you've accumulated during your lifetime.

Yet the ideal of equality of opportunity still operates. We acknowledge differences in the opportunities of children of migrant workers and corporate executives, but we also regard those differences as unfair—that is, they fall short of our ideals. For this reason we try out, often amid controversy, various social and educational programs intended to diminish the differences in people's opportunities. The existence and the validity of the ideal means that even people who *benefit* from the conditions that fail to meet it (i.e., those who inherited their advantages) must publically endorse the ideal and behave as if they were trying to fulfill it. The rhetoric of political candidates at election time bears witness to this.

Like every important ideal cherished by Americans, this one lives in perpetual tension with its contrary. Opportunities should be equal for all, but people should strive to give their children every advantage they can. Insofar as they succeed, opportunities will not be equal for all. We work to accumulate a fortune and succeed in reducing inheritance taxes, and then we're appalled at how widespread poverty is. There is a contradiction here, but the contradiction is not total. We don't believe that resources should be equal for all and we're encouraged to strive for as much as we can get. But most of us also believe that what individuals accumulate should not be preserved intact for their heirs. Much of the political history of the United States could be written in terms of the conflict between small but usually powerful groups seeking unconstrained freedom to accumulate wealth and pass it on to their heirs, and large but usually powerless groups seeking the constraints that would make opportunities more equal for all.

Some implications for education of the ideal of equality of opportunity were discussed earlier, but now they can be put more broadly. At one time in our history, equal opportunity for education meant that every child was entitled to the same education. People easily overlooked individual differences in talent and interest, because the religious, racial, and ethnic backgrounds of children who went to school were so similar. Now these group identifications are nearly as disparate as children's personalities themselves, and it is widely recognized that, if the *same* education were offered to *all* children, their opportunities would be very unequal. A few would benefit, and the majority would suffer.

After the first decade of this century, equality of opportunity was taken to mean different educational programs for different children, and schools offered a wide variety of curricular tracks.[11] But critics observed that such tracking systems in fact put children into programs that reflected the social and economic status of their parents. Children of working-class parents turned up in the vocational and commercial tracks, and the children of the well to do took college preparatory tracks. That situation still typifies American secondary schools, and it still violates the ideal of equality of opportunity.[12]

Later on (in Chapter 10), suggestions will be offered for a program that might help to equalize opportunities for children. For now, it is enough to see that schools have an obligation to work toward realizing this ideal, even if they cannot achieve it by themselves.

Equality before the Law and Equal Respect for All

Americans cherish the ideal of equality of opportunity largely because they regard themselves as equal before the law. In its narrowest sense this equality expresses an old Anglo-American legal tradition. In its broadest sense it expresses the even older Judeo-Christian tradition of loving or respecting others as equals. Equality is firmly built into the U.S. Constitution and its several amendments. But like equality of opportunity, this ideal confronts its contrary in both its legal and its moral senses.[13]

For example, equality before the law is taken very seriously, but we hope just as seriously to hire the best attorney we can afford. In a culture in which nearly anything can be bought, access to legal help is a function of private means. This is another contradiction, but again, not a total one. Those who cannot pay are provided counsel by the court at public expense.

The broader, moral sense of equality embodied in the ideal of respect for persons also meets its contrary in everyday practice. Western civilization, like most others, has traditionally been divided into classes of people. Slaves, serfs, and peasants were not respected or treated as equals by the aristocracy, the clergy, or the educated classes. These divisions and their inherent inequalities were explicitly abolished in the U.S. Constitution, but tradition doesn't die so easily. Blacks, members of many religious and ethnic groups, women, and gay people continue to suffer from discrimimation and are not regarded as equals by many white American males. U.S. history is highlighted by the efforts of these oppressed groups to achieve the equal regard promised in the Constitution.

Breaches in the ideal of equal respect for all are not limited to the treatment of readily identifiable minorities. Children are people, too, but they are often abused, exploited, and humiliated, in public institutions as well as in the privacy of their families. They have traditionally been told what to do, and most adults have found this convenient. "Why not?" they ask. "After all, they're only children."

The term "only" is a sign of contempt. It means that children are something less than adults, to be treated as inferiors. Children *are* inferior to adults in years, and in many areas of knowledge and skill. But since superiority and inferiority in these areas is irrelevant to the moral status of other adults, why should it be relevant to children? They are not inferior as far as their moral status is concerned, so they are entitled to respect just as any other person would be.

What sort of action does this respect entail? Is it possible to respect people and also tell them what to do all day long, without seeking input from them or permitting noncompliance? Can you respect adolescents and also tell them they are not permitted to leave the school grounds during lunchtime?

That children possess less knowledge than their teachers or parents is not a sign of moral inferiority. Nowhere is it written that one must complete a formal education in order to be worthy of respect or to be treated equally before the law. And from a purely practical point of view, people who are shown little respect when they are in school are not likely to have much respect for others when they're finished with school. What goes around comes around.

Like every ideal, respect for others as equals is subject to interpretation. But like other ideals it still offers guidance in our treatment of others, and it ought to offer some guidance in our treatment of young people in schools. It provides a touchstone for the criticism of present practices, even though we cannot define it to everyone's satisfaction. And we could not maintain our identity as a distinctive culture without it.

Freedom of Choice

Closely related to the ideals of respect for others and equality of opportunity is the ideal of freedom of choice in one's personal life. Having an opportunity implies being able to choose, and respecting others does not mean simply wishing them a nice day, but implies acknowledging the choices they make, however differently we might have made them. There is widespread agreement in America that people should be able to choose their friends and their mates, their jobs and their careers, their political, moral, and religious beliefs, their recreation and their entertainment. This ideal, too, is tempered by its contraries. A person may be penalized if his choice of friends includes people of another color. Some Americans would deny women the choice of whether to terminate a pregnancy, while others consider such a decision to be an expression of the ideals of free choice and respect for persons.

While freedom of choice is fundamental to American culture, it is often a contested ideal, especially with reference to the young. It would be rash to suppose that children were wise enough to make all of their own choices, but that's not a reason for denying them *any* choices. Then what sorts of choices should children have? Few questions are as fundamental as this one for the running of our schools, but not many educators have taken the trouble to answer it.[14] Some people have argued that schools permit the young no choices at all except trivial ones.[15]

Since the making of choices is crucial to the development of maturity, it's worth attending to the kinds of choices young people actually have. They do not choose to attend school, their major occupation for at least ten years. And most youngsters do not choose what to study in school, or how or when to study it. They exercise some choice in their leisure, although the school organizes many after-school ("extracurricular") activities and restricts students' choices within them.

Activities that were once entirely chosen by children are now, at least for middle class youth, organized and led by adults. Whether it be Little League baseball, Pop Warner football, or the pursuit of art or music, decisions are made by adults. These activities are treated as age-graded, organized learning experiences, on the model of schooling. The child may choose whether or not to join, but from that point on he follows rules and directions laid down by adults.

Elsewhere in America, the children of the cities don't have much opportunity to join Little League or take ballet lessons. These young people aim primarily to survive and at times to overcome the conditions that permit them a very limited range of choices. They do not choose to deal in drugs as if that were an alternative to playing Pop Warner football or working in their father's store. Some of the more enterprising of these youngsters discover that only dealing drugs provides needed income or the opportunity to exercise initiative and skill. Thus an antidrug program based on the belief that young people can "just say 'no'" assumes the existence of choices and the presence of alternatives (to which one might say "yes") that just don't exist.

Freedom of choice is an empty ideal if people can't conceive of alternatives, or, if ignorant or fearful of the consequences of choosing, prefer that others choose for them. If the young don't make significant choices as they grow up, they cannot mature. That is, they cannot develop the traits we normally associate with making choices: initiative, courage, discrimination, responsibility. It's true that some children are too inexperienced, immature, and just plain ignorant to make certain kinds of choices. But it's worth asking how the ideal of freedom of choice can be preserved in the wider culture if the young aren't allowed to make any significant choices at all.

Participation in Governance

Another ideal, equally prized, is narrower in scope. It is the belief that people have a right to participate in the making of the decisions by which they are governed. The narrowness of this ideal comes from two sources. On the one hand, we feel that decisions of government apply only to a fraction of our activities, leaving much of what we do untouched. On the other hand, we acknowledge the logistical problems involved in everyone's participating in all decisions of government. So we temper (some would say adulterate)[16] the ideal of participation with the device of representation.

The ideal of participation in governance, even through representatives, becomes vague and often debatable when we allow that governance includes much more than ordinary political decision-making. We're governed at work, too, and in our religious organizations, our recreational pursuits, our schools, and our families. Should governance in these institutions be participatory, too? There's not a lot of agreement here.

While participation is honored, there's little consensus about what it is we're supposed to participate in. Cynics can say that here's just one more vague ideal, yet it's an ideal that furnishes the leverage for social change in a world where change seems inevitable. The consequences of individual decisions are technologically amplified to affect people all over the world. Some of those consequences are devastating, and increasingly more people are demanding the right to participate in decisions, even in those made by private, commercial, and religious institutions. On a more intimate scale, these attitudes have been directed toward decision-making in families. However puzzling it may be, the ideal of participation is not an empty one, and it obligates those concerned with education to determine its relevance to the role of teachers and children in schools.

Getting Rich

The above ideals are almost universally accepted in America. People disagree about their meaning and application, but they don't reject them, and that's what distinguishes American culture from most others. But there is another ideal distinctive to the culture: the ideal of getting rich, of making one's fortune. This is not an ideal widely found in many nations, but it remains very powerful in America. It attracts immigrants and it is subtly employed to discourage children from dropping out of school. It drives the professional and managerial classes in their competition with one another, and it lures people of all classes into forms of criminal behavior, from insider trading to dealing crack. It powers lotteries all over the country.

But despite its power, the ideal of getting rich doesn't operate the way the other ideals do. The main reason for this is that it can't be shared. We can all be equals before the law and give and accept respect equally, but we can't all get rich together. If I get rich, then you can't, and neither can a lot of other people. Material wealth is finite, and if we choose to share it we must give up the ideal of getting rich.

Thus the ideal of getting rich occupies an ambiguous place in the culture. For one thing, many Americans no longer believe in it. They've seen what it takes to accumulate wealth, and they realize that they lack the background or the stomach for it. Furthermore, many Americans have abandoned the ideal not because it has become unattainable, but because they see it as unworthy. They see efforts to achieve the ideal as being responsible for the enrichment of a few at the cost of poverty for many.

Those who question the ideal of getting rich also believe it to be responsible for an endless and never-satisfied striving.[17] In this regard, the executive who works every weekend is not unlike the school principal whose achievement scores are never high enough. It is striking how the ideal of getting rich is paralleled in schools by the ideal of getting high grades. Many still strive for wealth and for A's, but a loss of faith can be found in school as well as in the marketplace. The widespread mistrust of these ideals is not characteristic of the ideals discussed earlier.

The United States Constitution

The last of the ideals we'll consider is related to the ones we've already discussed. The political, legal, and even the social and economic systems of the United States are based on a Constitution and a Bill of Rights. These have undergone little change since the nation was founded. Not all Americans are intimately familiar with these documents, and those who are engage in heated debate over how to apply them. Thus the Constitution itself is an American ideal—one which, like the others discussed here, commands universal allegiance while at the same time permitting significant differences in interpretation.

Unlike the other ideals, however, the Constitution is written down. While its prescriptions can be endlessly debated, it is regarded as a legitimate if not a sacrosanct document. Thus it serves as a kind of perpetual validator and control for our other ideals. In this regard, the Constitution serves an immensly important function. For while it guarantees the right of the people to participate in their own governance, it also guarantees that that participation will not be used to deny rights and freedoms promised elsewhere in the Constitution. In other words, it forbids majorities to deny the rights of minorities. Thus the Constitution maintains that the ideal of participation cannot be acted on so as to suppress the ideals of equality before the law, equal respect for others, equality of opportunity, and freedom of choice in one's personal life (which is often associated with the maintenance of personal privacy).

The Relation between Social Ideals and Personal Freedom

When we consider democracy and its common ideals we discover a paradox. For there really is no "way of life" common to all Americans. We live in many different ways, and that's how we want it. Our freedom to choose is precious.

But our concern to live *our* way, however different it is from our neighbors', makes it easy to forget that *only a particular kind of social order can protect and guarantee this individuality.* Most Americans are too busy to think much about what such a social order demands. Few see themselves as active political agents. We would as soon leave political action and political decisions to others.

This laissez-faire attitude toward political involvement might have been tolerable when America's wealth outstripped the rest of the world's. But to ignore the distinctive character of our society and the means required to maintain it can be dangerous when there is less wealth and fewer resources to divide up amongst ourselves. When we confront scarcity, unemployment, immigration, and high crime rates, our cherished freedoms—which allow the diversity of our ways of living—will disappear, unless we effectively maintain the ideals discussed here. Only mutual respect and equality before the law, equality of opportunity, participation in governance, and the Constitution itself will preserve our personal freedoms and maintain the diversity that characterizes the American way of life.

But these ideals aren't self-perpetuating. If they're not deliberately maintained, they'll disappear—even though their loss won't be noted in the newspapers. We can hope that our institutions will maintain our ideals, yet our ideals are needed to maintain our institutions. It's people and not institutions who have ideals, and ways must be found for people to pass these ideals on to their children. This isn't easy. It's not like conveying information, or teaching skills like penmanship or long division. It's a little like passing on a language: easy to do informally, without giving it a thought, but hard to do in a formal school setting. The kind of learning we'll be exploring, then, will have less to do with how we learn the multiplication tables or even the periodic table, and more to do with how we learn ideals—that is, with how we acquire certain dispositions.

A person's dispositions may also be referred to as "traits of character." Thus an education aimed at the cultivation of dispositions is an education of character. In what follows, however, we'll stick with the term "disposition"—partly because its reference is more specific than that of the term "character," and partly to avoid confusion with a contemporary movement called "character education."

While the dispositions considered here are typically thoughtful ones, "character education" is concerned with "obeying legitimate authority and satisfying appropriate responsibilities." Its proponents write, "The first moral need of the young is to learn to avoid ratiocination. Instead, they must accept the centrality of doing the hard thing without thinking about it . . ."[18] This, of course, is socialization, not education, since the inculcation of habit is being urged. This is also why we are not told what *makes* authority "legitimate," or what *makes* responsibilities "appropriate."

At this moment in history, schools are all we have for this difficult and important task. Yet schools are already charged with so many other things to do! Some of those things may have to be given up, for this conclusion is unavoidable: either we teach the young—or instill in them, if you like—the ideals that will maintain a democratic society, or we jeopardize the rich multiplicity of ways of life that we all cherish. Of course, there's room for disagreement about how democratic ideals should operate in school and in the lives of children. But there can be no disagreement *that* they should operate in these settings. The ideals of a democratic society must become the first priority of its schools: the one set of considerations that cannot be sacrificed to any other school aims or intentions, no matter how serious they may seem at the time.[19]

When we pursue the question of *how* schools might facilitate the operation and transmission of democratic ideals, we'll see that neither socialization nor education alone is sufficient. We'll also see that other educational goals are inextricably linked to the achievement of what might be called a democratic education. The rest of this book tries to answer the question, how do we achieve these goals?

We will confront the task of developing a democratic education by first looking at the problem of how people learn. This problem has been turned into a sort of riddle, because what ought to be obvious about it has been made dark and mysterious by generations of specialized, arcane academic research.

PART II

Educational Ideals: What's Possible, and How

3 Learning: The Acquisition of Dispositions

Schools aim to impart knowledge to the young. This is not an aim that can be achieved, but they try, anyhow. And while schools regularly fail, it's the children and the teachers who get stuck with the label "failure." Because this failure is perennial (and predictable), schools are periodically threatened with reform. Yet efforts to reform schools are typically driven by the aim of imparting knowledge. This kind of reform cannot succeed, no matter how hard people try, no matter how much they spend.

We will begin by examining the reasons for this paradox. We'll see why it's not simply *difficult* to impart knowledge to students, but actually impossible. We'll see why it is so paradoxical, if not quixotic, for scholars (of all people!) to demand that schools do better what they cannot even do at all. Some academic research will be cited to support this. But my main support will be based on common sense: on evidence that's available in everyone's experience. We'll have to free ourselves from the intimidation of educational research, which can bury understanding under a pile of numbers.

Once it becomes clear why we can't succeed in our relentless efforts to impart knowledge directly into the minds of students, we can seriously consider what the schools ought to try doing, instead. That will be the subject of the remaining sections of this chapter. When the impossible has been given up, we can see what young people *can* learn, with the help of teachers and schools.

Unless some things are learned, other things can't be learned at all. You can't learn to run until you've learned to walk; you can't learn to write if you haven't learned to speak. And you can't learn math (although you *can* learn some verbal habits) if you haven't learned to care how many there are. The concluding section of this chapter will show that the focus of schooling—what constitutes its ends and shapes its means—ought to be the development of inclinations to act in certain ways. These inclinations or tendencies to act will be called dispositions.

Acquiring Knowledge: The Impossible Dream

In the seventeenth century a Moravian bishop named Comenius drew up a plan for the comprehensive education of children and youth.[1] It covered the lowest levels of schooling all the way up to the university. It was designed to present in a sequential way all of the knowledge worth learning that had been accumulated by then. Comenius called his program "pansophism." The word means, literally, "all wisdom." This may seem to be a noble goal for education, but we'll discover that there is no hope of ever reaching it—or even of getting close. So it's not such a noble goal. It's not even a worthy ideal, for it generates only disappointment or cynicism, not serious effort or achievement.

There is no evidence that Comenius ever succeeded in teaching anybody his encyclopedic curriculum, yet it seems as attractive today as it was to Comenius. It could have inspired any number of state curriculum frameworks. In California, for example, a thick document details the history and the social studies that all students should be taught from the first grade through the twelfth grade.[2] This curriculum guide is truly awesome in its scope and detail. If teachers could teach it and students could learn it, we really would become a nation of scholars.

But no one knows whether anyone actually acquired the information contained in the state curriculum frameworks. That's partly because students are examined only for part of a year's work, never for what was supposed to have been learned over all twelve years. And it's also because students are tested right after a period of instruction, but seldom several years later, which is when it might matter. Despite the absence of evidence for its success, the aim of imparting a great deal of information to the young continues to dominate schooling.

Soon we'll examine what little evidence there is about how much of the curriculum is retained and how much is forgotten. But first we must ask, is there any reason why we should *expect* students to acquire and remember the knowledge imparted to them?

If you or I were asked to take an examination, tomorrow, on what we learned in grade school, we wouldn't be optimistic about the results. *We* know how little we remember. On the basis of our own experience, we should expect today's schoolchildren to remember about as much as we do. And we might ask, in a fit of candor, what's the *point* of working so hard to teach and learn all that information, if so little of it is remembered afterwards?

But our own experience is direct and unanalyzed. If we consult the investigations of theoreticians and researchers, we may find reason to alter our own unrefined conclusions.

The aim of imparting knowledge has guided school practice for so long that most people hardly bother to question its wisdom. Tradition shapes the aims of schools, and challenges to tradition are periodically turned aside by respectable educators. At the turn of the century, following Cardinal Newman's model for a liberal education, U.S. Education Commissioner William Torrey Harris urged that all children acquire the knowledge needed to fill the "five windows of the soul."

Progressive educators balked at this, but in the early twentieth century, William C. Bagley came to the defense of the ideal of imparting sequentially organized bodies of knowledge to schoolchildren. Henry C. Morrison carried on the tradition in curriculum theory, and the ideal seems as strong today as it was a century ago. New wrinkles are added to the old tradition, sometimes based on classical Western scholarship (e.g., Mortimer Adler), sometimes on scholarship derived from the thought of more recent and predominantly continental European scholars (e.g., Allan Bloom). E. D. Hirsch even lists the particular items of information that all schoolchildren should be expected to know.[3] The professional education establishment certifies this tradition by defining achievement in terms of tests that measure students' recognition of things that they read or heard before.

These writers all assume that it's possible to transmit virtually encyclopedic knowledge to the young. They allow that it might be difficult, especially for certain groups of students. But they never question whether it *can* be done. Their position on this matter was most clearly expressed by Robert M. Hutchins, who wrote this:

> I insist . . . that the education I shall outline is the kind that everybody should have . . . You cannot say my content is wrong because you do not know the method of transmitting it. Let us agree upon content if we can and have faith that the technological genius of America will solve the problem of communication.[4]

Thus educational thinkers perennially offer the wisdom that all students should acquire. And professional educators perennially devise new methodologies to transmit this wisdom. Their lack of success has not discouraged them from trying, again and again.

It seems strange that those who urge imparting knowledge to children have not undertaken systematic inquiry into the question of whether their goals are achievable. They simply assume that they are. *But we must question that assumption, since it is contrary to our experience.* Is there research to support the assumption that children can acquire and remember large amounts of information that was selected for them by others? Without such evidence, we should abandon that assumption—and along with it, the dominating school aim of imparting large bodies of knowledge to the young.

The target of our inquiry is the available research on the acquisition and retention of the kind of information found in ordinary school subjects. Like U.S. history, for example, or biology. Or the grammar and vocabulary of a foreign language, or the procedures of algebra.

What's most striking about this research is its scarcity. It's easy to find out what people retain when they study nonsense syllables or random sentences. There are lots of studies of people's recall of television ads and weather reports. But there are hardly any controlled studies of what people retain—a year later, or five or ten years later—from the subjects they took in school. There are studies that show how one technique of teaching math leads to better retention (on final exams) than another technique.[5] There are studies that show how material that's carefully organized is retained better (surprise!) than material that isn't.[6] And there are lots of studies of how particular instructional techniques can facilitate retention.[7]

But when one consults such volumes as *Fundamentals of Learning and Memory*,[8] or *Learning and Memory: An Introduction*,[9] one finds no discussion whatever of the retention of school subjects. These texts deal exhaustively with the recall of nonsense syllables, phrases, and even whole sentences. Educational psychologist Lee Cronbach writes, "Remarkably few controlled studies have measured the retention of school learning."[10] Little wonder that an article appeared in *Educational Researcher* entitled, "Enduring Effects of Schooling—A Neglected Area in Educational Research."[11]

An examination of several leading research journals in education over a recent five-year period yields similar results: not a single issue included a study of the retention of school subjects.[12] Despite this apparent lack of evidence, some writers are willing to say that "contrary to popular belief, students retain much of the knowledge taught in the classroom," and "although forgetting does occur, the amount lost is not as great as expected by popular belief."[13]

The above conclusions were based on an exhaustive search of the research literature, going at least as far back as 1930, on the retention of school learning. The investigators managed to identify ninety-six relevant research studies, although only thirty of them investigated the retention of knowledge for a period of a year or more. Of these thirty studies, *only two* focused on what we are concerned with here: courses in school below the college level.

It is staggering to consider that in a period of more than sixty years, only two studies could be found that tried to measure how much knowledge had been retained from courses taken in the public schools. And the evidence from those two studies was inconclusive. We might conclude, therefore, that the study of how much people remember from the courses they took at school is not a very hot topic among educational researchers. But the serious question is, *why* doesn't anybody investigate this? Is the issue so unimportant? That doesn't seem right, in the light of all the effort spent to get children to acquire and retain knowledge.

Do researchers neglect to study subject matter retention because students do in fact retain what they acquire? We've already seen that this is contrary to our experience. Since the aim is to discover how much is remembered *well after* instruction is over, a longitudinal study is called for, and such studies are inconvenient, time-consuming, and costly. A younger scholar whose advancement depended on the frequency of her publication might find her career jeopardized by research that took several years to complete. But established, tenured professors would be in no such danger.

Whatever the reasons, no substantial body of research exists to contradict the experienced-based claim that the vast majority of students in schools, including most of those who do very well, forget the bulk of the subject matter knowledge they were able to retain long enough to pass end-of-semester examinations. That there is little research available to either confirm or deny this claim is an indictment of the research community in education. Ulric Neisser wrote, "It is difficult to find even a single study, ancient or modern, of what is retained from academic instruction. Given our expertise and the way we earn our livings, this omission can only be described as scandalous."[14] Given what schools do, day in and day out, it seems incredible that there should be no clear evidence available to give anyone confidence that it's worth doing.

In the meantime, we find no reason to believe that the effort to impart knowledge produces any permanent result. Of course, we *do* remember some things from our school days. What our favorite teachers were like; who our friends and enemies were; how we could turn in our homework without actually doing it; and so on. But we don't remember the route or the cargo of the triangular trade; or the third law of thermodynamics; or the difference between a gerund and a participle; or how to factor an equation. Some of us do remember that there *was* something called a triangular trade and that there *is* a third law of thermodynamics. But it isn't clear whether those vague recollections serve any useful purpose.[15] Nor is it clear that it was worth spending all that time and effort in school just to accumulate vague recollections. Why is it that we recall so little?

Could it be that we're not smart enough to do any better? Or that we haven't tried hard enough? But if we weren't smart enough then, our children aren't likely to be smart enough now. And if we haven't tried hard enough, there aren't any new motivational techniques that haven't already been tried. So if either or both of these explanations should be correct, they suggest no remedies for forgetting. Teachers will keep on offering knowledge, and children will keep on forgetting it, once the exams are over.

A more likely explanation for our failure to retain subject matter knowledge is the fact that it just doesn't suit our purposes. The highly organized and very abstract studies of schools never did suit the purposes of children. But they were learned, anyhow, because children were warned about what would happen to them if they didn't learn. So they listened to their teachers, studied their texts, and crammed for exams. Most succeeded and went on to other teachers, other texts, and more exams. Even so, teachers at every level, from grade school through college, complain that the students they get when school starts in September are deplorably "unprepared." So what happened to the knowledge that enabled these young scholars to pass their exams, yet forget it the next semester?

Fans of cognitive psychology are likely to say that nothing at all happened to the knowledge: it's still there, in memory, waiting to be retrieved.[16] But that's just metaphysical speculation, because until the material is recalled, there's no way of getting evidence that it's "still there." And once it's been recalled, the claim that it had *been* there, all the time, is just an inference —not a testable claim about the contents of people's minds. In point of fact, there isn't any "there" in which knowledge could comfortably reside; a metaphorical warehouse has no space at all. For the moment, we only need to see why students tend to forget most of the information parceled out to them in school. When that's understood, we'll be able to see more clearly what sorts of activities and aims would be *worth* pursuing in schools.

If we find it hard to explain why we forget so much,[17] it's helpful to recall that we also remember a lot. Ordinarily, we remember our birth date, the telephone numbers of our friends, where we keep (most of) our tools, and what time the bus stops at the corner. We remember complex things, too. For instance, that grandpa is allergic to the dog, that the milk shouldn't be allowed to boil, and that what you paid the babysitter counts as a deductible expense if the sitter was required in order for you to go to work. Why do we remember such matters?

We're not seeking insight into the "mechanisms" of remembering: for the body parts that might be involved. But we are looking for an explanation that will help us to predict when other things will be remembered, and when they're likely to be forgotten. If the explanation is any good, it will help us understand the conditions that facilitate (or inhibit) remembering. This kind of explanation will be useful to educators, whose business it is to predict, explain, and arrange optimal conditions for the achievement of aims. Psychological or neurological explanations that refer to body parts—brain cells, neurons, chemical changes and electrical discharges—are not going to be much help, even if they are plausible. For when it comes to teaching, our focus is on interactions among persons. For obvious reasons, we're not going to fool around with their body parts.

Now we can ask, what have all these examples of remembering got in common? What is it about our birth date, the location of our tools, and the deductibility of the cost of the babysitter that makes them all memorable? To put it simply, we can't get what we want *unless* we recall those things. What they have in common (for us, but no one else) is their instrumentality for achieving purposes that are recurrent or important to us.

We are asked to write our birth date nearly every time we fill out a government or an employee form, and the recollection of our birth date controls our expectations about when we'll receive congratulations or gifts. To forget the date would result in a lot of inconvenience and would terminate some pleasurable anticipations. Because we use it often, our birth date becomes a verbal habit, and the same may be said of many of the phone numbers we know by heart. Our recollection of grandpa's allergy to dogs is not a verbal habit like "288-2205," but we consider it important that grandpa be comfortable in our home. Thus the memory suits our purpose and leads to putting Napoleon outdoors and running the vacuum over the furniture.

Knowing why we remember helps us understand why we forget. We remember our own birth dates, but we forget the birthday of almost everyone else. Sometimes this is embarrassing. But our purpose in remembering another's birth date—to offer congratulations—is a thin one. Most of us try to remember the birth dates of a few people who are important to us. For the same reason we remember the phone numbers of close friends, or people we call frequently. And we forget the numbers of those with whom we interact but little. And why not? We can always look them up.

We remember where we keep our tools, but we often forget where we put a tool we borrowed. We remember grandpa is allergic to dogs, but we forget what other allergies he has. Our purpose was to make grandpa comfortable, and we can put Napoleon outside. But we aren't in a position to do other things that might ease grandpa's other allergies. Now, you may have a dour, irascible grandpa whose visits you dread. He's allergic to dogs, too, but your family doesn't put much effort into making him comfortable. They usually forget about his allergies, leave the dog indoors, and remember his allergies only after grandpa begins sneezing and complaining about the dog. We remember that the sitter's expense is deductible, but we don't remember the exact number beyond which further deductions cannot be taken. The former, remembered fact enables us to gather appropriate information for our tax return. The latter, unremembered fact is one that changes yearly. There's no point in remembering it.

There are exceptions. Sometimes we're amused to have remembered some bit of trivia that's of no conceivable use to us. At other times we're mortified to have forgotten something vitally important. We are curious, inconsistent, and imperfect creatures. But we manage to survive in our complicated world because most of the time we remember what we need to remember in order to achieve our purposes, and we forget what no longer serves our purposes. That's part of the biology of survival. It's true of other animals as well as ourselves, although the term "habit" describes their behavior better than the term "remembering."

Now it should be clear why students forget the subject matter they learned in school. Once, they *had* a purpose for remembering it: an examination was imminent. After the exam was over, there was no longer any purpose for retaining the material.

Adults invent purposes in hopes of encouraging students to remember what they learned. They say, "You'll need it to do well in college." But this makes no impact on those who aren't going to college, and it's only half-believed by those who are. Or they say, "You'll need it to get a job," or "to be a good citizen," or "to enjoy your leisure in a worthwhile way," and so on. But students cannot understand how school knowledge could conceivably fulfil those purposes. It hasn't done so yet; why should it in the future? And so the knowledge disappears. For many, this happens as soon as the exam is over. For others, it takes a little longer.

Children will not *have* a purpose just because an adult assigned it to them. We remember what suits our purposes, but we don't remember what might suit the purposes that others assigned to us. When people devise curriculums for schools, they usually have in mind what the curriculum has always looked like. When they consider changing the curriculum, they try to imagine what might be important for people to know. They seldom consider the purposes that children have, or that they might be capable of developing with the guidance of teachers.

Once the curriculum is determined, other educational specialists set out to discover what might motivate students to learn it. They explore teaching strategies, interpersonal communication techniques, cooperative and competitive group methods, technological facilitation devices and, of course, rewards, bribes, threats, and punishments. Eventually, there is the exam. And after all that, the students forget it.

All that preparation, all that effort. All those hours, all that expense. And then the children forget it. This is the fate of knowledge that's imparted to the young. Students forget it because they have no purpose for retaining it.

What can be done about this? It would be easy to say, "impart knowledge that suits the purposes of children." But it wouldn't be easy to do. Children have wishes and desires, but they don't always have purposes. Furthermore, the school can't impart the knowledge that would help young people fulfill some of their purposes, like getting a job, and the school ought not to impart the knowledge that would help them fulfill other purposes, like buying and selling drugs. The relation of people's purposes to what they learn can't sensibly be ignored in a program of education, but it would be simpleminded to think that *all* the school needs to do is impart information that suits whatever purposes children have.

The problem, of course, lies in the school's aim to impart knowledge. *That's* the aim that controls the activities of schooling, and that's the aim that, when translated into curriculum and methods, produces the knowledge that everyone forgets. We can't conclude that schools should simply stop imparting knowledge, since there can't be any education without it. But my point has been to show that education becomes trivial and ineffective when the imparting of organized bodies of subject matter knowledge becomes the central aim of the activities of schooling. So we must ask, what activities other than imparting knowledge would it make sense for schools to pursue, and what other sorts of aims should guide those activities?

Attitudes and Skills As Educational Aims

Nobody's neutral about how they spend their time. Children have feelings about the time they spend in school, and they acquire attitudes about it. But the school is largely responsible for those attitudes, since those who acquire them are seldom active participants in the process of their formation. It's just something that happens *to* them. Unbidden and unannounced, attitudes shape our values and our dispositions, and we are often the last to realize that we even have them.

It takes a great deal of thought and effort to understand our attitudes, but acquiring them in the first place is not a thoughtful, rational process. For this reason, the fostering of attitudes is not an appropriate aim for education, although it *is* the focus of socialization. But we already saw (in Chapter 1) that schooling in a democratic society cannot risk making socialization its primary goal.

In the course of an education, attitudes will surely be formed, because socialization occurs whenever education is going on (processes that can be kept separate for purposes of analysis cannot be kept separate in the real world). When people are being educated they are necessarily becoming socialized to the practices and the values of the group within which their education is occurring. The formation of attitudes depends on nonrational and nonvoluntary factors that must be taken very seriously by educators. But they are not what an education aims at.

By way of contrast, the development of skills is not subject to the reservations we hold about attitudes. Skills can be acquired only with the voluntary participation of the learner, and it ordinarily takes some thought, or at least perseverance and attention, to acquire a skill. Attitudes can be acquired without a learner's realizing what's happening to him, but the case is different with skills. To be acquired at all, they must be practiced, and practice requires a learner's intentional cooperation. Since learners can see the role played by their own efforts in the acquisition of a skill, it is an activity appropriate to education.

Growing children need to learn plenty of skills, and a lot of them can be learned in school. But to acquire a skill, a learner must *want* to acquire it. In schools, many skills are taught that learners don't want to acquire. The result is often years of headaches for teachers, for children, and for parents.

You may have learned long division quickly, but lots of other students weren't so lucky. It took me two and a half years to learn it. I was miserable the whole time, my teachers were irritated, and my parents were humiliated. It was hard enough to divide with single digits, but when larger numbers were introduced, I balked. Besides being terribly hard, it seemed quite pointless to me. I couldn't imagine that I'd ever need to do long division, so why was I being put through this torture just to achieve something useless? On good days, I struggled manfully but lost track of what I was doing, and I fell into error. On bad days I talked back to the teacher and wound up sitting in the hall, or in the classroom after school.

I don't think my experience learning long division was that unique. But the irony is that long division isn't really that hard. If an adult who could count had to learn long division, how long would it take? Not two years, I'll bet, or even two weeks. What a pity to waste all that time struggling with an unwanted skill in school, and learn a number of bad attitudes besides! While some people don't mind wasting children's time (they are the same ones who lack respect for children as persons), they might blanch to see what it costs taxpayers to waste so much of the teacher's time trying to teach skills students don't want to learn.

By way of contrast, consider a skill that's difficult to learn: riding a bicycle. While it must be a hundred times harder (and more risky) to ride a bike than do long division, most children learn it a lot faster than long division. But children don't wonder what the point of riding a bike is. Their friends do it, especially the older ones. And they look like they're having a good time. If you want to be where they are and go where they go, you've got to ride a bike. So children are eager to learn. They try over and over and they survive falls, embarrassment, and bruises. Some children become better riders than others, of course, but the point is that virtually all children learn to ride bikes without formal lessons, without being graded, urged, or threatened, and with a minimum of mental anguish. They acquire the skill because (like long division) it's within everybody's reach, and because (unlike long division) they want to acquire it.

The skills offered by schools are usually more abstract than bicycle riding, and a lot less attractive. If children have no interest in learning those skills, the school cannot *make* them. For no human being, child or adult, can persist very long at a task that is abstract, seemingly pointless, and difficult to do. Take reading, for example. The parents of some first graders have been reading stories to them for years, but others in the same class have never had a story read to them. Other things being equal, those in the former group respond far more quickly and successfully to reading instruction than those in the latter group. Children who are accustomed to listening to stories and who enjoy them *know* what reading is for, and they know what they'll be able to do once they learn to read. They have strong reasons for wanting to read.

If we are to succeed in teaching skills, learners must want to acquire them. Schools have traditionally used extrinsic reinforcers to teach skills—rewards such as good grades, honor rolls and deans' lists, and punishments such as bad grades, humiliation, and loss of eligibility for after-class activities. The result for countless children has been years of wasted time, resentment and apathy toward school studies and, most ironic of all, the development of thoughtless, mechanical, low-grade skills. People are astonished at the number of illiterates and poor readers produced by schools. They tend to blame children (not trying hard enough) and teachers (poorly trained and willing to accept what's mediocre). But the real culprits are reading materials that *no one* would read unless they were forced to, and a system that relies on extrinsic rewards. For regardless of what the reward is, it cannot make the activity of reading interesting—that is, make the experience of reading a high-quality one. Lacking that, the pupil can only go through the motions.

Why would anyone want to acquire a skill, especially if it were difficult? There's no mystery here. We're willing to do it if the act of practicing it—even as a clumsy beginner—is itself pleasant. And we're willing to practice if we can clearly see how learning the skill will help us achieve other things we want. Practice that is enjoyable falls under the heading of intrinsically valuable experience; in the first chapter it was called high-quality experience. When we can see how a skill will get us other things we want, practicing to learn it becomes an instrumentally valuable experience.

Because they understand its instrumental value, children struggle to master bicycle riding, even at the cost of pain or embarrassment. People who want to write, or who are aiming at certain kinds of jobs, will practice at the keyboard of a word processor even though it's dull work. And people whose schedules don't allow them to watch their favorite television shows learn the skill of programming a video cassette recorder. It's not as risky as learning to ride a bike, or as boring as learning to type, but for many people it has its own unique sorts of frustrations that make it an off-putting experience.

Teachers hope that students will dutifully practice the skills involved in reading and math for similar instrumental reasons: "You need to be able to do this," they say, "so you'll be able to get this, or do that . . ." But what seems obviously instrumental to teachers is often opaque to children. They're too young to see the connection, and all *they* experience is boredom or frustration. That's why teachers need to arrange for students to have high-quality experiences when skills are being taught. Otherwise they'd be well advised to abandon at least temporarily the teaching of those skills.

A lot of people, children as well as adults, enjoy reading, writing, and even math. Those who enjoy them tend to do them rather well. It's not hard to see what this implies for educational policy. If the school is to succeed in teaching these subjects, it must help learners to enjoy them. This is not an endorsement of permissive psychology or "soft pedagogy." It is confirmation of the importance of these school studies, and recognition of the fact that there is no other effective way to teach them.

A Defensible Aim for Education: Acquiring Dispositions

Once it's clear that the teaching of skills is a legitimate educational undertaking, you might wonder *which* skills should be taught? It's easy to make a list of worthwhile skills. There are the "basic" ones, of course: the three *R*'s. Then there are study skills, library skills, problem-solving skills. And there are subject-specific skills, like laboratory skills, inductive and deductive skills, bibliographical skills, speech skills. Not to mention interpersonal skills, like leadership skills, listening skills, negotiating skills.

Before the list gets overwhelming, and before we're tempted to think that a school curriculum could be based on the varied skills we'd like children to learn, we must note something common to all of them. Regardless of how they may be practiced, they are never exercised alone, in a "pure" form. When any of the above skills is exercised, it happens within a broader, more inclusive activity. The skill in question is only a contributing part. We can contrast this with a skill like tightrope walking, which can be exercised before an audience as a "pure" skill.

But we don't simply "read" in the sense of deciphering or decoding words on a page. We always confront written materials with an aim in mind, and we read in terms of fulfilling that aim. Confronted by a poem or a newspaper editorial, our aims determine whether we'll even start reading, and whether we'll continue to read once we've begun. We read the poem and the editorial in different ways. The poem, for meaning and intrinsic satisfaction; the editorial, critically and judgmentally. Reading isn't just the exercise of a skill, nor even the exercise of several skills. It's a complex human activity involving skills and dispositions, and it is governed by aims, intentions, attitudes and understandings. If reading were taught *simply* as a skill, you might enable a child to decipher words on a page. But if that's *all* the child could do, you wouldn't called him a "reader" unless you qualified what you meant.

The same could be said of all the other skills on our list. A person with "laboratory skills" or "leadership skills" has not mastered a single, simple technique, but has acquired a large number of related skills, not to mention attitudes and dispositions without which the skills would be useless. And just as the skill isn't exercised in a "pure" form, it's not learned in a simple, pure form, either. We saw earlier that the successful teaching of a skill demands either that the learner enjoy practicing it, or see the connection between having it and getting something else she wants. Now we see that most skills, unlike tightrope walking, are embedded in broader and more complex activities. To say that learners should understand the instrumental value of a skill, then, is to say that they must be directly aware of how it is embedded in a broader and more encompassing activity that they either enjoy or find useful.

This means that if we want to teach a child reading skills, piano playing skills, or math skills, we'd better be sure that she *enjoys* reading, piano playing, or math. And if she doesn't enjoy those activities, we'd better hope she finds them useful. In either case, we'd like the child to have a disposition to read, play the piano, and do math. For if the child lacks those dispositions, she can't effectively learn the skills embedded in them. This amounts to saying that educational aims must shift from the acquisition of knowledge and skills to the acquisition of the dispositions for which that knowledge and those skills are needed. Skills just can't be introduced into persons the way a pacemaker is surgically introduced into a human heart.

Let's pursue the example a little further. However useful it might be to teach children phonics or word lists, the children will not become readers unless they become disposed to read. This disposition can be acquired only if children enjoy reading or see some useful purpose in it. Since beginning readers at ages five and six have few purposes that could be served by the skill of reading, they'd better enjoy it. This sets a clear task for teachers: to cultivate in pupils a disposition to read by creating classroom conditions that enable them to enjoy it.

What a Disposition Is

Teaching skills is important, but it's not practical to express educational aims in terms of long lists of skills. We've also seen that educational aims can't sensibly or defensibly be conceived as the acquisition of knowledge or of attitudes. But it does make sense to speak of educational aims in terms of the sorts of dispositions we'd like young people to acquire. When those dispositions have been identified, we'll know what kinds of understandings and skills will be relevant to acquiring them. We'll also have some clues about the kinds of activities that will promote the learning we're after. Given the centrality of dispositions to educational aims,[18] we need to make clear just how we're using the term "disposition."

When a person is said to have a disposition of a certain sort, what's meant is that he can be expected to act in certain kinds of ways in certain settings. If we say Karen is careless (i.e., disposed to be careless), we mean that she might not straighten the sheets when she makes the bed; she might not even make the bed at all. She might omit the zip code on her letters, or even omit the city to which she's sending a letter. She might put too much oregano in her spaghetti sauce, or leave it out entirely. We could also speak of more limited dispositions. We might not call Karen a careless person, but speak only of her being a careless housekeeper. But in any event we refer to the way she does things.

Thus, to say one "has" a disposition is to use a metaphor. We don't have a disposition in the sense that we have red hair, or a Buick sedan. A disposition always refers to how we act, not to what we possess. This linguistic point has practical implications. If you "possessed" an unwanted disposition, getting rid of it might pose a real problem. But when a disposition is conceived as a way of acting, an undesirable disposition can be dealt with by acting differently. Dispositions can thus be distinguished from habits, which operate more automatically and are consequently more difficult to change.

If the distinction between a possession and a way of acting is still not clear, consider the fact that intelligence is a disposition and not something we possess. If it were a possession, our intelligence would be fixed at a certain level (perhaps indicated by a test score),[19] and it couldn't be increased or diminished. But if intelligence is conceived as a way of acting, we can imagine learning how to act more intelligently in many settings (even IQ scores are readily changed with instruction). This is important to educators, who aim to help students act more intelligently. This aim can be expressed as changing students' dispositions, which involves changing the way they act, not exchanging one "possession" for another.

The term "disposition" refers not to a particular act but rather to patterns of action, or to the probability of an act. To say that Patricia has a generous disposition is not to imply that she'll make a contribution to the United Fund. It means that she can be expected to make charitable contributions greater than those of someone whose disposition could not be described as generous. Speaking about a person's disposition is like speaking about a character trait.

Less regular and predictable than a habit, a disposition is open-ended, flexible. It can intensify, change, or disappear. But you can't know whether a person's disposition has changed until an occasion arises where it would be appropriate to exercise it.

Because dispositional terms refer to probabilities, they are often used to explain or predict people's actions. "Why did Max strike her?" "Because he's a short-tempered bully." "Will he deny that he did it?" "Probably not, because he's honest." How do we know these answers are accurate? We have reason to trust them if the speaker has observed the person about whom he is speaking on a number of relevant occasions in the past. In this instance, if the speaker had often seen Max lose his temper and bully others, and if he had observed Max telling the truth in a number of settings where it wasn't to his own advantage to do so, we'd have reason to trust his explanation and his prediction.

But if Max didn't tell the truth, it doesn't necessarily mean that the dispositional statement was incorrect. It may only mean that a reasonable prediction failed to materialize. Glass is correctly described as brittle, and we can confidently predict that it will shatter every time we strike it with a hammer. But human behavior, less consistent and more flexible, is less predictable. Because a person is honest is not a reason to believe that he'll tell the truth *every time* he is asked awkward and difficult questions. We deal with people more or less effectively because we get to know what they're like—that is, what their dispositions are. But people are not programmed, and only a person who is disposed to be foolish would act as if he always knew just what his friends (let alone strangers) would do next.

Dispositions As the Focus of School Activities

There are several reasons why it makes sense to conceive the aims of schooling in dispositional terms. To begin with, dispositional change (unlike the acquisition of large bodies of knowledge) is an aim that is achievable. We know that doing things in certain ways in a supportive environment increases the likelihood that things will be done in those ways in the future.

In the second place, dispositional change is readily testable. We can tell when a disposition is undergoing change by watching or listening to the students we know. Paper-and-pencil tests of dispositional change are notoriously hard to construct, but experienced teachers can tell at firsthand whether their students' dispositions are changing. (Ms. Jones is pleased that Sally listens to the suggestions of other students now; last fall Sally just did what she pleased and ignored what the others said. Ms. Jones thinks this change in Sally's disposition is more important than her being able to find Wyoming on a map of the United States.)

A disposition once acquired also lasts a long time. This contrasts sharply with formally organized knowledge, which doesn't last much beyond examination day. Thus if schooling aims at changing students' dispositions, it aims at something that is achievable, observable (over a period of time), and fairly stable.

There's another reason for conceiving the activities of schooling in dispositional terms: most people agree about many of the dispositions the young should acquire. This contrasts with the way people disagree about what knowledge to teach. Should anthropological, sociological, artistic, and psychological understandings be included in the subject of history? Or just political and military ones? And what history should be studied? The history of Europe? Of Athens? Or of Central and South America, Africa, or Asia?

Should algebra be required in high school? Or should it be replaced by statistics? Since it's hard to tell what other people's children need to know ten years from now, we usually end by having them study what we studied when we went to school. The fact that the curriculum is surprisingly similar to the curriculum of a century ago[20] suggests that the aim of transmitting knowledge has locked schools into a tradition of teaching obsolescent and irrelevant material. Thus the empirical question of *whether* children remember that material may be of less moment than the fact that it *doesn't matter* whether they remember it.[21]

Casting educational aims in terms of dispositions takes us beyond the traditional curriculum and the doubts expressed about its content. For when we speak of dispositions, many come to mind that most people would agree are worth acquiring. For example, few people would object to fostering thoughtfulness in students.[22] Without trying to define the term, we may suppose that thoughtfulness includes a tendency to avoid impulsive behavior in problematic situations, and to avoid repeating unsuccessful behavior. A thoughtful disposition would also include a tendency to "size up" a problematic situation before acting, a tendency to question the adequacy of information, a tendency to seek and accept help from a variety of sources, and a tendency to try out ideas imaginatively before acting on them. And thoughtful people try to correct for their own biases and recognize their own mistakes.

How would you teach a person to be thoughtful? This question will be explored in detail in the next few chapters, but some preliminary observations can be made now. Being thoughtful is not a disposition that's saved for special occasions, so it ought to be fostered in everything that's done in school. Thus the worth of any activity sponsored by the school can be judged according to its contribution to the development of a thoughtful disposition in students. If a classroom activity doesn't promote thought, we have a right to ask why the activity is being carried on at all.

The school promotes academic studies, but it's also a place where large numbers of people have to work in a very restricted space. For this and a lot of other reasons, the school has the obligation to foster in its students sensitivity to others.[23] Like being thoughtful, this kind of sensitivity involves a wide range of active tendencies. Since it includes listening to others and responding to what they say, it can't be fostered in classrooms where students aren't permitted to talk to one another (having to listen and respond *only* to the teacher is more likely to promote obedience than sensitivity). Among the many dimensions of sensitivity are the consideration of the consequences for others of what one says and does; the giving of help when another needs it, and inquiry into the kind of help that's needed; the recognition of one's own shortcomings and the acknowledgment of other peoples' responses to them.

Like the disposition to be thoughtful, the disposition to be sensitive to others is another criterion for judging the value of any school activity.[24] If what's happening in a classroom isn't developing students' sensitivity to others, it's probably promoting the opposite traits. For example, a student's recitation in class ordinarily promotes boredom and inattention (rather than thoughtfulness) in other students. But it also fosters envy when the recitation is successful, and disregard or even contempt when it is unsuccessful.[25] Thus when sensitivity is not under cultivation, its contraries often are.

Thoughtfulness and sensitivity are only two among many dispositions that people will readily agree are worth cultivating in schools.[26] Among the others are responsibility, thoroughness, persistence, single-mindedness, curiosity about the world, honesty, and loyalty. And people also agree about less profound traits that nonetheless smooth the way for everything we do: promptness, neatness, courtesy, and so on.

Dispositions that are worth cultivating cannot, like academic subjects, be parceled out and studied for discrete time periods during the school day. Traits of character can't be turned on at 9:40 in the morning and turned off at 10:35. Just as dispositions become a part of people's character, their exercise suffuses all the activities that take place in a school day. If dispositions like the ones mentioned above are cultivated, many young people will see the point of academic studies, and they'll pursue them with more care and enthusiasm than otherwise would have been possible. When these dispositions are absent, academic studies have to be imposed. Then students undertake them mechanically and often resentfully.

The sorts of dispositions worth cultivating in schools will render people more cognizant of the world, more receptive to it, and more able to deal effectively with the challenges it keeps presenting. These dispositions may be contrasted with others often acquired out of school, which they are intended to replace: capriciousness, stubbornness, carelessness, impatience, deviousness, selfishness, insensitivity to others. These latter dispositions isolate people from the world and from others, and render them ineffective in dealing with novelty. In contrast, dispositions worth promoting in schools enable learners to keep on learning, in school and after school is over.

We may not know exactly what knowledge the young should acquire, but if what they do in school develops the sorts of dispositions discussed here, we'll be able to trust them to make their own choices of what to learn about. This is another reason why educational activities are likely to make more sense if they aim at dispositional goals instead of the accumulation of knowledge. Organized knowledge remains, of course, the stock-in-trade of schools. But its acquisition doesn't compete with the learning of dispositions. Rather, the acquisition of knowledge, secondary to the fostering of dispositions, is guided by the sorts of dispositions we seek to cultivate.

Summary

Educational goals aren't worth aimimg at if they disappear soon after they are met, or if they can't be met at all. That's why the acquisition of knowledge has to be rejected as an educational goal. But educational goals should also enlist the intelligent and voluntary participation of learners, and that's why attitudes must be rejected as goals of schooling—even though they remain essential to socializing the young. And while many skills must be acquired in the course of an education, their selection depends on the dispositions to which they are expected to contribute.

Although American society has become racially, ethnically, and ideologically diverse, most of its citizens would agree about a large number of dispositions that would be worth cultivating in the young. For these reasons, and because aims need to be cast in terms that indicate the sorts of activities that will achieve them, it has been urged that educational goals be expressed in dispositional terms. This point was elaborated in a discussion of several particular kinds of dispositions worth cultivating in schools.

Now we're ready to examine how these dispositional goals can be achieved; that is, how we can arrange conditions to enable young people to acquire the dispositions we're aiming at. We'll see that educational methods are implied by the ways in which we conceive our aims, and qualified by our understanding of how learning occurs.

4 Educational Method I: The Primacy of the Aesthetic

Educational methods are usually treated as means to ends. We assume that human learning can be understood and controlled on the basis of direct cause-and-effect relationships. The effect is what we aim at; the cause will be our educational method.

But education cannot be explained in the simple cause-and-effect terms that work so well for billiard balls. People are not inert objects, simply to be manipulated. They are active centers of energy, participating and not simply reacting to the events happening around them. Insofar as education is more than socialization or the mere inculcation of habits, it's not something that can be done *to* learners. It demands that learners participate in their own learning. They have to *do* something.

This chapter will examine what people do when they learn. It's about educational method insofar as method is understood as the arrangement of the conditions for this doing. I will try to show that, in order to learn, the activity undertaken by learners must be felt as satisfying to them, and must also involve some form of thought. When experience has these features it is called aesthetic.

The term "aesthetic" is usually associated with the arts, but its reference is acknowledged to be wider than that. Our response to the beauty of nature is aesthetic. So is our response to a game well played. But aesthetic qualities characterize experiences even more varied than these. They are felt when we work effectively and productively on nonroutine tasks, and they are felt when curiosity and puzzlement is followed by understanding. This chapter and the next two will discuss what these varied sources of the aesthetic have in common, what the conditions are that enable aesthetic qualities to appear in experience, and how experience that is aesthetic in quality is associated with learning.

This chapter will examine the aesthetic in contexts that are familiar: in activities that are undertaken because we expect them to be fulfilling, satisfying. The fine arts typify such activities. But many other activities are pursued for the sake of their aesthetic satisfactions: preparing and eating meals, drinking fine wines, fishing and camping, playing games, and so on. In the next two chapters we'll examine activities that aren't usually pursued because of the aesthetic satisfactions they offer, but which offer them anyhow: work, when it isn't merely routine; the solving of problems wherever they may appear; the pursuit of curiosity when it's undertaken without regard to practical outcomes.

Aesthetic qualities that appear in this wide range of settings will be explored in relation to learning. We'll also examine how our understanding of these relationships can be put to practical use in schools. By "practical" I mean this: since learning (defined here as the acquisition of dispositions) is a consequence of experience that is aesthetic in quality, *we want to know how to establish, in schools and in classrooms, the conditions that will foster aesthetic quality in the experience of students.*

At the Heart of Learning: High-Quality Experience That Is Aesthetic

The aim of socialization is getting people to conform to the practices and values of the group. Education, on the other hand, focuses on individuals and on developing in them unique abilities, understandings, and dispositions. For this reason, educators have to be concerned with the quality of the experience of individual learners.

The kind of experience from which most of us typically learn is intrinsically valuable to us. When our experience is high in quality we're absorbed in it, whether it's a lecture or a camping trip; an evening with a lover, a good friend, or a book; or an afternoon preparing our rosebushes for winter. People can learn from bad experiences, too—from mistakes, from being bored, from being mistreated. We tend to put these experiences behind us as quickly as we can. When we do this, we don't learn much from them; in extreme cases this is called suppression. But when these bad experiences lead to learning, it's because we reflected on them afterward. The tendency to undertake this kind of reflection is a trait of character—a disposition—which is worth fostering in schools. But there's no reason to assume that it already exists in our students. That's why our first concern must be to create conditions that will help students have experiences of high quality.

But we've already seen that the high quality of an experience is no assurance that learning will take place. We enjoy popcorn or a warm bath, but we don't learn much from them. The reason for this is that the kind of learning we're after—the learning of dispositions, not habits or items of information—requires thought from the learner. When an experience is high in quality and *also* involves thought, it is aesthetic in quality.[1]

Eating popcorn and taking a warm bath are high-quality experiences, but it's the absence of thought that distinguishes them from the high-quality experiences of writing a letter or listening to Mozart. Without getting too picky about a definition for "thought," we can at least rule out activity that's capricious or random, or merely habitual or routine.

Capricious activity is relatively thoughtless—it involves no expectation of consequences. What happens, happens. The experience is shallow because it's cut off from the past and the future. It may be pleasant, but it has little depth; we would not call it aesthetic.

Routine or habitual activity, performed with a minimum of awareness, is hardly perceived as experience at all. We often cultivate habits (e.g., preparing and eating breakfast) just so we can give our attention to other things (e.g., reading the morning paper, planning the day's activities). Because habits call for neither thought nor even attention, they cannot be experienced aesthetically.

To say that thought is involved when experience is aesthetic is to say at least that the experience demands our attention; it's not incidental or routine. But because the forms of thought are varied, we mustn't confine ourselves to a narrow conception of it that's bound by traditional, language-oriented limitations.[2]

Thought doesn't always require the logical, discursive symbols characteristic of language or mathematics. Thought is expressed by an artist in the wielding of his brush, and in the physical adjustment of a basketball player when he tries to block a shot. It is undertaken by a teacher when she realizes that a discouraged student needs some sympathy rather than admonition. And it is involved in the shock of recognition felt by a reader who suddenly realizes it is her own experience about which the poet has written.[3] Thus while the sensitivity, anticipation, and effort involved in thought can occur symbolically *before* overt action, they can all occur nonsymbolically, too, as an indistinguishable component of action.

A skeptic may ask, "what makes you think that getting people to act *this* way will develop dispositions in them?" Well, there's no guarantee that it will. But this is where the process starts. Once children become willingly and thoughtfully active, they need support and encouragement so they'll continue to act that way.[4]

Persistence is needed because dispositions aren't learned all at once. Traits of character are acquired gradually, so certain ways of behaving must be repeated consistently and in a variety of settings. Since many youngsters tend to give up when things get sticky, some people urge that they simply be required (i.e., forced) to persist. With the right rewards and punishments, force does work, and habits are learned. But we're aiming at intelligent dispositions, not habits. That's harder, because the quality of the learner's experience is important. That's why support and encouragement (sometimes) works, and force doesn't. Force, threats, and bribes are used in the absence of education. There may be times when this is necessary. But it's important to know what we're getting and what we're giving up.

Now we're ready to explore how various kinds of thinking are initiated. The sections that follow will show the close association of thinking with the aesthetic, and the association of the aesthetic with learning. The import of all this for schooling will be discussed in the last section.

An Overview of Thinking and the Aesthetic

We have discarded the fiction of the learner as a passive receptacle for knowledge, storing it in memory like a squirrel stores nuts. We aim to treat our students as active individuals, responsive to their social group yet growing in power to make discriminating judgments. For this growth to occur, they need to act thoughtfully in ways that are characteristic of experience when it's aesthetic. We'll begin by surveying what initiates this kind of thoughtful activity.

First, let's recall what won't initiate thought. My third-grade teacher used to tell us, "Put on your thinking caps." This advice never did much good. What would you *do* to put on a thinking cap? What *is* a thinking cap? Teachers with less grace or less patience simply tell their students, "Think!" That doesn't work either. But there are plenty of occasions when people do think. What are those occasions?

To begin with, there must be something to think *about*. Taking a warm bath can be relaxing; it can free us to think about many things. But we don't think about the bath itself. A bath, like a bowl of popcorn, doesn't give us much to think about. We may be given a great deal of information about, say, the political strategies that resulted in the election of President William McKinley. But most people won't think about that, either—and for the same reason that schoolchildren fail to think about most of the things their teachers tell them. There is a flood of information, but there doesn't seem to be anything to think *about*. We haven't the foggiest notion of what to *do* with the information. At least the bath and the popcorn were experienced with satisfaction.

What *do* we think about? Broadly speaking, two different sorts of occasions trigger our thinking. First, there are times when we consider things that we want, or things that are simply pleasant to think about. This sort of thinking is not a response to what's around us. It's self-generated, in the sense that it is developed from our past experiences. It often takes the form of fantasy, daydream, and reminiscence. Life would be impoverished without this kind of thinking, but we won't pursue it any further here. Schools have no obligation to deal with these thoughts, and it would be intrusive of them to try.

Another kind of self-generated thinking is the development of purposes and plans. The distinction between a fantasy and a plan is not a sharp one. Some of our fantasies turn into plans, while some of our plans may be little more than fantasies. But unlike fantasies, purposes and plans are intended to be acted on. Making a plan, no less than acting on it, involves dealing with obstacles to its achievement. And when obstacles come to our attention, we encounter the second sort of occasion for thinking: the appearance, in the course of our planning or in the world around us, of something we didn't anticipate—of a discrepancy from what we expected.

Some discrepancies appear in the course of our goal-seeking activities; they may trigger problem-solving behavior. When we aren't practically occupied, the appearance of a discrepancy in our surroundings may prompt us to look into it further—that is, to pursue our curiosity about it. Or we may attend to it more fully just for the satisfaction it yields. This renders experience dominantly aesthetic. But whatever the conditions are for its appearance, a discrepancy attracts our attention.[5] We can always ignore it and carry on with whatever we were doing (which in some situations might be disastrous). Or we can stop what we're doing and do something else. But if we try to resolve the discrepancy we'll be embarked on a course of thinking.

Because the learning we aim at demands thought, it's not enough to offer learners activities or presentations that provide them experiences of high quality. What we offer must also depart in some way from what the learners expected. This discrepancy will give them something to think about and something to do. The doing involves resolving the discrepancy. The attractiveness or the perceived importance of the situation will make it worth resolving. And because anything contrary to what we expected defeats our attempts to act habitually, it can provoke an effort to act thoughtfully.

Up to this point I've used the term "discrepancy" in a general and abstract way. Now let's look at some examples of discrepancies to see what they're like and how they typically develop in experience.

Our habitual ways of seeing things, hearing things, and doing things all work pretty well when the world meets our expectations. Our habits work when conditions are fairly constant. But a discrepancy from what we expect thwarts our habits. When that happens, we feel it. Sometimes with mild surprise or slight irritation, at other times, with considerable shock. For example, when you drive to work you expect the driver behind you to keep a safe distance. If you are struck hard from behind, the discrepancy from what you expected and the consequent interruption of your habits is felt quite strongly. At a restaurant, you expect to be served what you order from the menu. When the waiter says, "We're out of the apple pie," your disappointment is only mild. There are other desserts to choose from.

The feeling aroused by a discrepancy might trigger an emotional outburst. Or it might just go away after a while. But it can prompt us to think. When it does, here's how it works. Imagine shopping for a shirt or a blouse, and eventually finding one you like. The style suits you and so does the color and the pattern. Pleased, you pick it off the shelf, but you find the cuff buttons dangling, about to fall off. You don't expect to find this in a new shirt, so you've confronted a discrepancy from what you expected.

Disappointed, you *might* just sigh and put the shirt back, hoping to get luckier next time. But you might instead say to yourself, "I like this shirt. Is this defect so bad? It wouldn't be much trouble to sew the buttons back on. Besides, I might get the shirt at a reduced price."

The example reminds us that the detection of a discrepancy doesn't require us to think about it or do anything about it. But the discrepancy is *what* we think about, if we do any thinking at all. The example also illustrates the relation between the attractiveness of a situation and the likelihood of thoughtful action. Imagine picking up the shirt, frowning, and saying to yourself, "The color isn't very attractive, but I don't mind the style . . ." and *then* discovering the defect. Right back on the shelf it goes, and we continue searching. Only if we think the shirt is attractive are we likely to deal with the discrepancy.

Our discovery of a defect in the shirt is a discrepancy within a practical activity. A purpose has temporarily been blocked. We can either give up the goal or deal with the situation in some way. The latter option is often called problem-solving.

The resolution of discrepancies ordinarily affords aesthetic quality to experience and results in learning. We resolve discrepancies by engaging in one of three broad types of activities, depending on the type of discrepancy encountered. If you run into an obstacle on the way to your goal, like the dangling button on the shirt, you may try to overcome the obstacle in the interest of achieving the goal. This is usually called problem-solving.

When you are at leisure, you often explore your surroundings (which is what people do on holidays). When something unusual—that is, unexpected—catches your attention, you may seek to understand it more fully, without necessarily doing anything about it. This is recognized as the pursuit of curiosity. It occurs when a person works on a puzzle, when a traveler reads an inscription in an old cathedral, when an astronomer wonders about the origin of galaxies.

Finally, when your attention is caught by something unusually lovely or attractive, you attend to it more fully in order to see it or hear it more clearly, as a unified and meaningful whole. Experience then is dominantly aesthetic in character. The aesthetic appears in the experience of all three of these types of discrepancy situations, but we're less aware of it when we're trying to solve a problem or satisfy our curiosity.

The activity initiated by these situations is aimed at resolving the discrepancy that was encountered. The resolution can occur quickly, utilizing intuitive and unverbalized understandings, as it does when we discover a pattern in a new piece of music. Or it can take years and call for the accumulation of data, sophisticated hypothesizing, and the planning and execution of elaborate tests—as it did when Copernicus worked out, mathematically, Tycho Brahe's telescopic observations. In every instance, a person's experience is aesthetic in quality because she is willingly *engaged* in it, and because the outcome is dependent on her own thoughtful effort. But a person's attention in such situations is not on the quality of her experience. It is on the matter at hand. Ordinarily we judge the quality of our experience retrospectively—after it happened, when we look back on it.

In sum, we begin with a situation attractive to learners that offers something discrepant from what they expected. Then we encourage them to resolve the discrepancy through their own efforts. Now we'll see if we can recognize what these conditions would look like in familiar settings, in order to understand why they contribute to learning. Although experience can be aesthetic when we try to resolve discrepancies of any type, the remainder of this chapter will deal with situations that are dominantly aesthetic. This will allow us to see more clearly the conditions that result in the aesthetic. When those conditions are understood, we'll be able to see in the next two chapters how the aesthetic appears in experiences where other concerns dominate, as in problem-solving and the pursuit of curiosity.

Conditions of the Aesthetic As the Conditions of Learning

When we understand what it is that enables experience to become aesthetic, we'll be able to foster it deliberately. The arts are particularly effective ways of engendering aesthetic qualities in experience, although we can't be sure which arts will appeal to which people. But art isn't the only way, for the aesthetic embraces more than the arts. So we'll begin by examining some everyday kinds of activity that foster aesthetic quality but have little to do with art.

Dinner at the Walker residence is usually served around six. The menu depends on what the local market has on sale. During the week, the Walkers are usually tired out from work. Television accompanies the meal as often as conversation. The Walkers tire of this routine, and on the weekend Ms. Walker introduces some variations. On Saturday she tells her husband, "I'm cooking a steak with a bearnaise sauce. Let's eat at eight tonight." For a change, Mr. Walker looks forward to dinner; he decides to take a shower and put on a clean shirt. In the extra time before dinner he goes to the store for a bottle of wine. He makes the wait more pleasant by preparing an appetizer. In these ways the Walkers interrupt and alter many of their habits: dress, mealtime, manners, and the menu. They enjoy the prospect of the meal as well as the meal itself.

Dinner for the Walkers on Saturday was a deliberate disruption of their habits and normal expectations. Disruptions often produce irritation, but not in this case. First, the couple's eating habits were not *just* interrupted. They *chose* to interrupt them. Because the discrepancy was of their own making, they were in control of the situation. Second, their goal (dinner) was not abandoned: the discrepancies they created were all resolved. Dinner was not canceled; it was only delayed and presented in a new form. The delay was experienced as pleasant anticipation, not frustration.

The Walkers' experience on Saturday evening was aesthetic in quality. What they did was intrinsically enjoyable, and the way they felt about it resulted from conditions that are akin to what is called artistic form. That is, the conditions of the Walkers' Saturday evening dinner were similar to the conditions that are present when people confront music or painting.

The satisfaction in playing games is also dominantly aesthetic. It's nice to win, but if satisfaction depended on winning, people wouldn't play. We enjoy games even when we lose. Vince Lombardi's famous dictum, "Winning isn't everything; it's the only thing," refers to people who play for money. But what's aesthetic about playing a game?

Let's take chess as an example. There is a set of rules followed by each player, and games develop according to more or less standard beginnings ("openings"). The conclusion ("endgame") also unfolds within standard patterns. Like a genre of art, chess has its forms, and every game constitutes a set of variations on that form. The experienced player is familiar with many different openings, midgames, and endgames. This player may also be familiar with her opponent's repertoire of moves. Thus the chess player enters a game with a set of expectations so vast she could never put them all into words.[6]

But no two games are ever alike. People play chess because what they expect never happens *just* as they expected it. They are always being surprised. If they were not, they would either find different people to play with, or they'd quit playing the game. Thus at the heart of chess (and of most games) is discrepancy: a strategy that throws us off balance, a move we didn't expect. The distinctive pleasure of chess is in devising strategies and moves that will surprise your opponent, and in solving the problems that arise when he has surprised you. New knowledge about chess is acquired in every game, but that's not why people play. And while problems are solved in playing, they aren't "real" problems, but only the puzzles involved in the mastery of sixty-four squares on a board. Thus the distinctive pleasure of chess (aside from the gratification to one's ego in beating a good player) is aesthetic. Like dinner for the Walkers, chess offers satisfactions parallel to those offered by art and music.

The satisfaction of watching a game is in some ways similar to playing it. There are of course many different ways of watching a game, including passive ones where the spectator treats the game as background for his own conversation, only occasionally noting the score. But let's consider what happens when an avid fan watches a football game.

In accordance with a set of rules, football presents a series of events ("plays") punctuated by intervals during which subsequent events are planned. Each interval allows a spectator to develop expectations about the next play. Those expectations are based not only on the rules of the game, but on the score, the time remaining in the game, the particular personnel on the field, ad infinitum. When the play begins, it may surprise the spectator—that is, it may in some respects be discrepant from what he expected. As the play develops, he watches with new expectations, and these are more or less fulfilled, or not fulfilled, as the play is carried to its conclusion. Thus attending to the game is full of anticipation, which we occasionally articulate to our companions. Despite our anticipation, we are frequently surprised, although seldom shocked (as we would be if a defensive player were to fire a weapon at the football in midflight).

The spectator's surprise at an unexpected play (third down and a yard to go, and the quarterback throws the football downfield!) is resolved with a feeling of satisfaction or dissatisfaction, depending on the outcome of the play. The spectator hopes that one team will defeat the other, but his enjoyment doesn't depend on the final score, any more than the reader's enjoyment is dependent on the mystery's last page. The pleasure in watching a football game is therefore dominantly aesthetic, for it exemplifies a high quality experience that is permeated by thinking. An avid football fan has a lot more in common with a dedicated patron of ballet, although neither one is likely to admit it (this comparison can be made without even mentioning how fans appreciate the graceful skills of professional players like Jerry Rice, Michael Jordan, or Wayne Gretzky).

When we turn to the arts, the exemplars of the aesthetic, we'll find that the way they arouse feeling is similar to the examples just examined: they present us with discrepancies from what we expect.[7] But unlike everyday events, and more like the Walker's dinner at eight, the arts allow us to resolve the discrepancies that they create. That accounts for their appeal. But in what ways do the arts offer us discrepancies? And how are they resolved?

All artists arrange materials—paint, words, sounds—in special ways. When the arrangement refers to things outside the work itself—that is, beyond the frame of the picture, or outside the theater—the art is called "referential." A painting of Henry VIII and a ballad about a faithless lover are referential works of art. We can learn something about Henry VIII and his times by examining the painting; the ballad refers to people and events like ones we may have experienced.

When an arrangement of sounds or colors makes no such outside reference, as in instrumental music, some decorative art, and some paintings, the art is called "abstract." The impact of abstract art is wholly dependent on a person's response to the arrangement, or pattern, of sounds, colors, shapes, and so on—that is, to what is called the *form* of a work of art. References to things in the world cannot be discovered in all works of art, but form is always present in art. Similarly, form is perceived whenever experience is aesthetic. What made the Walker's dinner aesthetic for them, beyond the flavors and textures of the food itself, was its form: its timing, the succession of courses, the presentation of the food. Chess games and football games are also based on formal structures, and the satisfactions they afford depend on the ways in which form is realized in the events themselves. When we see how form achieves its impact, we'll understand how experience becomes aesthetic. And we'll see how conditions of learning can be established.

The form of a referential work of art has an impact on feeling, and so does its *content*—that is, its reference to recognizable things and ideas. The stained glass in a cathedral window may thrill a viewer because of its rich colors and the ordered intricacy of its shapes. But if this pattern of colored glass *also* depicts people and events that have moral and spiritual significance for the viewer, then that too has an impact. In this case, the form of the art has enriched and deepened its content. Its referential and abstract qualities reinforce one another.

The impact of content in referential art needs no special explanation. We ordinarily feel strongly about references to what we care about. But why are we so absorbed by abstract arrangements of sounds or colors? Why are we strongly moved by things that don't refer to anything at all?

Most of the time, we're not moved. We hardly notice the wallpaper, which typically is an abstract arrangement of colors, repeated endlessly. To see a little of it is to know what the rest is like. Perception of wallpaper is habitual, and that's why we put in on the wall. We don't want it to arouse feeling, because a wall is *supposed* to be an unobtrusive background to whatever is in front of it. The same can be said about the patterns of sounds softly piped into restaurants, airports, and dentists' offices. They too are intended to be an unobtrusive and harmonious background. So when a pattern is quite regular—that is, when it has few variations and no surprises—we quickly become familiar with it and then no longer notice it. We don't have much feeling about it, one way or another.

What do Bach and the Beatles, Debussy and Dire Straits *have* that Muzak lacks? Why is it that the patterns of sound at a concert arouse feelings that are pleasant and sometimes intense? The patterns in Muzak and in a great deal of popular music are so regular that we know just what to expect as the music unfolds. We can take it for granted. But in the concert, the patterns are different. The musicians (or the composer) present patterns that are infinitely varied: they keep surprising us. A pattern always triggers expectations, but concert musicians keep presenting us with discrepancies—with a melodic variation, a change in instrumentation, an unexpected dissonance, a new emphasis in the rhythm. Like the Walker's dinner and a chess game, music can present discrepancies that thwart our habits of perception. Yet the same music allows us to resolve those discrepancies if we continue to attend to it. This is to say that an experience we regard as aesthetic in quality is never simply a matter of encountering something that is "inherently" artistic or beautiful. The felt quality is, rather, a function of *how* people with certain histories *interact* with the objects of their attention.[8]

The resolution of discrepancies calls for forms of thought that round out an experience and make it aesthetic. This thought also makes the experience a potentially educative one. Without thought there is only feeling—mild or strong, pleasant or irritating. In everyday settings feeling is seldom resolved. It dissipates as one event is replaced by another, for the things that arouse feeling seldom allow us to resolve it. The shock of being struck from behind in traffic gradually diminishes and is forgotten as we concentrate on what we'll do if we arrive late to work. The disappointment at missing the apple pie disappears as we look over the menu for another selection.

Thus the daily histories of our feelings differ from the development of feeling when experience is aesthetic. In the latter case, the same stimulus that was perceived as discrepant *remains focal*. Feeling is transformed—it becomes pleasant, satisfying, fulfilling—as the discrepancy is resolved. No wonder people actively seek out the arts and other kinds of aesthetic satisfactions that are found in games, recreations, and personal relationships. But the aesthetic also appears in practical affairs when we encounter a problem that is neither overwhelming nor trivial—a problem we can deal with and carry through to a satisfactory resolution.

What kind of thinking occurs in response to art? While some people believe that it calls for no thinking at all, we've seen that thought is demanded to discover and resolve the discrepancies presented in both the form and the content of art. But this thoughtful effort isn't easy to describe in words, because it is seldom undertaken in the medium of language. This kind of thought is undertaken directly in sounds and rhythms, in colors and in shadings of light and dark, in metaphor and imagery, in the nuances of an expression or a gesture. Painters and musicians, actors and poets necessarily think in these ways; so do the people who enjoy the work of these artists. Susanne Langer called such thought nondiscursive; John Dewey referred to it as "qualitative," to distinguish it from the thought that is conveyed in conventional symbols.[9]

Qualitative thinking is employed not just to resolve the discrepancies found in formal patterns. The content of referential art also offers discrepancies that call for resolution. For example, we expect the inmates of mental hospitals to be deviant, just as we expect the hospital staff to be "normal," sane. But the events in Ken Kesey's novel and the subsequent film, *One Flew Over the Cuckoo's Nest*, lead us to believe it might be the other way around: at times the inmates seem more sane than the staff. As we watch the story unfold, we don't deal with these paradoxes in a logical way. But we *do* resolve them, because that's the only way we can make sense of the work of art. And making sense of something requires thought—even if language isn't used.

The Walkers found Saturday's dinner especially enjoyable because it was delayed and specially prepared. They could resolve all the discrepancies they created. We enjoy a concert because we are able to recognize the theme (not everyone can) even though it is delayed, even though it appears in a different voice and in a new rhythm. Thus the same music that offers us discepancies within patterns of sound enables us to resolve those discrepancies in the recognition that is the reward of continued thoughtful attention. The Walkers approached their dinner deliberately and voluntarily, just as we do the concert. We all had to deal with novelties and discrepancies, but we were confident that our satisfaction would not be denied.

In its *immediacy*, experience that is aesthetic yields the satisfaction that's felt when the quality of experience is high. In its *con-*

sequences, it yields learning. The kind of learning is infinitely varied, since it depends on the kind of thinking undertaken to resolve the discrepancy. Thus utilization of the aesthetic becomes a powerful mode of education. For when teachers create classroom conditions that foster aesthetic qualities, students have the motivation that is provided by immediate satisfaction, while teachers are able to promote the thoughtful effort and learning that they were aiming at.

It is ironic that many teachers recognize the educational potential of games, yet ignore the educational potential of the arts. Ironic, because games are deliberately kept separate from the events of personal and social life, while the arts often heighten our awareness of those very events. Every teacher knows there's nothing like a game to perk up a listless class. What they don't recognize is that art, too, would have a similar effect if arts were chosen that appealed to students the way games do. Later we'll discuss why the familar school emphasis on "great" works of art can spoil the art for children and interfere with their education.

In the meantime, games remain a welcome, if often overrated, activity for the classroom. The pitfalls of misusing games for educational purposes are familiar. John Locke tells of using archery for the learning of Latin words that were placed on the target. Locke allowed that his pupil's progress in Latin was slow, although his archery showed considerable improvement. More recently, Jules Henry wrote about "spelling baseball," wherein the correct spellings of words enable students to make "hits" and score "runs" in their efforts to defeat students on the opposing team. Henry observed that the spelling gains were short-lived, although students learned a lot of other attitudes and dispositions that were contrary to many desirable educational goals.[10]

When teachers are clear about their aims, games can be fun and educationally worthwhile at the same time. For example, games can challenge students to solve a mystery. As they play, students learn about the uses of evidence and about some of the rules of inference. Games can be played in which students try to increase their capital through investments. They can learn something about how markets operate. Games can be played in which students try to discover the value of a variable. In such games, mathematics appears in its most attractive form. And games like chess and cribbage and bridge and kick-the-can can be played just for the fun of it. For learning to play any game means learning how to plan strategy, how to learn from your mistakes, how to win and how to lose. Even playing a silly game teaches these things.

The use of games and the arts in schools is the most direct way to foster the aesthetic. In the next chapter we'll note how the aesthetic can also be fostered through experiences that are not dominantly aesthetic. For now, we'll put games to one side and see how the arts foster learning.

Let's grant at the outset that a lot of art doesn't foster much learning. It holds our attention for a short time only and then is quickly forgotten. We expect it only to entertain us: to pass the time pleasantly but not to leave a lasting impression. Yet sometimes we're surprised. For example, in 1989 a lot of Americans saw the films *Driving Miss Daisy* and *Do the Right Thing*. They got more than they expected. *Driving Miss Daisy* explored the relations between an elderly Jewish woman and her black chauffeur in the South, in the early days of the civil rights movement. *Do the Right Thing* confronted tensions that lead to violence among members of ethnic and racial groups in a crowded northeastern city. Instead of simply being entertained, audiences were challenged to think freshly about people and situations they had often taken for granted. Thought as well as feeling was aroused. Instead of forgetting these movies, people thought about them, discussed them with their friends, sometimes argued about them, and even saw them again.

After we encounter works like these, we're not quite the same persons we were before. We learned from them. And we learned more than we bargained for: about other people, about ourselves, about the world. Thus our discussion of works of art is not intended to promote education about art, but rather education about *anything*. For example, *The Adventures of Milo and Otis* is a 1990 movie about a kitten and a puppy, created by the Japanese zoologist and nature writer Masanori Hata. The film is narrated by Dudley Moore. Drama and humor, exquisite photography and an intelligent script create endless surprises that capture attention, arouse feelings, and afford satisfactions for viewers of all ages. So rich is the film that literally hundreds of questions and speculations could be raised about it after people have seen it. Teachers of most subjects could, at any age level, explore the social behavior of animals, animal growth and development, botanical, climatic, and animal interdependencies, interpersonal relations at varied phylogenetic levels including the human, and so on almost endlessly. Art does not, of course, *answer* these questions, but it provides reason and motivation for asking them and for following them up.

Even abstract art has direct consequences for learning. Repeated and varied interactions with patterns of colors and sounds enable people to acquire greater sensitivity to those patterns, and thus a more sophisticated taste. And as people become more sensitive to patterns offered by the arts, they may come to see the world in new ways, gaining greater appreciation for the shifting and subtle patterns presented in nature.[11]

Learning results from the perception of artistic form alone, but a more profound kind of learning is initiated by art that refers to things beyond the work itself. The impact of referential art is especially strong when its formal features are well executed and reinforce its content. While it isn't always apparent in instrumental music, the combined impact of form and content is readily perceived when words and music are presented together, as in folk songs and blues, art songs and opera. Until recently, painting exemplified the union of form and content. Motion pictures now offer this union in its most complex and sophisticated form. In a movie an idea can be conveyed in many formal modes at once. The idea of an utterly effective threat was expressed by the actor Clint Eastwood when he aimed his pistol and said, "Go ahead. Make my day." But the idea was *also* conveyed by his pursed lips and narrowed eyes, the resolute extension of his arm, the light glinting from the barrel of his gun, the angle from which the scene was photographed, the sudden cessation of background noise in the soundtrack.

When it's well done, the form of art focuses feeling on its content—on its referential meaning. A person is thus confronted with ideas that are immediately felt as well as understood. Not that learning will result from a single line of poetry, or a single scene in a movie like the one mentioned above. We aren't speaking of lessons, but of the impact of a complete event: the whole poem or a collection of poems; the whole concert; the retrospective show of an artist's work; the whole novel or play. Imagine reading a magazine article about the attitudes toward inmates of mental hospital staff members. Then compare its impact with seeing the movie, *One Flew Over the Cuckoo's Nest.* Mere information has a limited impact, but presented in the form of art it strikes our feelings deeply and requires us to think. We cannot soon forget it.

The Aesthetic Is Not the Same for All

The conceptions of expectation, discrepancy, and resolution described above also explain differences in people's responses to art. What's familiar to one person is new to another. Thus what's perceived as a discrepancy in a formal pattern by one person is seen as simply baffling by an inexperienced viewer or listener who comes to the pattern without any expectations. Again, what's new to a person at one time becomes familiar after a while: a discrepancy that once demanded absorbed attention for its resolution is now easily resolved. Art which once demanded concentration and afforded intense pleasure may now afford only the satisfaction of easy familiarity. And when perception becomes easy—a habit—a person will no longer care in the same way for art or music she once enjoyed.

Even though the music remains the same, *we* change with each subsequent hearing of it. That's why no work of music (or any other kind of art) can be *inherently* interesting, and that's why a person cannot enjoy the same musical work in the same way for an indefinite period of time. A recording played repeatedly is eventually cast aside. But a person may never tire of live performances of the same musical work, since the emphases and variations introduced by the performers are virtually unlimited. For this reason a musician may not tire of playing a particular piece of music. Complexity in art increases the likelihood that its patterns will hold our attention for a longer time, since more patterns, and more complex ones, allow more chance for unexpected changes.

Arts that are abstract don't arouse feeling in everybody, and the arousal is seldom easy or automatic for anybody. Certain conditions must be fulfilled, and these conditions are equally important for the appearance of aesthetic quality in any kind of experience, whether or not art is involved. At issue is the question, How is a discrepancy to be discovered? What's most important for answering this question is the fact that discrepancies are not "out there," waiting to be found. A discrepancy is always a function of an interaction between some thing or event in the world and a person who witnesses it. Thus there can't *be* a discrepancy without a person to experience it. That's why two people can confront the same event and *both* be correct when one says "There's a discrepancy there," and the other says, "No, there isn't."

The discrepancies and resolutions in a pattern will not arouse feeling in a person whose posture toward it, whose frame of mind, is exclusively practical or instrumental. An instrumental frame of mind is concerned with uses and with outcomes, not with immediacies and consummations. A person in such a frame of mind, when confronted with an abstract work of art, will want to know what it's for, or what it means (in a referential sense), or what it's worth. A mind so occupied has little room for the perception of patterns. The same can be said about problem-solving. Too much attention to the goal, or to the need for a solution, blinds a person to the intricacies of the problem itself. Thus for experience to be aesthetic, a person's posture toward any work of art, but especially a work that is abstract, must be consummatory, not instrumental. A person's attention must be focused on the nature of the patterns themselves: on what they offer, not on what they promise.

Furthermore, patterns that are subtle or that are executed in an unfamiliar style will be hard to detect. They may arouse no feeling beyond mystification or slight irritation. A person sophisticated in the nuances of Italian madrigals may be at a loss when confronting the music of Bali for the first time. Thus art can seldom be enjoyed by a person unfamiliar with the style of which it is an example. This suggests a need for extreme caution on the part of educators eager to acquaint the young with art that connoisseurs regard as masterpieces. Even "great" works of art will bore people unfamiliar with their style.

Finally, the quality of experience elicited by patterns in a work of art may be limited by the nature of the work itself. A lot of art just isn't very well done. Artists vary in ability, and even skilled ones know there's security to be found in the familiar. Thus many artists produce works that offer little originality or variety in their form. This is a common feature of much art that is popular, whose familiar patterns capture a large audience but don't hold it for very long. The contemporary fine arts often err in the other direction, where formal patterns in art and music are impossible for most people to detect, having been sacrificed in the marketplace to a consuming quest for novelty. Their audience requires the guidance of experts: critics and the proprietors of galleries ("gallerists").

Before we pursue further the question of learning, let's review what's been said. Learning has been associated with high-quality experience, and some forms of high-quality experience were linked to the aesthetic. The aesthetic, in turn, is exemplified in the arts (as well as games), and all of the arts afford aesthetic quality in virtue of the way we respond to the patterns they present. This response is felt as satisfying, because of the way that discrepancies from what we expect are perceived and eventually resolved.

But a person's experience won't be aesthetic if she doesn't perceive those discrepancies. That perception is dependent on three conditions. First, a person must come to the work of art in a consummatory frame of mind. She must be ready to attend to what is immediately before her, instead of subordinating it to considerations of utility, worth, or referential meaning. Second, the person must have some familiarity with the style or genre of the work. Without this, she won't know what to look for or what to listen for; patterns and their variations will be difficult to detect. Third, the work itself must present patterns in rich, varied, unique and yet intuitively intelligible ways. Wallpaper is ordinarily bland and repetitious because it's intended to serve as a background. For that reason we don't give it our full attention for very long, any more than we give our full attention to potboiler novels, or to banal melodies carried in monotonous rhythms.

The arousal of feeling is not in itself a learning experience. But when that emotion results from a confrontation with art, and particularly referential art, much more than feeling has been aroused. For the distinctive impact of art—or of any experience having aesthetic quality—results from *thought* having been engaged. Thought is required to resolve discrepancies that appear in experience or in the form and content of art. Earlier we spoke of the effort required to resolve discrepancies in presented patterns, or to discover patterns that were initially unseen. Only thoughtful effort will yield these resolutions and discoveries. Not the discursive thought that's conveyed in language, but thought undertaken directly in sounds, rhythms, colors, or movements of the body.

The experience of art is a special kind of high-quality experience because art arouses feeling and at the same time provides the material with which thought can work in order to resolve that feeling. That's what enables the arts to foster learning. Not necessarily the kind of learning that can be tested by multiple-choice items on standardized tests, but the kind of learning that's revealed in what a student thinks about, what she talks over with her friends, and what she comes to believe is important. These are matters that indicate gradual changes in the focus of a life, and it is on these things that the arts have an impact. But the arts don't teach lessons. Their teaching is, in Matthew Arnold's words, a "criticism of life":

> not directly, but by disclosure, through imaginative vision addressed to imaginative experience . . . of possibilities that contrast with actual conditions. A sense of possibilities that are unrealized and that might be realized are, when they are put in contrast with actual conditions, the most penetrating "criticism" of the latter that can be made. It is by a sense of possibilities opening before us that we become aware of constrictions that hem us in and of burdens that oppress.[12]

The Arts in Schools As Exemplars of the Aesthetic

Insofar as they act as a "criticism of life," the arts have an impact on people's learning. They surely don't require the intervention of teachers or schools, which seem pale and ineffectual when compared to the vitality and dynamism of art. But while the arts are integrated with people's daily lives in some parts of the world, they do not function that way in Western culture. In the West, especially in the United States, styles and fashions in the arts change so rapidly that its audience has been reduced to the relatively small groups that can keep current with the changes. The production of this art as well as its style is governed by a commercial market that readily sacrifices matters of form and meaning to considerations of sales.[13]

For these reasons, and because they can have so great an impact on learning, the arts should systematically and extensively be introduced into schools. Educators would be able to select works whose impact fosters learnings they hold to be worthwhile. Young people would get acquainted with arts they otherwise might dismiss as foreign and strange. And schools would be less prosaic places.

The arts in American education have traditionally been justified on the grounds that they provide wholesome recreation, salutary therapy, the cultivation of taste, or vocational preparation.[14] These are not bad reasons for teaching the arts, but they are not compelling enough to keep them from being among the first school studies to suffer when budgets are cut. The justification offered here for the uses of the arts in schooling is a different one. It doesn't deny that the arts can help to cultivate taste and develop creativity, although it allows that both can be developed in many areas outside the arts. And it recognizes that an education in the arts contributes to the education of feelings and the development of a healthy and stable emotional life.

But there's a more fundamental reason for bringing the arts into the schools. The arts teach. Whether or not it was the artists' intention, people learn from the arts. And they learn not just about the arts, but about the world. This teaching is attractive, seductive, and often compelling. Since schools are undeniably intended to teach the young about the world, the arts belong in schools because they are an incomparable means of doing the school's job.

Many specialists in arts education object to this justification for the arts in schools.They admit that art can make historical understandings come alive, that art can reveal the beauty of nature that science investigates, and that art can bring significance to the problems that sociology examines. But they claim that children who are exposed to art that is used in these ways will remain unaware of the intrinsic worth of art. As other learnings are pursued, the art itself will be dismissed, once its utilitarian role has been fulfilled.

This objection ignores the fact that most of what we call "fine art" was, when it was originally created, a way of enhancing religious, political, and social values. The epic poetry of ancient Greece and the altarpieces of the Renaissance were not intended to be valued or enjoyed for their own sakes—that is, purely as works of art. They were intended, *then* (and as I am urging, now), to call attention to issues and to celebrate values that their respective cultures deemed important. Thus a work of art is not misused or trivialized when it's employed in the service of other learnings and other aims. That has always been the role of the arts.

But those who would protect the purity of the arts and their independence from other school studies also miscalculate the impact of art on its audience. If a work of art could have an impact strong enough to enable a group of young people to give serious consideration to a scientific curiosity (How *can* a bee fly?) or to a social issue (What is to be gained by putting people who are "different" in segregated institutions?)—if art's impact is that strong, then the art won't be dismissed once the scientific or sociological study is under way. To think that art *could* be so easily dismissed is to misunderstand why the art worked in the first place. It helps students focus on a scientific or a social issue *because* its impact is aesthetic, and that's why it will not and in fact cannot be dismissed or overlooked by students.

Of course, a teacher can call the attention of students to the reasons why the art in question had such an impact. That would be an occasion for the formal analysis of style and its relation to content. That's surely worth doing, although some teachers may not have the background or the inclination to do it. But it would be foolish to insist that inadequately prepared teachers analyze form in art when they might more effectively have pursued other directions of study.

The distinction between the arts and the aesthetic helps us see more clearly the role of the arts in the schools. Since the aesthetic is relevant to some of the most important forms of learning, and since the arts are but one way of fostering the aesthetic, the primary justification for bringing the arts into schools lies in their capacity to foster qualities of experience that will enhance a very broad range of learnings. Thus the primary justification is *not* that the arts are needed to foster education in the arts. That's an important aim, of course, but so is education in math, history, and science. All of them are important areas of human achievement, and career interests can be cultivated in any of them. But just as science transcends the boundaries of any scientific subject because it represents an attitude and a method of thinking appropriate to all human concerns, so art transcends the boundaries of art education because it exemplifies a method of fostering learning appropriate for all school studies.

Education in the arts is as important a responsibility of schooling as education in math or science. A rich literature is available that treats the goals and the methods of education in the arts,[15] but this is not central to the present discussion. Whether and to what extent the various arts can enhance emotional stability, critical thought, or achievement scores can all be debated. But it cannot be denied that the arts are for many people unique sources of immediate enjoyment. And since art is not always accessible and not always easily understood, these are reasons enough for an education in the arts. Reduced to its simplest terms, the arts enrich people's lives, and education in the arts contributes to that enrichment.

Our concern is with education in the broadest sense of the term, and about how it can be enhanced when the quality of students' experience is aesthetic.[16] In the next chapter we'll see how the aesthetic is fostered by experiences having little to do with the arts; here we'll see how the arts can be employed to foster the aesthetic qualities that are associated with learning. The focus is on anything worth learning in schools, and on how the arts can contribute to that learning.

Room for the arts can easily be found at the elementary level of schooling. Herbert Read put it this way:

> . . . Those activities which we denote by such words as 'imaginative,' 'creative,' 'originating,' 'aesthetic,' do not represent a subject with definite limits which can be treated like any other subject and allotted its two or five or seven periods in a competitive time-table . . . Our aim is not two or more extra periods. We demand nothing less than the whole thirty-five into which the child's week is now arbitrarily divided. We demand, that is to say, a method of education which is formally and fundamentally aesthetic, and in which knowledge and manual ability, discipline and reverence, are but so many easy and inevitable by-products of a natural childish industry.[17]

In saying this, Read meant far more than simply bringing works of art into the classroom. He believed that children's play, fostered in school, could be developed into drama, design, dance, music, and crafts. Because these are all artistic activities, they can bring aesthetic quality to the experience of students. They can also develop into studies which, while remaining aesthetically worthwhile, are no longer dominantly artistic. Drama fosters reading and can lead to the study of communication. Dance and music may lead to other forms of physical education. Design involves all forms of graphic representation, and crafts require measurement (leading into mathematics), and can readily be developed into gardening, biology, and some elementary physics and chemistry.

In the terms of the present discussion, the activities urged by Herbert Read are ideally suited to be the foundations of elementary education: they require thought and they have a strong appeal for children. Nearly a century ago John Dewey recognized the appeal of such activities when he urged that education be based on what he called four natural impulses or instincts.[18] Two of these impulses were for the expression of feeling and for making things, which when encouraged will result in arts and crafts and (what is often overlooked but combines both art and craft) cooking. The other two impulses, for investigation and for social intercourse, will be explored in subsequent chapters.

Both Read and Dewey make it clear that school learning suffers from the imposition of academic exercises that demand external forms of discipline and control. Instead, they urged that schools institute activities naturally attractive to the young because they afford aesthetic quality to their experience.[19] More recently, Seymour Sarason cited strong empirical evidence for the value of artistic activities. Participation in creative writing and the graphic arts fostered emotional and intellectual growth among groups of people on whom some educators had given up: the mentally retarded, ghetto children, and the aged and the terminally ill.[20]

The pursuit of artistic activities in school can be reinforced and enriched by giving children opportunities to enjoy and study a variety of art works created by others. The aim is to open a wide range of issues and topics to learn about. Teachers who read stories to children have been doing this for a long time. When well-written stories that appeal to children are chosen, reading is learned more readily than it is from drills, and children can learn virtually anything about the world, about other people, and about themselves. Stories, plays, and movies, not to mention poetry (including song lyrics) and all of the graphic arts, are endlessly rich in content—that is, in the range of their references. Because elementary school teachers can use their time in flexible ways, these media can be explored in whatever directions may be suggested by the particular ways that students react to them.

At the secondary level, the school day is divided into equal periods of time to accommodate separate academic subjects. Hardly any students are interested in all of these subjects, but whatever interests they might have are ignored when bells arbitrarily terminate their studies and send them elsewhere. This literally anaesthetic form of organization is all the more reason for bringing the arts and artistic activities into secondary schools.

While the literary arts are normally a part of English classes, other forms of art are usually absent from the rest of the curriculum. This would be bad enough if it simply left school dull and colorless. But matters are worse than that, for it indicates failure to employ an effective instrument for learning. A multitude of videotapes made for public television is available for the teaching of science. It would be hard to think of a better way to fire the imagination or stimulate the inquiries of the young about the habits of animal life than to show tapes like these.

For example, our conception of a bird's flight has been formed by a lot of experience watching robins, sparrows, and blue jays. Most of us know little and care less about ospreys. But to watch the graceful flight of this bird, to see its wings folded back as it dives from high in the air to catch a fish below the surface of the sea, and to see the osprey carrying its prey back to its young in the nest can be an experience of genuine aesthetic quality. The flight and the habits of this unfamiliar creature are a constant source of surprise (i.e., discrepancy). We'll return to this example in the next chapter, when we see how curiosity is aroused. For now, we can see how the film naturally raises a host of researchable questions that can lead to a far more valuable sort of learning than the imposition of other people's answers to other people's questions.

The teaching of history and the social sciences can seem academically distant and forbidding when it is made up solely of textbooks, data, and exams about anonymous, faceless people and events. Yet many teachers will bear witness to a transformation in their classes when literature was introduced. Since people must be interested in the past before they can profitably study it, historical novels—from *The Three Musketeers* to *The Color Purple*, from *A Tale of Two Cities* to *Trinity*—can create the possibilities for experiences that naturally lead to inquiry and to a wide variety of learnings.

While drama and literature have been available to teachers of academic classes for generations, the technology of the late twentieth century has multiplied the possible uses of the arts. Film and videotape rentals bring another form of the aesthetic to learners, whether or not they are proficient readers. Secondary students were not yet born when the Vietnam War was fought, and they don't feel as strongly about it as their parents do. But feelings will be aroused in students who are shown John Wayne in *The Green Berets*, Jane Fonda in *Coming Home*, and Oliver Stone's *Platoon*. Such films can be discussed as works of art, but they also present viewers with incompatible facts and conflicting interpretations. The arts are not in the business of supplying answers, but the unsettling visions they offer of the past, the present, and the future almost demand further exploration.[21] At the theater on Saturday night, accompanied by friends and popcorn, even provocative movies may only entertain. Shown in school, they can still be enjoyed, but they can also stimulate serious discussion and inquiry with the help of teachers.

All of the arts have a place in the teaching of subjects ordinarily considered academic. Textbook generalizations about other cultures often fail to arouse interest. But what people looked like, how they lived, and how they felt, become immediately perceptible in the graphic arts of Mexico's Orozco or Rivera, of Japan's Hokusai or Hiroshige, or of the printmakers of America's "ashcan school." The arts are thus a powerful, perhaps indispensable means of multicultural education. "Barriers are dissolved," wrote Dewey, "limiting prejudices melt away, when we enter into the spirit of [the arts of other cultures]. This insensible melting is far more efficacious than the change effected by reasoning, because it enters directly into attitude."[22]

Any arts introduced in schools should be *enjoyed*. Without enjoyment, the experience for students is not high in quality, and without that it cannot be aesthetic. When the aesthetic is absent from the experience of the arts, not only will learning be unlikely, but students will have no idea why "art" itself is thought worthy of their attention. Thus it's not enough that schools offer masterpieces to the young. Ignorant of artistic traditions, they will not know what to look for or to listen for, or what to expect. While education *in* the arts is intended to broaden perception and refine taste, education *by means of the arts* must operate at the level where children are found. This means that schools must employ forms of art with which the young are familiar—in many cases, the popular arts.

Academicians belittle arts that are widely popular, and accuse those who would use them in schools of pandering to the tastes of the uncivilized. But there is no good reason to suppose that, because art is popular, it must be superficial, tawdry, or bad. The evidence indicates that Homer was popular in his day. Shakespeare was popular, and so were Verdi and Louis Armstrong. And the profound art of Ingmar Bergman, Akira Kurosawa, and Spike Lee has reached a wide audience.

No better case for the use of the popular arts in schools has been made than the one offered by Vincent Lanier. He wrote:

> Motion pictures, television, photography in popular magazines . . . all of these possess in small or large measure not only some art qualities, but also those art qualities art teachers have been taught to revere. But . . . these popular visual arts forms exist only outside the school. Inside the art room, the models of artistic worth are Massacio, Mondrian, Motherwell . . . For as we teach, we tell them in effect, that the rich life of the popular arts they enjoy outside of school is worthless. For many thousands of our school children, this attitude must be another intolerable indignity. We teachers do not like their speech; we don't like their dress or their grooming . . . and we don't like their taste in the arts. If they don't submit to this barrage of hostility, of course, we call them "alienated youth," subtly transferring the burden of guilt to the children.
>
> Part of the cure might be to focus our attention on the popular . . . arts as content for the school.[23]

Lanier notes that by beginning with art that's familiar to students, we can "teach them why and how they enjoy what they already appreciate. From this knowledge may come the ability to transfer some insights to the fine arts." But whether or not we succeed in cultivating an appreciation for de Kooning by bringing to students the more accessible figures of Orozco, the latter's prints can directly show young people how it feels to be members of an oppressed peasant class. And if it is important for teachers to help the young understand the conditions under which whole classes of people are oppressed, then it is important that the young be reminded of how oppression *feels*.

Summary

A serious consideration of the aesthetic in education is not just for the sake of getting the young to appreciate the arts. Because the aesthetic is a quality of experience that fosters learning, to consider it seriously is to consider the transformation of all of the methods of schooling. This transformation is aimed at providing students with experience that is high in quality and that also provokes thought. Such experience is found when the young engage in activities that are attractive to them and that present them with discrepancies that call for resolution. Such activities can also foster curiosity and the solving of problems. These activities can be initiated by games and, even more effectively, by utilizing the arts throughout the school curriculum.

Subjects that are required of all students are often referred to as "solids." That label also suggests, to students, that they are impenetrable. The arts are usually elective subjects, but they ought to be widely used in connection with every subject. There's much to be gained by this, if only the enhancement of the quality of students' experience in school. But it's also likely that the feelings and concerns aroused by means of the arts will encourage students to try penetrating the so-called "solid" subjects themselves. Under conditions of study like this, "scholarship" would no longer be reduced to the obedient and routinized pursuit of isolated subjects. Rather, it would become a strongly motivated inquiry into problems and issues that matter to students and to the cultures of which they are members.

5 Educational Method II: Curiosity

Thinking, the Aesthetic, and Learning: A Reprise

We saw in the last chapter that in order to learn, people have to *do* something. This doing must be felt as intrinsically satisfying, and it must involve some kind of thinking. When experience has these traits, I've called it aesthetic. This is a broad use of the term, but it's not contrary to ordinary usage. "Aesthetic" always connotes something satisfying. That it should also imply some thinking reminds us that even simple pleasures don't always come thoughtlessly. When they do—as in the pleasure of a warm bath—they're more properly termed "sensuous" rather than "aesthetic."

Even so, the coupling of thought with the aesthetic may still give trouble, so let's examine another case of experience that has aesthetic quality: a ride on a roller coaster. You may think this is an odd example. Children and the simpleminded can enjoy a roller coaster, and the standard response of anyone is to laugh and shout. So where's the thinking? And what's aesthetic about it? Isn't it stretching an idea beyond credibility to put roller coasters in the same category as plays by Shakespeare?

Not at all. In fact, the roller coaster ride illustrates perfectly what it is for experience to be aesthetic in quality. First, let's see where the thinking comes in. To take a ride on a roller coaster—even your very *first* ride—is to embark on an adventure about which you have prior information. You've been told about it: that it's exciting, that it's (absolutely!) safe, that it's enjoyable. You've also been told that it's very fast, that you'd better hold on, that you mustn't stick your arms out. And you saw the roller coaster before you ever rode in it. You've seen the passengers, too—holding on, shouting, laughing. You are probably aware of how slowly the cars climb the first steep grade, and of how quickly they accelerate when they descend.

So you know a lot about roller coaster rides before you get on one for the first time. This means you have very explicit expectations. If there's any doubt about this, have a look at the faces of the roller coaster riders (especially the children) before the cars begin to move. The operator pushes the lever and the cars begin their slow ascent. You *knew* you'd be carried up slowly. Just what you expected. You also expect to start moving very rapidly after you reach the peak of the first hill; you've seen how steep the decline is, and you've watched the cars go down. Slowly you are carried higher and higher. You look over the side of your car. The park is spread out below. People are foreshortened; they're getting smaller and smaller. You're full of anticipation.

Now the cars have reached the crest. They are poised, almost motionless in that moment between climbing and dropping. You clutch the retaining bar tightly, because you know what's coming. And then the descent. You accelerate quickly. You're going fast now. You expected it. *But not that fast*! NOT THAT FAST! You're shouting, along with the others, because what you got wasn't *just* what you expected. The roller coaster had a surprise for you: a discrepancy from your expectation. And it's not over, either. You've reached the bottom of the hill and the track ahead of you rises gradually and makes a broad loop. The cars will have to slow down a little, and you relax. But no! The cars *tear* along the curve, seeming to pick up speed even as they ascend! Another surprise, another discrepancy, and you're shouting again!

When the ride is finally over, you're very pleased. You got what you came for: not just a fast ride, but a ride that took your breath away because it wasn't just what you expected. Certainly a satisfying experience. But was it thoughtful? Of course it was. For your satisfaction was possible only because of your prior knowledge and because your expectations weren't met as you thought they would be. Consider the situation if you *didn't* have prior knowledge, if you didn't have a definite set of expectations. Your experience would probably have been one of pure terror—if you could have been persuaded to go on the ride in the first place.

The roller coaster ride was satisfying because it involved a form of thought. The experience of it was aesthetic. Of course, it wasn't just like watching a performance of *Hamlet*. Neither is cleaning the mag wheels on your Corvette, nor watching waves break against rocks. What's aesthetic doesn't feel the same as anything else that's aesthetic. What *is* common to anything experienced aesthetically is the appearance of a discrepancy from what you expected, and a satisfying resolution to that discrepancy.

We also saw, in the last chapter, that these experiences result in learning. Outside school, learning is seldom what we aim at when experience is aesthetic. Yet learning is one of its consequences. This is even true of the roller coaster ride. We're usually a little hesitant before our first ride; sometimes we need to be persuaded. Afterward, most (but not all) of us feel differently about it. We don't need to be persuaded the second time. Now we're ready to consider rides that before we'd refused even to think about. What we learned may not be as profound as the Secret of Life, but it's not trivial, either. We learned to be a little less afraid. To be a little more disposed to try something new, to take a chance. If you haven't had this sort of experience, spend some time at one of the rides the next time you visit a theme park. Pick out a first-timer or two, and see how they behave when the ride is over. And hang around. See what they do next.

We don't always learn "from life," but we do learn out of school when our expectations aren't met, and when we thoughtfully try to resolve the discrepancies. If formal education is to succeed, it must deliberately establish conditions like these in schools. They're not always obvious, but these are the conditions under which all learning takes place.

In the last chapter we focused on the fine arts (and to a lesser extent, on games) as exemplars of cues to aesthetic experiences that might result in learning. We also noted, in passing, that problem-solving and the pursuit of curiosity were ways of resolving other kinds of discrepancies, and that these events can also result in learning. Curiosity and problem-solving can also effectively promote the acquisition of knowledge, but problem-solving is even more important for the development of organized, goal-oriented thinking, and for the kinds of dispositions that develop when students consistently think this way over a varied range of conditions.

Some features of curiosity and problem-solving are ordinarily overlooked, but they are vitally important to our interest in learning. Solving problems and following up curiosity, when they are not done carelessly, haphazardly, or abortively, demand thought, but they may also yield intrinsic satisfaction. It follows, then, that the solving of problems and the pursuit of curiosity can render experience aesthetic in quality, just as games and the fine arts do. Not aesthetic in the limited sense of "beautiful" or even "pleasing to the senses." But aesthetic in the sense that underlies our entire discussion: satisfying and thoughtful.

What follows is an examination of educational method, but you will not find here a long list of pedagogical ploys and strategies: computer simulations, role-playing exercises, arts activities, illustrated lectures, demonstrations, raids on the library, field trips, labs, ad infinitum. These strategies have productive uses, but they can be misused, too. Lectures, field trips, and games can be stimulating, but they can also be boring. We are now seeking not the specific, but the general: the form of activities that help students learn; more precisely, the conditions that foster aesthetic quality in the experience of students. For when experience is aesthetic, it *cannot* (by definition) be boring: it cannot fail to have an impact. And while we seek conditions for educational practice that are general, we intend at the same time to show how an understanding of general conditions helps to generate specific activities worth trying out in a classroom.

Planning, Problem-Solving, Curiosity, and the Perceptually Attractive: Common Elements

We're about to examine curiosity (and, in the next chapter, problem-solving) in order to discover how it can be employed in school classrooms. But curiosity is not a unique kind of experience, nor is it unique to certain kinds of people. So it will be helpful to begin by examining from another angle what's common to the various activities that result in learning.

In contrast to acquiring a habit, learning demands thought. We saw in the previous chapter that occasions for thinking appear when we want something and when we try to get what we want. (The negatives of these conditions also initiate thought: when we want to avoid something, and when we try to avoid it.) Wanting may go no further than fantasy or reminiscence, but when we begin to lay plans for what we want, our thinking becomes disciplined because it's directed by a purpose.

A plan becomes thoughtful when we imagine what can go wrong with it and then try to figure out what to do about it. This planning can itself yield satisfaction. Since it is thoughtful, it can be experienced aesthetically. Planning something pleasant, like a holiday trip, can be intrinsically enjoyable. But even planning something we want to avoid, like overdrawing our bank account before the month is out, yields some satisfaction as the plan emerges.

All this thinking remains hypothetical until we actually put the plan into operation. Action proceeds smoothly until we run into an obstacle we hadn't foreseen when the plan was under development. An unforeseen obstacle is, of course, a discrepancy from what we expected. At this point, a number of possibilities appear. Suppose you've left home in the evening to have a prescription filled, but you find the pharmacy closed. You might abandon your plan altogether, or (more likely) delay it until tomorrow. Or you might keep driving around the neighborhood, looking for a pharmacy that's open. That's a form of (relatively thoughtless) trial-and-error behavior. Or you might try to locate a telephone book, look up nearby pharmacies, and make some phone calls until you find one that's open. This latter option is called problem-solving. If the obstacle can be overcome (i.e., if the discrepancy can be resolved), you'll certainly experience satisfaction at the solution. You may also find satisfaction in problem-solving itself. For despite our practical aims when we solve problems, the process itself when thoughtfully undertaken can be experienced aesthetically.

There are also occasions for thinking (hence learning) when we're not up to something—that is, when we're neither acting to achieve a purpose nor planning an action. We may be at leisure. We may simply be waiting for something or for someone. We might daydream or fantasize, but we might also pay particular attention to what's around us. This is more likely to happen when we're in an unfamiliar environment: in a new restaurant, in the home of a new acquaintance, on holiday in a foreign country. When we have time to explore our environment, we often encounter something that surprises us—something we didn't expect. A discrepancy of this sort doesn't constitute a problem for us because it doesn't block our purpose. But it does arouse our curiosity. To pursue curiosity is to engage in thinking, and since we're not confronted by a problem, we undertake such thinking only if it's intrinsically satisfying. Curiosity can be extinguished scarcely a moment after its arousal, but when we actively pursue it, our experience is aesthetic in quality.

Chapter 4 focused on occasions when attention is held by something perceptually attractive: layered colors over a setting sun,[1] a calico cat curled in a corner, a work of art. Unlike the settings described above, this kind of experience may be dominantly aesthetic. We saw that what attracted our attention in the first place was something seen (or heard, smelled, tasted, or even felt) that was discrepant from what we expected. If we remain attentive to what attracted our attention, we engage in (usually nonverbal) forms of thinking that can resolve the discrepancy. In experience like this, aesthetic quality is focal—although an artist, unlike her audience, is involved in practical problems as well.

Here's what's common to all the activities we've been considering. Planning, problem-solving, the pursuit of curiosity, and attention to the aesthetic all involve thought. In each case, we approach a situation or entertain an idea with a particular background of information and understanding, and we have certain expectations about what we'll find. Thinking is our response to a discrepancy (real or imagined) from what we expected. Thinking is intended to resolve the discrepancy: to improve the plan, to solve the problem, to satisfy the curiosity, to discover the pattern that was difficult to discern. When the effort to resolve the discrepancy is successful, or looks like it will succeed, the thinking is experienced as satisfying. All these occasions for thought can foster aesthetic quality in experience. All of them can result in learning.

There is another similarity among these activities: the thinking that appears in each is a type of problem-solving. Because problem-solving is undertaken in so many different ways, this may not be immediately apparent. In planning, our problems are imagined ones, so our problem-solving is hypothetical—it occurs in imagination. The problem-solving that occurs when obstacles get in the way of our purposeful activities is straightforward, and is the subject of the next chapter. Curiosity is hardly more than a mild feeling unless it develops into problem-solving, even though the "problem" is not one that impedes our purposes or blocks our activities. Finally, the resolution of discrepancies that appear when experience is dominantly aesthetic is also a form of problem-solving—often unrecognized because usually nonverbal. All of these forms of problem-solving can be enhanced when undertaken in a social setting—that is, when people do it together. The impact of other people on an individual's learning will be examined at greater length in the next two chapters.

It's pretty clear why a problem should be an occasion for thought; that's why some educators urge that the dominant focus of schools should be on problem-solving. The reasons for and against this approach to schooling will be considered in the next chapter, when we develop a conception of problem-solving more adequate than the one that underlies this dispute. But first we consider the merits of curiosity as a way of initiating learning activities in schools. Curiosity, too, fosters problem-solving, but the "problems" with which curiosity deals are often more manageable in school settings than the more pressing problems that complicate the lives of children and youth.

Curiosity

As we examine curiosity and the kind of thinking to which it leads, we need to keep this general principle in mind. If a learner isn't *attracted* to something (which can render experience aesthetic in quality), isn't *concerned* about something (e.g., the adequacy of a plan or an action), and isn't *curious* about something, *then there isn't anything for her to think about. And if there isn't anything to think about, there isn't anything for her to learn.*

Every day, students in schools are engaged in activities that offer them nothing to think about. They are told to read, to listen, and even to "solve problems." Yet within these activities there may be nothing that's attractive to them, nothing that they care about, and nothing that they're even curious about. This leaves students with nothing to think about beyond their own private concerns. All they can gain from such activities is the satisfaction of performing them correctly. That thin reward is no substitute for the aesthetic quality of experience when activity has been productively thoughtful.

If we expect success from any of the hundreds of available strategies for initiating learning, they must have the immediate appeal typical of the arts, the capacity to raise problems relevant to students' genuine concerns, or features likely to provoke curiosity. A scholar can learn without these initiating cues because she already *has* interests that guide her scholarly work. But young people in schools aren't yet scholars, and most of them never will be. The school's task is to help the young discover and develop interests and dispositions of their own. This can be done only in settings that are both attractive and thought-provoking.

There are only a few ways to initiate learning, and the generation and pursuit of curiosity is one of them. Parents and educators say they hold curiosity in high regard, yet it is rarely found in school settings. This is a serious problem for schools (and not just a matter of curiosity!).

How do we know when a person is curious? Ordinarily, when she asks a question or wants to find out about something. But not always. We've already seen that in the course of our practical activities there is much we need to find out. But this need should not be described as curiosity at all. It's driven by our desire to achieve a purpose or solve a problem. The more a person's behavior is dominated by a strong goal or drive, the less likely is that person to be curious.[2] Curiosity stands apart from our practical activities and goals. If someone asked us a question and we said, "Why do you want to know?" we'd suspect the person wasn't simply curious if he said, "So I can get there before they close," or "Because I only have ten dollars with me." *Those* answers suggest that the asker of the question is dealing with practical affairs.

Questions intended to initiate or maintain social intercourse—to keep a conversation going—also fail to indicate the presence of curiosity. We typically ask and respond to such questions when we find ourselves interacting with people we don't know well. "What kind of mileage does your Camaro get?" "Do you think the Dodgers will win it all?" "Have you noticed how many homeless people there are downtown?" "What college did you go to?" In many social settings, these questions don't have any practical import; they're intended to maintain a conversation. Many people learned when they were young to ask "why" as a way to maintain the conversation—not because they were curious.

That many questions don't indicate curiosity can be inferred from the fact that the person who asks them is likely to forget the answer in a few moments. People reputed for their grace and facility in social settings are adept at remembering the answers to questions like these. In such cases, it's not the answer that matters, but the fact that the answer was remembered. The role of information in social settings bears an almost eerie resemblance to the role of information in schools. The student preparing for a test knows that it's not the answer that matters, but whether or not she remembered it.

Curiosity, then, is a matter of wanting to find things out apart from the demands of practical affairs or social intercourse. It appears when we don't *need* to find out something. Then why should we even bother? Why would anyone want to know something if she didn't have any reason or need to know? What makes people curious, anyhow?

When a person is neither making plans nor pursuing a goal, neither interacting with others nor asleep, she can be said to be at leisure. Nothing has to be done. Yet when there's nothing to do, it's very seldom that people do nothing! Research in physiological psychology indicates that a lack of stimulation, felt by people as boredom, triggers strong activity in the nervous system.[3] Bored people *look* for something to do. Children in a classroom who have finished their assigned work, or who don't understand even how to begin the assignment, are the ones most likely to disrupt class.

Animals, including humans, are not passive organisms simply waiting to respond to external stimuli. They are naturally active, and when there's nothing at the moment they need to do, they'll do something anyhow. Animals explore.[4] People telephone a friend, read a book, see what's on television, take a look in the refrigerator. Psychologists refer to all this as exploratory behavior. Those who engage in it aren't responding to external pressures, and they aren't certain about how their explorations will turn out. A deliberate seeking after the aesthetic falls under this heading, and so does some socializing. Curiosity, too, is a form of exploratory behavior.

Aristotle may have had curiosity in mind when he said, "All men by nature desire to know." He believed that people are naturally curious about the world and interested in finding out how it works. The development of philosophy, the sciences, and history, which has produced a vast store of settled, verified knowledge, is driven as much by curiosity as by practical needs. But Aristotle overgeneralized. Not everyone exhibits curiosity. The achievements of science can be attributed to a small number of people, and even scientists aren't curious *all* the time, or curious about *everything.* So if we consider a person at leisure, relieved of goal-driven pressures, we have to ask, under what conditions will such a person become curious?

Let's start with our own experience. Ask yourself, "What have I been curious about recently? What made me curious about it?" If your experience is anything like mine, the following story may sound familiar. I'll describe a situation in which I became curious, and in which I had an opportunity to follow it up. Then I'll indicate why I became curious. We may not be curious about the same things, but you can judge whether the *conditions* that aroused my curiosity match the conditions that arouse yours. We want to get as clear as we can about these conditions so we can arrange for them in school classrooms.

I recently went to Papa B's for dinner. The restaurant opened a few months ago just a couple of miles from the university, and it serves a good pizza and excellent ribs. This evening the place was empty except for one other diner—just like the last few times I ate there. I ordered the ribs and they were delicious. But I wondered why business was so slow. How could they even pay their rent if they served only a couple of meals at the prime dinner hour?

I told the manager (with whom I'd spoken before) how good the ribs were, and I asked her if she knew why her place was so empty when the food was so good. She said she hoped just to survive over the summer, because she expected her clientele to increase when the students returned to the university in the fall. What made me curious about the sparse patronage at Papa B's? Why did I wonder whether they'd be able to stay in business? Can answers to these questions help explain why you become curious?

To begin with, I was at leisure. After I ordered dinner I had no goals to pursue, no problems to solve. Second, there was nothing there to distract me from attending to my immediate environment: no telephone or television, and nothing to read. And I was alone. I was in a pleasant situation, and I was hungry and looking forward to a good plate of ribs. These are conditions that make curiosity *possible*. But there still needs to be something to be curious *about*. Another condition is needed.

When I'm in a restaurant that serves good food, I'm used to a crowded dining room. If I have to wait for a table, I'm not surprised. Papa B's serves good food, but it was almost empty. That's discrepant from what I expected, and that's why I wondered where the customers were. Just as one sort of discrepancy (from an expected perceptual pattern) serves as a potential cue to the aesthetic, another sort of discrepancy (within a familiar state of affairs) is a potential cue to curiosity. When I also wondered whether Papa B's would be able to stay in business, a practical consideration entered the picture: if they went under, I'd lose a pleasant and convenient place to eat.

Psychological research supports this interpretation of the conditions that foster curiosity. McClelland has shown that a person's curiosity about something depends on how much or how little her expectations about it are satisfied. If the events that follow an expectation are perceived *just* as they were expected, interest wanes and boredom or inattention is likely to result. At the other extreme, when events are totally unexpected, we're more likely to be astonished or uncomfortable rather than curious. Berlyne wrote that organisms strive to maintain "intermediate arousal potential"; in Helson's and McClelland's terms, they respond to small discrepancies from the level to which they are adapted.[5]

When I pursued my curiosity by speaking with the manager, my aim was not to solve a problem by changing a state of affairs. I just wanted to gain some information, because that's all that is needed to resolve this kind of discrepancy. In everyday situations, we can satisfy curiosity by asking a question, doing some reading, and sometimes by just looking a little more carefully.

Thus curiosity, like the appearance of aesthetic quality in experience, is the consequence of having perceived a discrepancy from what we expected. The aesthetic can result from a discrepancy in an expected perceptual pattern of sounds or sights (or events, as in the case of the Walkers' dinner). But curiosity results from perceiving something discrepant from what we understand. Experience can become aesthetic when we simply attend further to what aroused a discrepancy (assuming that the stimulus—a poem, a painting, or a thunderstorm—possesses the requisite formal features). But this will not work in the case of curiosity. Simply to continue attending to what is contrary to understanding will not usually satisfy our curiosity. We have to do something. But unlike the problem-solving we undertake in our practical affairs, the successful pursuit of curiosity need not alter the situation that originally produced it. Curiosity is satisfied with a good answer to our question, wherever we find it. Sometimes it's satisfied just by taking a better look.

The curiosity of a scientist is far more sophisticated and specialized than ours, and answers are much more difficult to find. A scientist can't simply ask a friend or look up the answer in an encyclopedia. Her inquiries make changes in conditions, just to acquire the needed information. Yet the scientist does not change conditions the way a goal-oriented problem-solver does, for her goal is simply to understand something—not change it. Paradoxically, experimental scientists have found that they have to change a situation simply in order to understand it. An example of scientific curiosity will make this clearer, and at the same time show how science is but an informed, professional extension of the ordinary sort of curiosity you and I occasionally have, but seldom have the skill or the time to pursue. This example is from the the Curies' discovery of radium, and it cannot be expressed more clearly than in Marie Curie's own words:

> During the course of my research, I had had occasion to examine not only simple compounds, salts and oxides, but also a great number of minerals. Certain ones proved radioactive; these were those containing uranium and thorium; but their radioactivity seemed abnormal, for it was much greater than the amount I had found in uranium and thorium had led me to expect.
>
> This abnormality greatly surprised us. When I had assured myself that it was not due to an error in the experiment, it became necessary to find an explanation. I then made the hypothesis that the ores uranium and thorium contain in small quantity a substance much more strongly radioactive than

either uranium or thorium. This substance could not be one of the known elements, because these had already been examined; it must, therefore, be a new chemical element.

I had a passionate desire to verify this hypothesis as rapidly as possible. And Pierre Curie, keenly interested in the question, abandoned his work on crystals (provisionally, he thought) to join me in the search for this unknown substance.

We chose, for our work, the ore pitchblende, a uranium ore, which in its pure state is about four times more active than oxide of uranium.

Since the composition of this ore was known through very careful chemical analysis, we could expect to find, at a maximum, 1 per cent of new substance. The result of our experiment proved that there were in reality new radioactive elements in pitchblende, but that their proportion did not reach even a millionth per cent!

The method we employed is a *new method in chemical research based on radioactivity*. It consists in inducing separation by the ordinary means of chemical analysis, and of measuring, under suitable conditions, the radioactivity of all the separate products. By this means one can note the chemical character of the radioactive element sought for, for it will become concentrated in those products which will become more and more radioactive as the separation progresses. We soon recognized that the radioactivity was concentrated principally in two different chemical fractions, and we became able to recognize in pitchblende the presence of at least two new radioactive elements: polonium and radium. We announced the existence of polonium in July, 1898, and of radium in December of the same year.[6]

It should be noted that Madame Curie's language in describing the turning point of this research is quite similar to the language used in the present analysis of curiosity. Thus, "their radioactivity . . . was much greater than the amount . . . had led me to *expect*." And, "This abnormality greatly *surprised* us." And then, ". . . it became necessary to *find an explanation*." What followed after that, which will be discussed later, is the procedure ordinarily called problem-solving. But that's not *all* that was important to the Curies in their laboratory. For the quality of their experience was aesthetic. This will be shown in the next chapter, when problem-solving is the focus of our attention.

Curiosity in Schools

Schools can offer two kinds of situations in which young people might become curious. One is simply the provision of a rich environment, some leisure, and some encouragement. The other results when teachers systematically try to provoke curiosity. The first of these situations seems rather unlikely in American schools in the late twentieth century. But it's worth examining, anyhow.

By a rich environment I don't mean oriental carpets on the floor and a silver tea service at break times. Despite America's private wealth, most American public schools can't afford any sort of carpet, and they're hard pressed to provide milk out of cardboard cartons. But an educationally rich environment is simply one that provides a wide variety of stimuli, and this needn't cost a lot. A classroom needs a multitude of *things* that have potential interest to children. Books, first of all, of every sort. Used books are cheap and they sell for small change at secondhand stores. Paperbacks cost a dime and a full set of (old) encyclopedias can be bought for a few dollars. Copies of *Life* magazine a half a century old sell for a quarter. Adults are delighted to page through them. Why not schoolchildren?

Other kinds of things that contribute to a rich classroom environment readily come to mind. Toys, tools of all kinds including the tools of the arts, costumes, cookware, cuisinaire rods, animals (small enough for pens or cages), games, athletic equipment—there's no end to the list. Since the growth and institutionalization of garage sales and flea markets, it's conceivable that the ingenuity of America's school administrators could create channels through which the flotsam and jetsam of our upper and middle classes might flow into our school classrooms.[7]

But at the time of this writing many of our classrooms are overcrowded, and there's hardly room for all the students. So in order to provide children with a rich environment, we'll also have to take them out of the school and into the community. For the moment it's enough to note that the community is one of the more important things about which children have to learn, and that it would be inefficient, ineffective, and plain silly to try to confine all of that learning to school classrooms.

Providing a rich environment in or out of the classroom is the easy part. The hard part is providing the leisure that's needed to take advantage of it. As we saw, curiosity is nurtured by leisure and thwarted by practical pressures: by a demanding schedule of goals. Yet nowhere can goals be found in richer abundance than in public schools. (Thousands of school classrooms are still expected to achieve "behavioral objectives," which are typically expressed in the following way: "Given a human skeleton, the student will correctly identify at least forty bones from the following list . . ." A classroom might be governed by hundreds of such objectives.) Instructional goals, rarely chosen by the students who are expected to meet them, come with explicit time schedules for their achievement. Every day in school is a busy day as children move from scheduled activity to scheduled activity, from class to class. Nothing could be more detrimental to arousing curiosity in children.

Why should school classrooms be so busy? Why should they be so imperiously governed by such a multitude of immediate and long-range goals? Here we encounter what must be regarded as one of our civilization's Great Paradoxes. We are told that the seventeenth century settlers of New England were dominated by a strong work ethic, a consequence of the Reformation-inspired belief that worldly success was a sign of one's predestination. Two centuries later that ethic, combined with a series of brilliant inventions, unregulated capitalist expansion, and twelve- to sixteen-hour workdays, created the most productive industrial and economic system the world had ever seen.[8] Output per worker increased to the point where fewer workers were needed. Child labor laws at the turn of the century may have had regard for the welfare of children, but they were also designed to keep hundreds of thousands of young people out of the labor market.[9]

The dedicated application of the Protestant work ethic, compatible with unrestrained greed, meant setting more ambitious, expansive industrial goals, and the more systematic organization of the labor force to achieve those goals. Among other things, this enterprise created an unprecedented amount of leisure time for the nation's youth. Time for what? Adventure, exploration, public service, or the pursuit of curiosity? No: it turned out to be time spent in school. As child labor laws were passed, the states also tightened their compulsory education laws and made sure that children stayed in school longer. The work ethic that powered industry now began to dominate schools. As the school population increased, educators developed new curriculums and aimed at a wider range of more specific educational goals.[10]

The Great Paradox lies in the fact that schools are not industries and do not in any literal sense turn out salable products. They are intended to promote learning. But insofar as learning involves the pursuit of curiosity, the transference of an industrial and entrepreneurial frame of mind to the school becomes an enormous obstacle to learning. Another aspect of the paradox lies in the fact that most people extend themselves in their work *in order* to get adequate leisure to enjoy the fruits of their labors. But the leisure won for children by increased productivity in industry was soon turned into a form of work (schoolwork). There is a perverse logic behind this paradox. Since the goal-dominated, schedule-dominated organization of schools reflects corporate and industrial organization,[11] learning becomes an incidental concern of schools, and socialization becomes the major function. Schools socialize the young into working at a pace chosen by others for the achievement of goals chosen by others. Successful students make a smooth transition into jobs and careers. Meanwhile, we forget that for the ancient Greeks (whose civilization remains an inspiration for our own), the word for "school" also meant "leisure."[12]

All this suggests that it won't be easy to get schools to provide more leisure for students. Idle hands have long been regarded as the devil's workshop, and productivity and hard work have become the idols of a business culture. But traditions change, even old ones. The resources of the planet are seriously threatened by the unlimited growth of productivity. This same tradition, transplanted into schools, is an equally serious threat to the development of children's minds.[13] Politically and economically inspired commissions and blue-ribbon panels periodically come up with new reforms, new sets of goals and more demanding schedules for schools and schoolchildren. In the name of "reforming" education they urge programs that would only make schools more dismal places in which to work.

A rich environment and the provision of some leisure will result in some children becoming curious about some things. But curiosity is fragile and needs encouragement to stay alive. A competitive classroom climate is disastrous to curiosity because a curious child simply drops out of the competition. Highly specific and frequently administered tests require productivity in students and, again, discourage curiosity. And the very specific time frames for the achievement of specific learning goals is also a great inhibitor of curiosity. It can even be discouraged by a teacher whose intentions are just the opposite. Too facile an answer to a child's question may be a convenience for the child, but it doesn't encourage her to follow up her own curiosity. Teachers, then, should encourage children to answer their own questions—by taking those questions seriously and providing the sort of guidance that might be helpful in exploring them.

If curiosity is to be aroused in our schools, more will have to be done than simply providing a rich environment and hoping that nature will take its course. By the time they get to school many children have already learned that it doesn't pay to ask too many questions. But curiosity will appear if teachers set up situations intended to arouse it. This can be done in a lecture, in a laboratory situation, in the selection of a story to read, in the use of a computer, in organizing a field trip, and in countless other ways.

All of these approaches need to offer students something a little different from what they expect, for that's what provokes curiosity. Of course, a teacher needs to know what her students are likely to expect. This is easier for a teacher who is experienced and well acquainted with the students. She'll also know what her students expect if in her planning she deliberately sets up expectations in her students. Even so, not everyone gets curious about the same things. In the pursuit of curiosity, just as in the experiencing of the aesthetic, a class will seldom be able to act as a unit. In the next chapter we'll examine the reasons why different individuals and groups in a class can learn better by pursuing different activities.

A few examples of intentionally provoking curiosity in classrooms will make the point clearer and bring theory back down to earth. These activities won't demand exceptional skill from teachers; they're the kinds of things many good teachers have been doing all along. What matters is to see why they help to promote learning, so they can be more frequently and consistently employed.

Richard Suchman's work in inquiry training provides a classic example of the arousal of curiosity in the teaching of science. A group of students is gathered around a pot of boiling water, into which the instructor dips a strip of metal. She withdraws the strip and the students watch as it bends downward. The instructor asks for an explanation and the students claim that the heat caused the metal to contract. The instructor suggests that they try it again, as a check on their hypothesis. Once again she dips the strip in the water and pulls it out, but this time the strip bends upward! This mystifies the students, and they begin to speculate about the reasons why. After the second dip they had expected the strip to bend the same way it did previously, but what they saw was discrepant from what they expected. The discrepancy aroused their curiosity. The instructor encouraged them to follow it up by participating in their speculations and raising key questions. This helped them eventually to discover that the strip was made of two metals that respond to heat at different rates.

The more heat-sensitive metal contracted again after the second dip in the water, causing the strip to bend. But the instructor had rotated the strip 180 degrees, and that resulted in the strip's bending upward instead of downward.[14]

In Chapter 4 we examined the school use of a video on the habits of the osprey. That discussion focused on the grace of the bird's flight and on the power and accuracy of its fishing expeditions. Attention was directed to the video's artistic features, but we should also note that in cases like this, what initially attracts attention because of its aesthetic appeal may hold attention longer if it arouses curiosity. The flight of the bird is strikingly beautiful, but students will also be surprised that a creature hundreds of feet in the air can spot a fish below the surface of the sea and then snag it in one powerful, precise plunge. Such accuracy is discrepant with anybody's expectations, and curiosity about the physiology that makes this possible is easily aroused in many students, and is certainly worth pursuing.

The field of mathematics is full of curiosities, and curiosity is the reason why some people become mathematicians. Since the math that's useful in solving everyday problems is relatively simple (and often learned as readily out of school as in it), common sense would suggest that curiosity serve as the focus of math education. But math is also a matter of abstractions, and not everyone finds abstractions interesting. This is hardly news, but it does help explain why so many students find math even more boring than it is difficult. What's hard to understand is why our school systems (from college professors of mathematics on down) demand that all children in schools study math virtually every day for at least ten and often twelve years of schooling.[15] Is it education or is it children that they don't understand? Are they confused about what's helpful in the living of a normal life? Or do they persist simply to maintain the employment of thousands of teachers and professors of mathematics? These are potentially practical questions. At the moment, I'm just curious about them.

Mathematical games and puzzles—which are abundantly available to teachers—are rich resources for the arousal of curiosity. But curiosity can be aroused in other ways, as well. A local teacher occasionally gives to her students a list of numbers for their homework assignment. "These are the answers," she says. "Your task is to make up problems that will have these answers." That assignment is certainly discrepant from what children expect from math homework, and their curiosity is evident from the kinds of questions they ask. "We can't be wrong, then, can we?" "Are we allowed to come up with anything we want?" "Do we all have to make up the same problems?"

When discussion in a math class showed that several different answers were being offered as the solution to a problem, philosopher and former math teacher John Schulte would say to his class, "This is a democracy, isn't it? Then why don't we vote on the answer, and accept the number that wins?" This turns out to be much more than just a math lesson, since it raises epistemological issues like the nature of truth and evidence. Yet these issues are vitally important for an understanding of mathematics, and children are quite capable of examining them. But only if discussion is initiated by curiosity. Schulte aroused curiosity by offering students ideas that were discrepant from what they'd come to expect from a math lesson.

When the history teacher Bill Bigelow was about to begin teaching a unit on the voyages of Columbus, he confronted some disconcerting facts. The history textbook's discussion of Columbus was sometimes false, it omitted important and relevant material, and it was altogether misleading about what Columbus was up to and what he achieved. Furthermore, he knew that students ordinarily believe whatever is printed in a text (why else would teachers *test* them on it?). So Bigelow introduces the unit by taking a purse off a student's desk and announcing that it belongs to him. This seems quite unfair, if not absurd, to the class, and lively discussion follows each of Bigelow's purported reasons for claiming that the purse is his. Finally, Bigelow asks, "What if I said I *discovered* this purse? Then would it be mine?" Before long he is able to ask the class, "Why do we say that Columbus discovered America?" By now the class is ready to begin a more analytical and critical investigation into the enterprises of Columbus. As in the above cases, the momentum of this inquiry is generated by the students' curiosity, and their curiosity was a function of their perceiving something discrepant from what they expected in a history class.[16]

After making sure that the children have copies of the textbook at their desks at the start of a new semester, a social studies teacher of my acquaintance begins the class by holding up her own copy and saying, "OK, here's our textbook for the year. Where would you like to begin?" Of course the pupils expect to begin at the beginning; they don't expect to be asked where to begin. But the teacher's question is a serious one, because she knows that it doesn't really matter where you begin, and that there might be better reasons for starting someplace else than page one. So she pushes her question, and urges the children to make suggestions. The ensuing discussion sometimes goes on for days. It teaches children what a table of contents and an index are for, and it helps them to discover what their own interests are, and how they might be followed up. All of this is crucial to an intelligent examination of social studies. And it was provoked by the curiosity aroused when the teacher raised an intriguing possibility that was very discrepant from what the children were used to.

Insofar as the subject of English (or any other language) is mainly concerned with the examination of language and ideas by means of language, curiosity can significantly be employed. Most literature is intended to arouse curiosity as well as aesthetic quality in experience. If teachers are familiar with their own students as well as with literature, they should be able to select material that embodies both these kinds of appeal. Then literature itself can be trusted to have its own valuable impact. Besides offering appropriate selections and choices, the teacher need only raise some provocative questions about the reading and ensure that students have opportunities to talk over with others what they're reading. A teacher may have to take a more active role to arouse the curiosity of younger students that will draw them into books. A final example will illustrate this.

My fourth-grade teacher, Mrs. Karsten, read us a story nearly every day. But on some days she would stop well before the end and ask us how we thought it would end, or how we thought it ought to end. This usually led to animated discussion and sometimes to strong disagreements. Then Mrs. Karsten would ask the disputants to offer reasons for finishing the stories as they did. On some occasions she would ask us to write out our own endings, and read them to the class the next day. Looking back, I realize now how much we learned from those sessions. Figuring out the logic of a story's plot, seeing the integrity of its characters, considering alternatives, backing up our own views, and articulating our own ideas verbally and in writing were all developed by Mrs. Karsten's lessons. And all of this happened because she provoked our curiosity. Of course, the *art* of the original storyteller got us involved in the story, but it was the discrepancy created by Mrs. Karsten that provoked our curiosity. For the story would stop before we expected it to. And when our teacher asked us, "How do you think it will end? How would *you* end it?" we unexpectedly became authors ourselves.

Problem-Setting and Problem-Solving

Once a student has become curious about something, it's reasonable to ask, "where do we go from here?" All of us become curious from time to time, but usually we don't do much about it. *Just* to arouse children's curiosity without allowing and encouraging them to follow it up would be a pointless exercise. The above examples were mainly intended to show how curiosity can be *aroused*; they only suggested that this arousal was followed by certain kinds of discussions, inquiries, and explorations.

Curiosity is a fragile thing, easily dissipated by more pressing concerns unless it's encouraged and guided into subsequent inquiry. The crucial moment when curiosity is either developed or dropped is the point at which a problem is articulated. It is the moment when "I wonder what . . ." is replaced by, "What if I . . . ," or "Why don't we try to . . ." We can put this more formally: in order for curiosity to be educationally productive, it must be turned into problem-solving. This transformation occurs when a problem is set. Problem-setting is the process by which a matter of curiosity is articulated in such a way that it becomes amenable to inquiry that is relatively systematic.

Thus problem-setting turns the pursuit of curiosity into problem-solving. We saw in the previous chapter that attention to formal, perceptual features of the environment is also a kind of problem-solving that renders experience aesthetic when it resolves discrepancies in what is perceived. Yet this isn't easily recognized as problem-solving because it occurs intuitively, sometimes very quickly, and seldom by means of ordinary, discursive language. (For these reasons educators, mental testers, and others have failed to acknowledge the thoughtful dimensions of the aesthetic.) The problem-solving that ensues after curiosity produces problem-setting is easy to recognize because it's ordinarily conducted in language. When experience is aesthetic, the quality of experience is a person's dominant concern. But discovery is the dominant concern when curiosity is pursued into problem-solving.

When action is blocked, when something gets in the way of what we're doing, the utility of problem-solving is obvious. But problem-solving can also result from affairs that have little to do with our purposeful activities. In discussing the arts and the aesthetic we saw one way problems are solved in a setting that's not instrumental or practical. Curiosity also appears in nonpractical settings; when a problem is set, it too can lead to problem-solving. But aside from our examination of aesthetic contexts, we haven't yet confronted the question of how problems are solved. That will be the topic of the next chapter.

Summary

The indulgence of curiosity isn't just a pleasant pastime. It can lead to the development of lifelong interests and careers, and it has advanced the arts and sciences that are distinctive of our civilization. But simply *telling* children about the arts and sciences isn't likely to make them curious. Information in and of itself has no power to arouse curiosity, and the expectation of being tested on the information is likely to suppress it. Thus the consequence of taking curiosity seriously in schools leads to the paradox of not taking so seriously all that we plan for children to learn.

The next chapter will examine problem-solving, to which curiosity often leads. Problem-solving is often undertaken individually, and schools tend to encourage children to work alone. But we'll see that problem-solving in schools can most productively be undertaken in groups. The next chapter will focus on two topics that can hardly be understood independent of one another: the nature and uses of problem-solving, and the indispensable role of peer groups in schooling.

6 Educational Method III: Thinking as Problem-Solving and the Role of Groups

For an image of a thinker, you couldn't do much better than Rodin's famous sculpture: a man seated, shoulders hunched forward, chin resting on his hand. But repose of that sort is the exception, not the rule. Most of our thinking occurs as thoughtful action, as rapid adjustments to changes in our physical and social settings. We shift our luggage without dropping it so we can reach the ticket in our pocket; we make a droll remark to calm an angry spouse; we pass the ball to a teammate who's in a better position to take a shot. The thought involved in all this usually goes unnoticed because it's unpremeditated. It's *how* we act, not something we do before we act. We don't look much like Rodin's *Thinker*, yet it would be a mistake to believe that our thoughtful actions are simply "automatic."

There are times when the complexity, the novelty, or the seriousness of a situation calls for a delay of action. Then thinking becomes conscious: we *feel* it as a process: as difficult or smooth, as frustrating or satisfying. At those times we engage in problem-solving. In this chapter we'll see that all extended thought is a form of problem-solving, that in daily life, much of our problem-solving is done in concert with others, that a great deal of educationally valuable problem-solving will be done by students working together, and that the most significant educational consequence of problem-solving in school has little to do with the problems that get solved.

The value of school is often conceived in terms of results, the products of students' behavior. These products—exam papers and test scores—are of particular interest to school administrators and college admissions officers. The rest of us, teachers and parents and citizens, are interested less in those products than we are in the kinds of *people* schools produce. Schools that encourage problem-solving are organized so that the student goes after the all-important solution. But what *we're* after is a more thoughtful, a more educated person. Problem-solving aims at solutions, but the point of having students do it is to get them to acquire certain intellectual skills and dispositions. And since success involves the help of others, we also aim to have them acquire certain social skills and dispositions.

The Meaning of the Term, "Problem-Solving"

Problem-solving is a practical activity. We do it when something gets in the way of what we're doing. But while everybody solves problems, not everbody does it well. That's why it's worth having children do it in schools: practice brings improvement. The young learn valuable attitudes and skills, and they acquire some knowledge as well.

But the term "problem-solving" is so widely used among educators that it's come to mean just about anything short of memorizing passages from a text. Students trying to figure out how to reduce chaos in a school cafeteria are said to be problem-solving. But so are students working through a list of math problems assigned by the teacher. These activities have little in common. If we call both of them "problem-solving" and try to discover how we can help students become better problem-solvers, we'll find ourselves heading in two different directions. In the cafeteria example, members of a group seek to arrive at a unique solution to a problem that irritates everyone. In the math example, individual students seek predetermined answers by following a teacher's directions. To call both activities "problem-solving" suggests they are similar when in fact they are quite different. So a choice must be made about how to use this term.

The first half of the term, "problem," referred in earlier chapters to whatever interfered with someone's purpose. If I am thwarted when trying to achieve my purpose, I have a problem. Students who wanted to eat lunch in a quiet and relaxed atmosphere were frustrated in a noisy, chaotic cafeteria. They had a problem, and they recognized it as their own.

Now consider the students who were given a page full of math problems to solve. In most cases it wasn't *their* purpose to solve the problems. It was the teacher's purpose. Had the teacher not assigned the problems, the students wouldn't have tried to solve them. That's because most students don't aim to learn math; it's not their purpose. Whether or not you think it's deplorable that students lack such a (worthy) purpose, its absence means that there's nothing that can interfere with it. In other words, if a person's purpose isn't in jeopardy, he doesn't have a problem. Students who lack a problem can't engage in problem-solving.[1] What can they do?

This brings us to the second half of the term, the part about "solving." For the moment we'll take "solving" in the conventional sense of being a thoughtful and not an impulsive or habitual activity. We can be more precise later on, but in this sense of the term, the cafeteria problem could be solved thoughtfully, while the math problems could not. The cafeteria problem is too complex and too unique to be solved by mere habitual activity, but the math problems could be solved by exercising a habit. For if the students are *told how* to solve the assigned problems, they simply have a task to complete. If they don't know how to solve the assigned problems, they can act impulsively or wait for help. In neither case will they engage in problem-solving.

There is an exception to this analysis, wherein problem-solving *could* be applied to the list of math problems. Consider Mary, who knows how to solve the assigned problems but gets stumped by a tough one. She can engage in problem-solving if she accepts the solving of that problem *as her own purpose*. If Mary doesn't adopt that purpose as her own, she'll try something else: write an answer impulsively, ask a neighbor or copy from her, or just leave the item blank. Teachers are familiar with all these responses. They'd prefer that their students try some problem-solving, but they don't know how to get them to acquire the *purpose* of solving those problems. So they simply tell them to solve them. Backing up this telling (or more accurately, commanding) is a whole system of rewards for those who try and penalties for those who don't. But to get the rewards and avoid the penalties, Mary has a lot of options besides the arduous one of problem-solving.

A problem doesn't become our own just because someone assigned it to us. What would prompt Mary to have a go at problem-solving? When she's stumped by a tough one, Mary might decide to test her mettle by trying to figure it out. That's a decision to adopt a purpose that happens to be congruent with the teacher's purpose. Now the problem is Mary's problem, and she can engage in problem-solving.

It can be satisfying to finish a page of math problems. It's not the satisfaction of doing a job well, but the satisfaction that attends completing a task: we're glad it's over. But when Mary is working hard on a tough problem, she can gain the kind of satisfaction that attends the thoughtful solving of a problem she accepts as her own. We've already encountered this kind of satisfaction: it is aesthetic in character. We're invigorated when we deal with difficulties in the course of our planning because the plan is *our* plan; we enjoy a new piece of music because the perceived discrepancy was a function of *our* experience. Similarly, we find it stimulating to pursue a problem that emerged from curiosity because it was *our* curiosity. When purposeful activity is blocked, we can take satisfaction in dealing with the obstacle because we see it as *our* problem that stands in the way of *our* purpose.

In sum, "problem-solving" in the discussion that follows refers to an activity thoughtfully conducted to overcome obstacles to the achievement of one's purpose. If the purpose belongs to X, then the obstacle is perceived as X's problem. This is a fairly common use of the term, although it excludes a lot of activities that are often called problem-solving. Because it's an activity that is personally relevant, problem-solving can be experienced with satisfaction, although we may "lose ourselves" in the activity because of its immediacy and intensity. In the same way, we lose ourselves in reading a novel, becoming aware of our satisfaction only when we put the book down. While it ordinarily lacks the sensuous features characteristic of the arts, problem-solving, like the experience of art, can be aesthetic in quality; both can be thoughtful and satisfying. But they are pursued with different aims in mind.

Problem-solving and the aesthetic can be considered as two ways of describing a single phenomenon. If you are interested in the cognitive or practical aspect of this phenomenon—that is, in coming to know something or in achieving a sought-for outcome—then you describe it as "thinking" or problem-solving. But if you are interested in how a person feels—that is, in the quality of his experience—then you describe it as an experience that may be aesthetic in quality. When it is effectively under way, problem-solving is experienced aesthetically. And even when experience is dominantly aesthetic, one is solving problems. Progressive educators working in the Deweyan tradition focused almost exclusively on the cognitive and practical aspects of problem-solving, and virtually ignored its aesthetic aspects. Thus they failed to take account of a rich set of conditions (discussed at length in Chapter 4) that can foster learning.

On the definition of problem-solving offered here, much solving of problems that goes on in schools isn't problem-solving at all. Assigning a page full of math problems won't produce much problem-solving. Asking students to answer the questions at the end of the chapter won't promote much problem-solving either, nor will asking them to identify the parts of a plant or the features of a frog's circulatory system, or a set of locations marked on a map. Because these assignments ordinarily aren't relevant to students' purposes, they don't offer problems students can perceive as their own. So they can't foster problem-solving—except by chance, as in the case of Mary, described above.

Problems cannot simply be *given* to us. They are usually what we discover when we run into trouble, or when we decide to pursue our curiosity. But we can't discover what's already been given to us. If a student doesn't see what's been given to him as *his* problem (which entails his having adopted the relevant purpose), it's just a riddle, a puzzle, or an enigma. Sometimes children enjoy puzzles, but most of the time what's offered as a "problem" is received as just another task. It's not usually an occasion for problem-solving because the student does whatever is expedient to get the task done.

It's not just splitting hairs to separate activities that count as problem-solving from those that don't. We may want our students to learn how to follow directions, obey orders, and complete tasks. Schools certainly give them plenty of practice. But in doing those things, they won't be learning to hypothesize, to test their ideas imaginatively, or to risk trying them out in practice. In short, they won't learn the skills and dispositions that are developed by engaging in problem-solving if they spend all their time just completing assigned tasks.

Now it's time to examine the process of problem-solving itself. We've already seen its generic form: the discovery and resolution of discrepancies from expectations. When experience is dominantly aesthetic, we've seen how the process becomes thoughtful, and how it yields satisfaction to those who engage in it. Now we'll follow the process as people pursue it in practical, goal-directed settings.

We're still clarifying the *meaning* of problem-solving. We're concerned with how problems are ideally solved, not with how people typically solve them. In their daily affairs, we are by turns sensible and silly, wise and foolish. Sometimes we search for relevant evidence and make careful inferences. Sometimes we act on hunches, get stubborn, and hope to get lucky. What we want is not an account of everything that happens when people tackle problems, but what an ideal model of problem-solving would look like. Since we aim to guide the young, we want to know how problems are most effectively solved—that is, how we ought to solve them.

But we're not seeking an abstract model of pure rationality. The way problems are ideally solved is in fact the way people sometimes really do solve problems. The clearer we can get about this, the more confidence we'll have in the process, and the better guidance we can offer the young. I'll borrow heavily from John Dewey, who by turns referred to problem-solving as the "complete act of thought," "reflective thinking," and sometimes just "thinking." I'll continue to speak of "problem-solving," and reserve the term "thinking" for more discrete and less context-dependent settings.

The first condition for the appearance of problem-solving is a person's being involved in an activity intended to achieve her own purpose. This was called a "purposeful activity" by progressive educators, an "actual empirical situation" by Dewey. Such activities, he wrote, "give the pupils something to do, not something to learn."[2] These activities can be likened to a stage on which some obstacle must eventually make its appearance. As we've already seen, a problem can't even be conceived unless some purposeful activity has been blocked or disrupted in some way.

Activities that are free of problems can be pursued without much thought. We can act habitually, doing what we've already done before, or simply follow directions or a plan. Many of our daily activities follow this pattern. But when activity doesn't produce what we expect, habit is interrupted; the plan breaks down. In the terms of the earlier discussion, we now confront a discrepancy from what we expected. But this is a discrepancy that's different from the kind described in the last chapter. When the aesthetic is dominant, we encounter a discrepancy from what we expected to see or hear. But now we perceive a discrepancy from a course of events we expected (or hoped, or intended) to occur. We say to ourselves, "*That's* not what I thought would happen!" Or, "That's not what I planned!"

Discrepancies appear in experience unannounced. They lead nowhere until they are interpreted. Since problems are things that people try to solve, a perceived discrepancy will not lead to problem-solving unless a person sees the discrepancy *as* a problem. That is, as worth solving and as susceptible to a solution. Some discrepancies are trivial and allow us to go on with what we were doing. The oil pressure is low, but we're only a block from home. "No problem," we say. Some discrepancies are so great that, instead of trying to deal with them, we discontinue activity altogether. Clouds gather as we pack the horseshoes and the food for the picnic, and it begins to rain before we finish loading the car. "No problem," we say, unloading the car. "We'll play some Monopoly and have lunch at home." And some discrepancies are so great that we can do nothing about them at all; we suffer them as best we can. A cramp during a race, a betrayal by a friend, are not problems to be solved. We can only feel the disappointment and try to control our feelings.

Once we've decided that a discrepancy is worth dealing with and that it can be dealt with, we've identified a problem. Problem-solving can thus be seen as occurring within clearly marked boundaries. Dewey characterized them this way: "The two limits of every unit of thinking are a perplexed, troubled, or confused situation at the beginning and a cleared-up, unified, resolved situation at the close."[3] But before the process starts, a troubled situation must be recognized as a problem. Problem-solving is what happens between the identification of a problem and its eventual resolution.

In the simplest kind of problem-solving, a person gets an idea and tries it out imaginatively. If it seems acceptable, he acts on it in order to resolve the original discrepancy. I'm driving from Davis to Crockenburg on a tight time schedule when I see a road sign announcing that the main road is closed for repairs. There are several alternate routes. One is quite direct and goes through the towns of Hot Springs and Sandoval. Another follows the river without passing through any population centers. A third route takes me a greater distance but offers a freeway. I consider my options and decide that the longest route will take the shortest time, so I head for the freeway.

Compared to the other options, taking the freeway seemed like a good idea. But I didn't *know* it was a good idea until I actually drove to Crockenburg. The drive became a successful test of my hypothesis, because I arrived in Crockenburg on time. This isn't a complicated example, but it contains the essential features of problem-solving: a purposeful activity (my trip to Crockenburg), a discrepancy (the road was closed), a problem (I can't reach my destination in the usual way), an idea or hypothesis tried out imaginatively, and finally, action that turned out to be a successful test of the hypothesis: it solved the problem.

Consider the difference between problem-solving and other, less thoughtful courses of action. I might have acted impulsively. I could have turned off the highway at my first opportunity and taken the first alternative that presented itself. But I would have needed some luck to get to Crockenburg on time. Or I could have acted from habit. Before the main highway was built I used to take the road that went through Hot Springs and Sandoval. If I had done that I'd have been late. Problem-solving didn't guarantee success, but it did increase the chance of reaching my destination on time. In a contingent world, the best we can hope for is to increase the probability of success. Problem-solving does this.

What distinguishes this simple form of problem-solving from impulsive or habitual action is the generation of an idea, an hypothesis. Other forms of action follow *directly* when a problem has been identified. They are literally thoughtless. But when action is based on problem-solving, an hypothesis is interposed between the problem and the act.

To foster this simple kind of problem-solving in schools, we would ask our students to "stop and think." By that, we'd mean, "don't act impulsively; don't just act on habit." We'd be asking students to tell us (or tell a friend) what they were going to do before they did it, and tell us why they thought it would work. If students acted this way consistently over a long period of time, they'd experience more success and more satisfaction than they could by any other means. They would then become *disposed* to act that way—that is, to "stop and think" when they encounter a discrepancy in the course of pursuing a purpose.

Thus extensive experience in problem-solving develops a disposition to act with forethought, to let ideas guide one's actions. It also disposes a person to avoid impulsive action, to recognize when discrepancies constitute soluble problems, and to confront problems and deal with them rather than withdrawing from them and prematurely giving up otherwise worthwhile activities. These are all dispositions worth having and worth cultivating in schools. They can't be learned from lectures or from lessons. They can only be acquired as a function of regular and repeated engagement in problem-solving activities. The crucial role of these activities in learning has recently been rediscovered and rechristened "cognitive apprenticeship."[4]

Problem-solving situations aren't always as simple as the example just described. We don't always know enough to formulate a testable idea. In the example, I drew on past experience to formulate an hypothesis and try it out imaginatively. But when Polly Jones, a newcomer in town, discovers that the main road is closed, her only idea is, "I'll have to find another way." But that's just a fact—not a hypothesis to be tested.

Polly doesn't know any other ways to Crockenburg. She needs information before she can formulate a testable hypothesis. She can look at a map or make a phone call. Eventually she'll acquire some alternatives and generate a hypothesis to act on.

A lot of our problem-solving calls for information. Getting the information so it can be used in solving a problem is a meaningful undertaking, in contrast to acquiring informatioan just to be able to answer questions on an exam. When problem-solving involves the acquisition of new information, additional dispositions are fostered: respect for information and the disposition to seek it wherever it can be found. These dispositions contrast sharply with the distaste often developed in the young when information is imposed on them. They also contrast with students' inclinations to seek information only in standard, approved places: textbooks, teachers, and in cases of extreme need, encyclopedias.

We don't always succeed, even when we act on a carefully worked-out idea. I had decided to take the freeway to Crockenburg because it was a faster route, but if *everybody* who found the main road closed had the same idea, we might all be caught in a traffic jam, and I'd have been late. If my work involved several more trips to Crockenburg, I'd have to reject my first hypothesis and try another one.

In typical school settings, a wrong answer simply means a lower test score. Students try to avoid wrong answers at any cost, and they avoid taking risks for fear of getting it wrong. Over time, such experiences discourage originality and generate conservative dispositions. But when problem-solving situations are regularly pursued in school, learners come to understand that being wrong is not necessarily a fault but is sometimes an unavoidable step in the process of reaching an effective solution to a problem. Thus problem-solving develops additional dispositions when ideas fail to pass the test of acting on them: the courage to try out ideas, willingness to recognize and admit error, and persistence in the face of setbacks.

These simple examples of problem-solving illustrate the components of the process. Here is a more complex example, drawn from the medical research of the physician Ignaz Semmelweis. If we compare this case to that of Mme. Curie (in Chapter 5), we'll see that scientific inquiry does not always proceed from curiosity to problem-setting to problem-solving. In this case we'll see how a genuine problem, not just curiosity, can initiate the sequence of events that constitutes problem-solving.[5]

As a member of the medical staff of the First Maternity Division in the Vienna General Hospital, Semmelweis was distressed to find that many women who were delivered of their babies contracted a serious and often fatal illness known as puerperal fever or childbed fever. Between 1844 and 1846, the death rate varied between 6.8 and 11.4 percent. This was even more alarming because, during the same period of time, the death rate in the adjacent Second Maternity Division was much lower: between 2.0 and 2.7 percent.

Semmelweis rejected some explanations because they were incompatible with well-established facts. That there were "epidemic influences" was rejected because the Second Maternity Division was spared the illness rate of the First, and also because very little childbed fever occurred in or around the city of Vienna. For similar reasons he rejected the idea that the fever was due to overcrowding, or to differences in diet or general care.

Psychological explanations were tried. For example, to bear the last sacrament to a dying woman in the First Division, a priest had to pass through five wards before reaching the sickroom. The appearance of the priest, preceded by an attendant ringing a bell, was held to have a terrifying and debilitating effect on the patients in the wards, making them more likely victims of childbed fever. This adverse factor was absent in the Second Division, since the priest had direct access to the sickroom. Semmelweis tested this hypothesis by persuading the priest to come by a roundabout route and without the ringing of the bell, so he could reach the sickroom silently and unobserved. But the mortality in the First Division did not decrease.

Semmelweis formed a new hypothesis when he noted that in the First Division women were delivered while lying on their backs, and in the Second Division, on their sides. "Like a drowning man clutching at a straw," he tested this hypothesis by using the lateral position in the First Division. Again, the mortality remained unaffected.

Early in 1847, an accident gave Semmelweis the decisive clue for the solution of his problem. A colleague, Kolletschka, received a puncture wound in the finger from the scalpel of a student with whom he was performing an autopsy. Kolletschka died after an agonizing illness that displayed the same symptoms that Semmelweis observed in victims of childbed fever. Although the role of microorganisms in such infections had not yet been recognized, Semmelweis realized that "cadaveric matter" that the student's scalpel had introduced into Kolletschka's blood stream had caused the fatal illness. The similarities between the illnesses of Kolletschka and the victims of childbed fever led Semmelweis to the hypothesis that his patients had died of the same kind of blood poisoning. He and his colleagues and the medical students had been carriers of the infectious material, for they used to come to the wards directly after performing dissections in the autopsy room, and then examine the women in labor after only superficially washing their hands, which often retained a characteristic foul odor.

Semmelweis hypothesized that if he were right, then childbed fever could be prevented by chemically destroying the infectious material adhering to the hands. He tested the hypothesis by requiring all medical students to wash their hands in a solution of chlorinated lime before making an examination. The mortality from childbed fever promptly began to decrease. In 1848 it fell to 1.27 percent in the First Division, compared to 1.33 in the Second Division. Further support for the hypothesis came from the fact that patients in the Second Division were attended by midwives, who did not participate in the dissection of cadavers.

This classic case of problem-solving has all the features discussed to this point. Semmelweis encountered an obstacle to the successful pursuit of his medical practice: an unacceptably large proportion of mothers in the First Maternity Division was becoming ill and dying. Since a similar death rate could not be found elsewhere, Semmelweis acknowledged the presence of a problem. He rejected some proposed solutions (i.e., hypotheses) on logical grounds, and he rejected some other hypotheses after they failed experimental tests he had devised. New information enabled him to formulate yet another hypothesis, and he devised a test that produced the result the hypothesis had predicted. (As Semmelweis himself later found out empirically, a test that affirms a hypothesis does not prove the *truth* of that hypothesis. But it's a step on the way to an inductive generalization. And it's the way an immediate problem gets solved.[6])

Problem-solving is the way people survive and prosper in a world that doesn't just give us what we want. Yet this eminently effective procedure is rarely found in schools, since it requires that students be engaged in activities that are purposeful for them. The structure and organization of schools doesn't encourage purposeful activities. How, then, could problem-solving be conducted in school classrooms?

Problem-Solving in Schools: The Role of Groups

A couple of things about school classrooms distinguish them from other environments in which we learn. In the latter, we learn on our own or with our associates. But in school, we are expected to learn in the midst of a group of two or three dozen others of the same age. Moreover, a single adult is expected to be in control of all of these learners. The size of the learning group discourages individuality in the learners, and the responsibility given the adult encourages him or her to behave in an authoritarian way. These tendencies interfere with learning. Further, the structure of the classroom itself creates its own pedagogical problems.

We've already seen that what attracts one person may not appeal to someone else, and what piques a person's curiosity may be of no concern to another. And because a problem is a function of an activity in which a person is purposefully engaged, a problem for one person may not be a problem for another. So it's hard to offer something in a school classroom that will foster learning *for everybody*. But teachers try to do it anyhow. Everybody is given the same assignment and is expected to learn from the same lecture and the same books. And everybody takes the same exams. In these classes, little is offered that might render experience aesthetic, or provoke curiosity, or permit students to identify it as *their* problem. Most students will do what they think is necessary to satisfy the assignment, but they won't learn much.

Traditions do have a life of their own. But like weeds in a garden, their vitality and their ubiquity aren't sufficient reasons for tolerating them. When there are several dozen learners in a classroom with very different backgrounds, abilities, and interests, it isn't good sense to try to teach them all the same thing, in the same way, at the same time.

Here's a frequently suggested alternative: have each student pursue individual learning tasks. But how do you manage this in a class of thirty? A student doing something no one else is doing won't get much help from others, and others aren't likely to care. The teacher is the only one who can help. But when everyone is engaged in a different task, it's difficult for the teacher to give significant encouragement and criticism to them all. Even to try would leave the rest of the class unsupervised as they worked at their own individual assignments. But without supervision, the rest of the class becomes restless, finding it hard to keep concentrating on their assigned, isolated tasks. These kinds of problems have been enough to thwart most attempts to radically "individualize" instruction.

A room full of thirty or forty heterogeneous people defeats traditional modes of classroom organization and instruction, and efforts to group students by ability do not eliminate their heterogeneity.[7]

Only when a presentation or an activity has an unusually broad and rich appeal can whole class instruction promote learning, and there are hardly any circumstances in which individualized learning programs will succeed. There is but one alternative remaining: to conduct learning activities in small groups.

The large size of classes would be reason enough to put students in small groups for purposes of instruction, but other reasons for doing it are strong enough to justify small groups even if class size were reduced by half. To begin with, tough problems are more readily solved by people working together than working alone. Second, schools are expected to cultivate certain kinds of attitudes and dispositions toward others. But such attitudes can be learned only in the company of others. The nature of these attitudes will be quite different, depending on whether students are working at individual tasks within a large group, or working with each other in smaller groups.

Finally, the school is expected to socialize its students as well as educate them. Socialization, which promotes adaptation rather than independent thought (see Chapter 1), happens to the members of groups whether we like it or not. Thus it makes an enormous difference whether students are socialized to a large, impersonal, authoritarian group, or to a smaller, interacting, democratic group. Long before students are old enough to engage in the analysis or criticism of social groups, they will function as members of groups. And they will become habituated to the customs of those groups and to the way they are controlled. As responsible adults in a democratic society we cannot avoid choosing the character of the groups to which we want our children to become accustomed. Since in schools we socialize as well as educate, we must choose the kind of society within the school into which our children will be socialized.

Everything the school does is enhanced when students are organized into groups. The development of effective thinking is fostered when students solve problems cooperatively as members of groups. The development of democratic attitudes and dispositions can be fostered in democratically organized groups. And since people are socialized simply by virtue of their membership in groups, socialization is defensible when groups are responsibly organized. Yet however important the formation of groups may be, the activities undertaken in them have educational value only insofar as they generate problems. For problem-solving must become the dominant focus of the groups.

Up to now we've discussed problem-solving as an activity undertaken by individuals acting alone. But we'll see before long that without the support of others, few people are likely to become adept problem-solvers. Thus a crucial role for the small group in the classroom is to help its members acquire the skills and dispositions needed to solve problems.

Thus far the discussion of problem-solving has treated its components—hypothesizing, data-gathering, testing—as if they were simply steps to be ticked off in a mechanical procedure. Little has been said about the attitudes and dispositions people must have if they are to succeed at problem-solving. But since problems keep us from getting what we want, we often find them unpleasant and difficult. We seldom greet problems cheerfully. We often get stubborn and fall into bad habits, lose our temper and act blindly, get frustrated and blame others. Or we turn sour and just give up on what we're doing. Solving problems isn't just a mechanical procedure; it calls for more than a set of skills. It requires attitudes and dispositions—like the courage needed to acknowledge the existence of a problem that has to be dealt with; the patience and persistence required when a problem isn't easily resolved; a willingness to risk, to seek help and to give it, to accept personal responsibility, and to admit error. These are some of the most prized traits of character people can have. They are among the most important outcomes of education.

But if you need these traits of character to be a problem-solver, where are you going to learn them? This question brings us to one of education's most daunting paradoxes: *the attitudes and dispositions that are among the chief outcomes of education can be acquired only by doing the things that depend for their success on the presence of those attitudes and dispositions*. Aristotle made this clear more than two thousand years ago:

> For the things we have to learn before we can do them, we learn by doing them, e.g., men become builders by building and lyre players by playing the lyre; so too we become just by doing just acts, temperate by doing temperate acts, brave by doing brave acts.[8]

We want Johnny to learn to stick with a task, even though it's difficult and it looks like it'll take a long time. The only way for Johnny to learn this disposition is to engage in difficult, time-consuming tasks. Yet if Johnny *lacks* the required disposition at the time he engages in the task, what will *keep* him engaged so he can both finish it successfully and develop the dispositions we're aiming at?

There are two answers to this question. The first returns us to what's necessary for problem-solving: an activity that's purposeful for the student. The second answer brings us to a more detailed consideration of the role of groups in learning. We'll consider these two matters under the headings (1) activities that are purposeful, and (2) shared purposes and problem-solving in groups. In the next chapter, the question, "How shall these groups be composed?" will be raised, and we'll consider the criteria for the establishment of learning groups. Those criteria will return us to issues of democracy, and some representative and successful examples of democratic schools will be discussed.

1. Activities That Are Purposeful

The dispositions we hope to foster in the young are never entirely absent when we begin instruction. For example, good work habits may *seem* to be lacking when we ask students to do our assignments. But out of school, when those same people undertake activities of their own choosing, they exercise some of the very dispositions we think they lack. We assign a difficult academic task and wish Johnny had a disposition to stick with it until he was done. But when he practices his shots in basketball or plays a video game, he *does* stick with it until it's finished to his own satisfaction. Thus we seldom have to "implant" a disposition that doesn't yet exist. Instead, we need to *develop* a disposition that's already there, but which may be narrow in scope or insufficiently strong.[9]

Even the very young stay with an activity as long as it's immediately rewarding or promises a desirable outcome. But tasks assigned in school often lack these features. Then attention wanders and work becomes careless. Adults behave the same way; that's why they seek work that brings immediate satisfaction or at least a reward. Adults become accustomed to working at hard, monotonous, even offensive tasks. But they get paid for it. Children, too, will learn to perform distasteful tasks if we pay them. It may be fortunate that we lack the resources to do that. But we must still ask the awkward question, "Why would we *want* to dispose the young to perform difficult, monotonous, or otherwise distasteful tasks?"[10]

While most people might not wish to bore children or make them suffer, many believe that material has been identified that all children *must* learn. They admit this material isn't very exciting.

When children have to study it anyhow, they get (predictably) bored or offended. In consequence, they learn to resent teachers and schools, to display a solicitousness they don't feel, and to acquire work habits—like rote repetition, imitation, copying, and cheating—that are just the opposites of the ones we'd like them to learn.

It's no secret that if we want students to exercise and develop their good habits and dispositions, we should offer them tasks that interest them and appeal to their purposes. This approach is often called "soft pedagogy": indulging the young so they won't resent us. But there really isn't much choice here. Regardless of their age, humans simply can't work effectively for very long at aimless and uninteresting tasks. It is not "realism" to ignore this fact of life; rather, it is to abandon pedagogy altogether and turn schools into mindless labor camps.

If academic material worth teaching holds no interest for learners, then it becomes necessary to "make" it interesting. To do so we promise rewards (or punishments): grades, eligibility for football or the drama club, a place in the college of one's choice. But rewards don't make a task interesting. They simply offer something desirable for completing an uninteresting task. Since learning is a function of the activity undertaken—that is, the task (and *not* the reward), undesirable learnings take place anyhow. What's needed is to encourage activities that are themselves interesting because they appeal to purposes.

The arousal of curiosity and of the aesthetic in experience generate both interest and purpose. But schools need not depend exclusively on these approaches. For young people *already have* some purposes of their own, and they can be helped to develop others. These purposes can become the focus of problem-solving activities. Thus in addition to arousing and pursuing curiosity and the aesthetic, teachers can utilize the existing interests and purposes of children to develop activities that will stimulate thinking and experimentation.[11]

There are several useful ways of initiating problem-solving in schools: (1) Some students aren't dealing effectively with obstacles that block their purposes. Schools can help them turn these obstacles into problems that are soluble. (2) Some students fail to achieve their purpose because they are unaware of what's blocking it. Schools can help them discover what the obstacle is. (3) An absence of purpose marks the lives of many students, which may be an unacknowledged cause of discontent. Schools can help them acquire some new purposes that will generate activities and inevitably encounter obstacles.

Next, we'll look at some activities that exemplify these three approaches to problem-solving. We'll also see that these activities can effectively be pursued within small groups. Thus our focus on the role of students' purposes in learning is broadened to account for the fact that many purposes are or can be shared.

2. *Shared Purposes and Problem-solving in Groups*

(a) Dealing with obstacles that block purposes. More than half of secondary school students work after school. Some need the money, others just enjoy having it. But many young people live a long way from where job opportunities can be found; the distance is an obstacle to getting a job. In many American cities, public transportation is unreliable or nonexistent, so you need a car to get to work.

But cars cost money, and without a job you haven't got the money to get the car to get to work. Adolescents are willing to explore this problem because cars, money, and jobs suit their purposes. It's not an abstract, textbook problem for them; it's a very practical one. But even a used car seems out of reach.

Most teachers know from their own experience that the price of used cars far exceeds their value. They also know that market forces don't encourage the young to spend money in a thoughtful way. But the influence of the school ought to be in the opposite direction. Through discussion in class, a teacher could encourage a group of students to formulate an idea something like this: it's possible to find a used car in good running condition at a price a youth in this neighborhood could afford. *That*'s an hypothesis a lot of high school students would be willing to test.

You may wonder what this has to do with academic learning, but that's not at issue here. We've seen that merely presenting knowledge won't produce learning, so we aim now to stimulate some problem-solving in order to develop dispositions—in this case, dispositions about buying and selling, and about the economic organization of our world. Of course, a great deal of knowledge will also be acquired in the course of this problem-solving, and other dispositions will be acquired, too: toward research, toward their peers, toward working, and so forth. Students' dispositions toward owning and using cars may even change. And their inquiry will uncover areas of academic study that may become attractive to some of them. Let's see, then, how the inquiry might develop.

The aim is to find an affordable used car in good running condition. But you can't just go out and *act* on the idea. Information is needed. To begin with, students will have to decide what they mean by "in good running condition"; how far from perfection will they be willing to go? To decide this is to get clear about what's being sought, so inquiries must be undertaken into the operating systems (the power train, transmission, etc.) of an automobile. Some of these systems must be intact; others can operate in less than perfect condition, and still others can be repaired at a reasonable cost.

Gathering relevant data can most efficiently be done by students working in smaller groups. Some students may get interested in the fields of physics and engineering, which are just beyond the boundaries of the present inquiry. Eventually, the information is pooled and then discussed by everyone involved in the inquiry (it's not likely to be the whole class). Then decisions can be made about the sort of car that's wanted.

The question of what's affordable raises a new set of problems. Students may have to examine varied sources of financing and the significance of differences in interest rates, and then see how all of this is related to their own resources. They might consider pooling their resources and financing one another, instead of limiting their search to commercial lenders. This inquiry into financing, like the search for relevant data about cars, might be daunting for someone working alone. But it can be stimulating and rewarding, both practically and socially, when it is undertaken with one's peers.

In the world outside school, the point of acquiring knowledge is to use it. In this school example, the point is the same: somebody in the class is going to buy a car. While some students examine the engineering features of cars and others investigate the economics of a purchase, others are locating places (e.g., classified ads and used car lots) where the right car might be found. The students may also decide that it matters what the car *looks* like, and this may precipitate another, parallel inquiry. Eventually, some cars will have to be seen firsthand. What the students find will be related to the more general features the class has decided are necessary or desirable in a used car.

Eventually, hypothesizing becomes specific: given its type, its age, its condition, its appearance, and its price, *this* is the car to buy. Is this the right answer? It surely won't be found in the back of the book. In problem-solving, the only way to test the value of an idea is to act on it. The car must be purchased and then driven regularly to work.

That's the culmination of this long sequence of activities called problem-solving. Not because exactly twelve weeks of work have been completed, or because six chapters have been read, or because an exam has finally been taken. It is a culmination because a problem isn't solved until a situation has been clarified and a purpose achieved. Activity is felt as culminating when it has produced a high quality experience that, like a drama, has a perceived beginning, complications, development, and a resolution.

This example may have been oversimplified. Some information is hard to get and some just isn't available. There will be disagreements among those who investigate, and interpersonal attitudes and skills will be challenged. Used cars that are available may not measure up to the criteria, so the criteria may have to be changed. And the car actually purchased may fall apart a week later; students need to be ready for this. Problem-solving can take a long time and it can be very difficult. And it still can fail. But failure to get what you want doesn't mean that useful understandings weren't gained, or that worthwhile dispositions weren't being formed.

Problem-solving is a rich educational resource. It develops a wide range of worthwhile dispositions and it organizes and interrelates diverse skills and large bodies of knowledge. It can also transform purposes that are distinctive to children and adolescents into characteristically adult purposes. For example, many young people prize cars that are new, smart-looking, and powerful. Advertising supports this. A car is seen as a symbol of status, a way of attracting friends. But purposeful inquiries into the mechanics and the economics of buying, using, and maintaining a car can help young people acquire more mature purposes.

(b) Discovering obstacles that block purposes. People often have purposes that remain unfulfilled because they don't recognize what's standing in their way. Many young people looking for a job would like one that's interesting and varied, that appeals to their intelligence, that accords them a measure of respect, and that pays well. But most of them aren't offered jobs like that, especially if they have a minority or low-income background. Instead, they are offered menial jobs that are dirty and repetitious, lack challenge, offer little chance of advancement, and pay the minimum wage without benefits like insurance and time off. Stock boy, kitchen help, janitor, cashier.

They'd like to work in sales instead of the stock room. To wait on tables instead of cleaning up in the kitchen. Many are convinced that only the narrow-mindedness and prejudice of their employers stands between them and the job they want.

If students' suppositions about their employment predicament were correct, there would be nothing they could do about it. Many of them believe this, and believe their alternatives are limited to a lousy job, no job, or illegal work (e.g., running numbers, selling drugs) that involves some danger but offers challenge, social support, and high pay. It's no surprise that a lot of smart and enterprising young people choose the latter course.

This issue may not be considered by some educators a fit subject of study, since it has no home within a standard academic subject. But if educators ignore the issue, they not only turn their backs on the serious purposes of the young, but they waste an opportunity for a powerful, liberating kind of education. It's a chance for some significant problem-solving, but only when a problem can be identified.

Whether a whole class or only a part of it is engaged, a teacher can, through discussion, help students see that if their assumptions about the stupidity and prejudice of employers are *correct*, there will be nothing that can be done about employment opportunities. But the correctness of those assumptions can be challenged—and it ought to be challenged, since it is a fact that *not all* employers are stupid and prejudiced. A teacher could ask if there is one student present who had at least one employer who wasn't stupid or prejudiced. The point, of course, is to create a context of discussion where it makes sense to ask the question, What *other* reasons might exist for the scarcity of desirable job opportunities for the young? Discussion in the group thus moves toward identifying a problem that will promote thinking and at least the first stages of problem-solving.

No two discussions will ever take the same course, but if the teacher has some background in the social sciences, she can help students understand that there are several sources of limits to their opportunities: the prejudices of some employers; some of their own shortcomings; and the nature of our social and economic structure. Students can learn through discussion, reading, observation, and testing, that our economic system demands the exploitation of the labor of those who work. It will confirm students' suspicions when they discover after objective inquiry that the young are among the most exploited of all workers, and that females, blacks, and ethnic minorities are among the most exploited of the young.[12] Apart from their particular vocational goals, it's important for students to learn why this is so, and what might be done about it. If school authorities maintain the pretense that opportunities are truly equal, and that all one needs to do is try, then they deserve the contempt that they get.

Obstacles to good jobs for the young are largely systemic; they're not easily discovered. For example, the more desirable jobs that are available to the young involve interaction with the public. This puts a premium on communication skills. But the speech of the young, and especially the young of minority groups, is not always clear to the wider public. This is in part due to the relatively recent creation of a "youth culture." This culture is largely isolated from the world of adults, partly because of a "youth market" (another form of economic exploitation), and partly because our economic system requires the parent, or both of them, to be away at work. Within the youth culture, a language is spoken that differs from that of most adults, and those differences are magnified by neighborhood segregation that reinforces speech patterns unique to members of lower economic classes and racial and ethnic minorities.[13]

This last point is a potentially liberating one. Unless a young person talks the way a white, middle-class person talks, he or she will be stuck with limited job opportunities. English is taught in school for twelve years, but only scholars (not ordinary schoolchildren) can learn to speak a language from teachers and books.[14] People learn to speak by speaking with others, and that's the first and the most profound fruit of socialization. That's another reason why students need to learn in groups. It's also a reason why segregation in neighborhoods and in schools is so disastrous for a democratic society: it's very hard to speak like a middle-class white person if there are no such persons around to speak with.[15] (We needn't consider whether there is such a thing as a "better" form of speech; our focus here is only on access to better job opportunities.)

But if students can find a purpose in changing some of their language habits, teachers can help them do it—even in segregated schools—through the judicious use of silent and oral reading and group discussion. Without the willing effort of learners, no change is possible at all. But if through a process of shared problem-solving (in this instance, the problem is about worthwhile jobs) a need for language learning is clearly seen, teachers have something to work with. Changes are possible when they're seen as effective means to desired ends.[16]

It's a long way from looking for obstacles to good jobs, to understanding how our economic system works and learning some new language habits. Not all classes or student groups will go the whole distance or take the same route. And for many, the initial problem will remain unsolved. But these aren't deterrents to the enterprise itself. (For comparison, consider that we teach millions of young people mathematics for ten to twelve years and produce only a handful of people who enjoy the subject or pursue it for a living.) Schools cannot be expected to solve problems that originate and are maintained outside the school. But they could hardly be called schools at all if they didn't acquaint the young with the sources of their major problems, and didn't enable the young to think constructively about making worthwhile changes in their lives and, eventually, in the structure of society.

(c) Developing new purposes. It has often been noticed, especially by parents, how bored and restless the young become during the summer months. Why does this happen? How is it that the delirious joy of being released from school in June is gradually replaced by a readiness to return in September? Why do so many young people find it so hard to find something to do in the summer? Could it be that in the preceding nine months of study at school they didn't acquire any new purposes that might have guided their summer activities? If the school did help its students acquire new purposes, why weren't they pursued during the summer?

All of these questions are answered when we acknowledge the very strong likelihood that schools do *not* enable their charges to acquire any new, vital purposes. But if a student hasn't acquired a new purpose, what could she *do* with all the new academic knowledge she was offered? Here is a serious failure of education, for absent the acquisition of new dispositions and new purposes, there would seem to be little point in exposing the young to new knowledge and skills. It would seem that a school has simply failed in its educational mission if its students leave it with the same purposes they had when they entered (along with some new ones they acquired out of school). But if schools and teachers take seriously the task of helping students develop purposes they didn't have before, then new avenues to problem-solving will be created that won't be dependent on the purposes that students already had.

Nearly a century ago, John Dewey served as principal of an experimental school on the campus of the University of Chicago. Within the school a number of informal organizations had developed, including a camera club and a club for discussion and debate. But as the chroniclers of that school wrote, the members of these groups were "sadly put to it for quarters. There was no spot which they could call their own, where meetings could be free from interruption and under their own control."[17]

Dewey observed that unless a person has formulated a plan to achieve an aim, he has not so much a purpose as merely a wish or a desire. There's a great deal that most of us desire, but only when we've considered what we'd have to do to get what we desire, and are prepared to act on those considerations, can it be said that we have a genuine purpose.[18] Because the children in the two clubs at Dewey's school wished they had some privacy and space of their own does not in itself indicate that they had a purpose. But the teachers at this school took seriously what their students wanted, and they provided the conditions that could transform wishes into purposes. Here is what happened in this school:

> Out of the actual, pressing, and felt need of the children the idea of the club-house was born—an actual house planned, built, and furnished by themselves. The two clubs joined forces, discussed the idea, consulted with the adults, and decided that the erection of a club-house was a feasible plan. Committees on architecture, building, sanitation, ways and means, and interior decoration were formed, each with a head chosen because of experience in directing affairs. The site for the building was chosen under the guidance of the teachers in the different departments; plans were made and the cost estimated. A scheme for decoration was worked out, designs for furniture made. The choice of a location was prefaced by a study of the formation of soil, the conditions of drainage, climate, exposure to light or wind, which must be taken into account in building a house.[19]

The club-house was eventually built, and before it was completed it involved all of the children in the school. Admittedly this was a grandiose project, not easily emulated in very many schools. But it shows how it's possible for teachers in a school to help students acquire new purposes and act on them thoughtfully. Here are some of the outcomes of the project:

> This enterprise was the most thoroughly considered one ever undertaken in the school. Because of its purpose, to provide a home for their own clubs and interests, it drew together many groups and ages and performed a distinctly ethical and social service. It ironed out many evidences of an unsocial and cliquish spirit which had begun to appear in the club movement. As children came to realize the possibilities afforded by the cooperation of numbers, this spirit changed from an exclusive to an inclusive one. The boys busy on the benches and the

> girls working on the cushions were brought together by a common purpose as they had not been for more than a year. . . . Another value of the project was that the children made contacts with a wide variety of professional people whom they consulted on their problems or from whom they purchased supplies.[20]

Problem-solving depends on having a purpose toward which activity is directed. Students already have purposes that, when recognized by schools, can serve as a focus for problem-solving. But groups of students can also be encouraged to develop new purposes. Some of these will emerge (as the club-house did in the above illustration) from what students already want. But children can also be helped to develop new purposes in the course of pursuing their curiosity, or in following inquiries that originated in experience that was initially aesthetic in quality.

In the above examples, emphasis was placed on the advantages of problem-solving in cooperative groups. When a problem is complex and difficult, the help of others can make every step in the process more effective. It makes success more likely, and it reinforces attitudes and dispositions of two distinct sorts: those that are germane to success in solving problems, and those that facilitate effective cooperation among partners. In the next chapter we'll shift our focus from problem-solving as a shared enterprise to the nature and composition of the learning groups themselves. Given the educational importance of these groups, it's worth asking how they can be established so as to afford the best possible chance of helping their members solve problems.

7 Educational Method IV: Learning Groups, Democracy, and Democratic Schools

In its more complex forms, human thinking requires the use of symbol systems, whether they be graphic forms, as in drawing and painting, or verbal language. Of course, no human ever worked out a symbol system all by herself. However those systems originated, they did so within the context of human groups, since symbols (unlike the *signs* that we and other animals make, like arching the back or gnashing the teeth), are intended to facilitate action with, and therefore have meaning for other people.

Just as symbol systems originated in groups, thinking itself originated within the activities of groups. Once more, the image of Rodin's *The Thinker* turns out to be misleading. Some humans do, some of the time, go off by themselves to do a bit of hard and protracted thinking.[1] But most of us do most of our thinking—that is, our problem-solving, in the company of others. Our associates can stimulate our thinking and make it richer and more productive. They can also discourage our thinking and virtually ensure that it will fail. We sometimes make erroneous judgments about our ability to think because of the unexamined influence of our associates; others who judge us make similar mistakes. Teachers often make and then record judgments about the capacities of a student without taking into account the influence of the student's peers, or even their own influence, on that student.

Since the influence of our associates has so much impact on our thinking, for good or ill, it can be disconcerting to think that *who* our associates *are* is often a matter of chance. As children, we don't choose our family, our neighborhood, or our classmates. And even if we did, it's not likely that we'd do much better than what we get by chance. But when adults undertake deliberately to educate the young, it would be irresponsible to leave such matters to chance. If the character of a person's associates is likely to have a strong and lasting impact on the character and quality of her thinking, then teachers are obligated to try to assemble groups of students in their classrooms that have promise of exerting a good—that is, a stimulating and helpful—influence on the thinking of their members. So we now attend to the criteria that can be employed for establishing productive and harmonious learning groups.

Criteria for the Establishment of Learning Groups

Mere membership in a group socializes a person. As long as you're a member, and as long as it's important for you to remain a member, you'll conform to the habits, practices, and values of the group. In Chapter 1 we saw how dangerous this process could be if it were *all* that schools fostered, for socialization has little use for thinking; it relies on habituation. But since to a greater or a lesser extent all groups socialize their members, the process can't be avoided, any more than breathing can. Thus educators are responsible for ensuring that *the groups in which the young are interacting are organized in ways that they think are socially desirable and morally defensible.* The reason should be apparent. Groups will develop in their members whatever attitudes and dispositions govern the operation of those groups.

Teachers often put their students into groups, but they don't always realize the importance of how they choose to form these groups. They often treat it as a routine matter, incidental to what they believe are more important choices about content or instructional method. But the choice of how to form student groups is among the most important choices that teachers make.

Some teachers believe that students should be able to have their friends in their groups. Others believe that putting friends in the same groups should be avoided because it might encourage behavior that's not task-oriented. Which belief makes more sense will depend on the circumstances, but those circumstances can't be intelligently judged until we have some defensible criteria for selecting people for group membership. These criteria are pedagogical, social and political, and moral. Whether friends should be put together or kept apart depends on the satisfaction of these general criteria. They can be discussed under three headings: (1) common interests and purposes; (2) inclusiveness; and (3) democratic functioning.

1. Common Interests and Purposes

The members of a group must have something in common. Otherwise it's not a group at all, but just an accidental collection of people. Most grouping in schools is based on achievement: if test scores or grades are similar, students are assembled in informal groups within classrooms, or more formally in tracks (or "streams") within a school. We'll show below, and later in Chapter 10, that this basis for grouping defeats our educational aims.

When discussing curiosity, problem-solving, and the aesthetic, we paid particular attention to students' interests and purposes. At the beginning of a class or a semester, those interests and purposes may be unknown or obscure to the teacher, and even to the students themselves. But once activities are begun—once a presentation has been made or a discussion is under way—interests and purposes become manifest, even though they may not be shared by everyone. Thus the first criterion for establishing a learning group should be obvious: its members should share a similar interest or purpose, because *that* will be the focus for whatever activities they undertake. This is a strictly pedagogical criterion. If learning is fostered best when students pursue what's interesting or purposeful to them, and if that learning is enhanced when people share those interests and purposes, then common interests and purposes should be a major basis for the formation of groups.

Since people have many interests and purposes, and since schools try to develop a wide range of these, students will be members of different groups at different times, and will probably be members of several different groups at any one time. But they won't always work *in* a group all the time that they're members of it. Students will often work individually, sometimes for extended periods, after which they'll bring the results of their work (or the problems they encountered) back to the group for consideration.

There are times when the number of people who share a common interest is greater than the number who can work together well. Then additional groups, all of which may pursue similar activities, need to be set up. The membership of these groups will be established on the basis of further criteria.

2. Inclusiveness

A second criterion for the establishment of classroom groups is also a pedagogical one, but it's a moral, a social, and a political one, too. Its pedagogical aspect is this: we can learn from others only if their experience, or if some of their interests, are different from ours. Although in our casual social groups we seek the easy comfort of people with backgrounds and interests similar to our own, usually we learn less from these associations the longer we maintain them. Thus when children are working in groups with common interests, they'll learn more from one another the more diversity there is among them.

Despite the educational advantages of heterogeneous groups, schools traditionally put young people into groups based not on differences, but on similarities: of IQ scores, of school grades, of racial and ethnic background, and of social and economic class. But this kind of grouping seldom enhances anyone's education. Students in the upper tracks don't ordinarily achieve more than they would if they were heterogeneously grouped; those in the lower tracks achieve considerably less than they would if grouped heterogeneously. What's worse, the members of all groups work in relative ignorance of what the others are like. The members of the upper tracks maintain unwarranted attitudes of superiority; the members of the lower tracks have difficulty maintaining self-respect, and they conceive a future that holds little opportunity. The extensive research on homogeneous and heterogeneous groups overwhelmingly supports these conclusions.[2] Thus for pedagogical reasons alone, the groups in which students learn should be as inclusive as possible of the widest variety of other students who are available.

The moral and sociopolitical dimension of the criterion of inclusiveness can be put in a precise way. Since (1) through the process of socialization people develop attitudes and dispositions about others that reflect the attitudes of their group, and since (2) in a democratic, pluralistic society we maintain ideals of tolerance and respect toward those who are different from ourselves, and since (3) attitudes about others are most effectively and defensibly learned in the company of those others, it follows that the most effective way of fostering tolerance and respect for diverse peoples is to engage in cooperative activities with them as members of heterogeneous groups.[3]

This aspect of the inclusiveness criterion for the formation of groups supports multicultural education. But it would be incorrect to call it a multicultural criterion. Here is why. The attention of educators to multicultural considerations sometimes ignores or obscures other kinds of differences among people that are just as important as far as the quality of their lives and learning are concerned. When diversity is at issue, it's not just racial and ethnic and gender differences that matter. Heterosexually disposed youth can learn from those who are homosexually inclined. Economically lucky children can learn from the disadvantaged. Loquacious, outgoing people can learn from the shy and the quiet ones.[4] People who are interested in books can learn from people who work best with their hands. People who are serene can learn from those who are troubled, and people who are able can learn from those who are disabled.

People who mistrust such diversity in learning groups fear that those who are different might "hold back" the others, might disrupt the progress of the majority. It's true that a student with cerebral palsy can't be treated as if she were no different from her classmates. And of course there should be times in a school day when she is separated from others in order to receive special kinds of help. But in a very fundamental way, the school must treat this child, as it treats every student, as a *person*: as one entitled not only to formal instruction, but also to the companionship and respect of others, and to the sense of belonging and well-being engendered by it, *without which formal instruction is largely ineffective.*

As for the others in the group, the so-called "normal" ones, the presence among them of someone who is different can accustom them to developing a sympathetic understanding without which the group will be unable to achieve its collective purposes. It may be convenient for those in power to segregate "deviates": the old, the young, the ill, the crazy, homosexuals, violators of the law, people of color. But segregation in the world outside the school produces misery for the members of these minorities and leaves everyone else ignorant and afraid. Segregation is a cancer that gnaws at the heart of a democratic society. It is unconscionable even to consider emulating it in schools.

Thus the principle of inclusiveness as a criterion for establishing groups in school has both a pedagogical aspect (people learn best in diverse groups) and a moral-social aspect (a democratic society honors diversity in its people). The second aspect of this criterion is independent of the first one, because it addresses the issue of socialization, not learning. The young will become socialized to *whatever* group includes them as members. So let us ensure that it will be a diverse, heterogeneous, unsegregated group. But we need to go further still. We need to ensure that the group functions democratically.

3. Democratic Functioning

When we're concerned about the educational consequences of being a member of a group, the most useful questions we can ask about it (whether it be a family, a nation, fellow workers, or students in a classroom) are these: What is it up to? Who's in it? How are decisions made in it? The first two questions were addressed in the two sections above. Now, in considering democracy as a third criterion for the establishment of groups in school settings, we focus on the question of how the decisions are made that guide what the group does.

Of the various aspects of democracy considered in Chapter 2, freedom of choice is most relevant to our present concern with decision making. Because the people in our school groups share interests and purposes, their choices must be shared, too. This means that in a group setting, freedom of choice implies participation in governance. But insofar as governance is shared, choices for individuals are not wholly free.

This is the hardest of the three criteria to act on. In the next section we'll see how it's possible to do it, and how it's been done in actual school settings. For now, we must get clear about (1) what participation in governance means in actual practice, and (2) why it must characterize the operation of groups in schools. We'll address these two issues in order.

1. The meaning of participation is confused and corrupted in a nation whose representatives have become unresponsive to its people. In the closing decades of the twentieth century, most eligible voters in the United States did not vote. Thus most Americans did not even participate in elections, let alone participate in governance. The many reasons for this cannot be explored here, but it would be fair to conclude that, while they maintain their allegiance to democracy, the American people have not acted on any common meaning for participation in governance.

But the meaning is much easier to discern if we limit it to the operation of small groups with common interests, instead of trying to apply it to a sprawling nation of two hundred and fifty million people. In a small group of students, participation can be taken to mean that all members are encouraged to express how they feel about what they have done, are doing, or are going to do, and that those feelings and points of view are taken into account when decisions about activities are made. This means that in *whatever* manner decisions are made, they be preceded by open discussion. It's worth emphasizing that participation is not achieved simply by voting. The mass media, and the consolidation of their ownership, have shown us how it is possible systematically to manipulate people's votes. And because voting can be manipulated even in a small group—without any help from technology—the importance for participation of free and open discussion becomes paramount.

Thus even when children are very young and it is wise for an adult to make some of the decisions for a group, the children and the adult have the right (and the obligation) to hear what the affected people think. This is not just for the sake of "blowing off steam." For if a teacher *consistently* makes decisions contrary to the feelings and ideas of children, and if open discussion makes this clear to everyone, pressures for change, both within and outside the classroom, are likely to develop.

When they are older, students can usually make their own decisions as members of a group. On some occasions they may vote, but discussion often reveals that a consensus makes voting unnecessary. Discussion also reveals disagreements. That may suggest the need for a vote, but it may also suggest a need for getting more information or advice before a decision is made. The necessity to make a great many decisions may lead a group to designate some of its members as decision makers within explicitly demarcated areas.

What it means to participate in decision-making in a small group seems clear enough. But it's just as clear that humans are not born with the understandings, skills, and dispositions that would enable them to do it effectively. This puts a heavy burden on classroom teachers. First and foremost, they'll have to model the attitudes and skills of democratic leadership. They'll also have to encourage students to participate in the governance of their groups, reinforcing those who imaginatively reconstruct existing choices, who broaden the range of choices, who accept without rancor the rejection of their ideas by others, and who become committed (and help others to become committed) to group decisions different from those for which they argued. They must also have the patience and understanding to live through and help correct the blunders, distortions, and outright sabotage that will inevitably occur, over and over again. This is a big order for teachers, yet it's one of their most important responsibilities—no less important than teaching children to read, write, or calculate.

2. Democracy is so fundamental an ideal in the United States that even violations of it are defended in its name. Participation in governance is a part of the meaning of democracy, although we've seen that on a broad national scale it's not always easy to tell just what it means to participate in governance. But in a group of schoolchildren there isn't any doubt. If adults believe in the value of democracy, even as an ideal not fully realized, then it has to be acknowledged as the preferred way of organizing the young when they learn in groups.

Objections to this are usually based on the belief that the young are too immature to govern themselves, and certainly too immature to make decisions regarding their own education. Some people regard even college students as too immature to participate in decisions about what they learn.[5] But this objection simply has no foundation. If people are too immature to make decisions about their learning activities when they are in school, then how could they be mature enough, after they've left school, to make decisions about *other* people's learning? By what mysterious means would people acquire this maturity *after* they leave school? Does nature provide some trick that has eluded the investigations of science? Does a mantle of maturity descend on us, unannounced, from heaven?

Those who object to the participation of the young in their own governance in schools apparently believe that maturity is not learned at all, but rather appears the way freckles do in old age. If we reject this foolishness as I think we must, we will recognize that maturity is learned, just like any other trait of character.

A disposition to participate *in a mature way* in the decisions made by one's group can be learned only by participating in making those decisions. In the process, students learn to express their own views, to consider the views of others, to support their opinions with evidence and reasons, to accept responsibility for their decisions, to recognize when they've made a mistake, and to reexamine decisions that lead to unexpected consequences. They also learn to consider what's good for the others in the group as well as what's good for themselves. And they learn that you don't always get what you want when decisions are made democratically. Teachers can help students to value the process and what it promises, so that they can live with the pain of losing and keep participating in the community, rather than withdrawing from it, as many adult Americans have done.

The mature dispositions just discussed cannot be learned by the young if governance is in the hands of someone else. If they are not learned, then other dispositions surely *will* be learned: dispositions of withdrawal—of allowing others to make decisions in which you had a right to participate, and dispositions of obedient acceptance of the decisions of others.

The possibility of everyone's learning the dispositions of docility, acquiescence, and withdrawal is a risk that cannot be taken in a democratic society. Democracy requires a citizenry skilled in the arts of shared decision making and disposed to act that way. But these attitudes and skills are not magically conferred on us. They must be learned in appropriate social contexts. The best time for people to learn them is when they are growing up—when their characters are malleable. And at the present time the best place to learn these attitudes and skills is in school, since only a few young people are lucky enough to learn them at home, and fewer still learn them on the streets. If they aren't learned at school, they're not likely to be learned at all.

Still, it can be objected that all this concern about the learning of democratic dispositions is overemphasized. We have our Constitution, it is said, and we have our laws and our traditions. Isn't this enough to preserve democracy? When the young enter society as adults, our laws and our traditions will protect them and guide their actions.

Like the belief in a divine gift of maturity, this belief is also based on little more than hope and ignorance. Because people spend much of their lives in groups, they cannot grow up without *any* attitudes and dispositions toward social organization and decision making. If they're not disposed toward democratic forms, then they'll be disposed toward undemocratic forms of organization. If the teacher or an elite group of students chosen by the teacher makes the decisions, then students, in acquiescing, will become accustomed to *that*. As they grow older, people who are accustomed to being told what to do become increasingly uncomfortable with democratic forms of organization. They become, in Jerry Farber's phrase, authority addicts.[6]

When people misunderstand or mistrust the law, when they haven't participated in making laws and can't even conceive how to participate, then laws can be upheld only through excessive legalism and force: massive police and military power and an ever-growing prison system. This happened in the United States at the end of the twentieth century.[7] The legal profession expanded even as it lost the respect of the public; the courts expanded yet were overburdened with case loads; police forces increased in number yet could not restrain growing crime rates; and the number of prisons mushroomed, although convicts were released early for lack of a place to put them. With a larger proportion of its citizens in prison than that of any other nation in the world, with the rest of its people in growing fear of violent crime, and with ever-larger numbers of nonvoters losing faith in political parties and in the political system, the future of democracy did not seem assured.

One thing was clear. In the late twentieth century, the United States faced staggering inequities, both absolutely and in comparison to other industrial nations, in the areas of health, education, and welfare. Yet the major share of the nation's resources were spent by the representatives of the people (irrespective of political party) on the military, the Central Intelligence Agency, the Federal Bureau of Investigation, local police and prisons, and on a massive arms industry that supplies them all.[8] These agencies depend for their existence and their effectiveness on force and on secrecy—precisely the traits which undermine and eventually destroy a democracy. A government in which citizens do not participate, in which they have no voice, will not stem the growth of its military and paramilitary institutions.

Democracy can survive only if people are committed to it: only if they have acquired the skills and the understandings, the attitudes and dispositions that foster participation in their own governance. But people are not born with this commitment, nor is it given to them along with their high school diploma. They must learn it. This difficult and most important of all learnings can be achieved only through many years of active participation in democratic forms: through the processes of socialization that result from mere membership in groups that are democratic, and through education itself, in which democratic processes are practiced, examined, questioned, challenged, tested, and judged. Perhaps new kinds of institutions are needed in which the young can learn the skills and dispositions of democratic citizenship. But for now, schools are all we have.

Democracy in Schools: Has It Ever Worked?

The discussion until now has been hypothetical and theoretical. Examples were offered of how problems can be solved in democratically organized groups of students, and the meaning of democratic participation was clarified. It was just now argued that the activities of schooling need to be organized in democratic groups, for two different sorts of reasons. First, students become socialized into the groups of which they are members. Since this socialization can't be avoided, I suggested that a society that values democracy arrange for the young to become socialized in groups that are trying to practice democracy. Second, effective participation in a democractically organized group calls for interpersonal skills and dispositions of an unusually complex and subtle kind (it's much easier just to give and obey orders). These skills and dispositions are not given at birth, and they aren't acquired through natural processes of maturation.

And since there aren't many occasions to learn them out of school, it was suggested that in school the young be educated in democracy as well as socialized to it.

But a skeptic could grant the theoretical plausibility of these arguments and yet still object to them. He might say that our students just can't handle this kind of organization. They need discipline. They need to be told what to do. Democracy is fine for grown-ups, but if you try it with children and youth, your efforts will end in chaos. And then you'll end by telling them what to do, anyhow.

The best way to meet this kind of objection may simply be to cite some cases where democracy has been successfully practiced in school classrooms. It's not necessary to show that it's been successful all over the country, because it hasn't been tried all that much. But it is necessary to show that it *has* been successfully practiced if we want to meet the skeptic's objection that it *can't* be successfully practiced. So we'll offer three illustrations of the successful operation of democracy in schools: (1) in a small school serving children from upper-middle-class homes; (2) in a school serving racially and ethnically mixed low-income children; and (3) in a school district serving predominantly low-income, minority neighborhoods. Other cases could be cited, but these examples are particularly relevant to current educational problems, and detailed descriptions are available. The purpose here is not to argue that all who try a democratic approach to schooling will succeed, or even that all who teach should try it. Rather, it is to show that *it's possible* for teachers to organize the learning activities of the young in democratically functioning groups. And that the consequences of such organization are very desirable from educational, moral, and social perspectives.

1. The Sudbury Valley School

Peter Gray and David Chanoff have described and analyzed the Sudbury Valley School, a fully accredited private day school in Framingham, Massachusetts.[9] The school has no admissions standards and it admits anyone aged four or over. Between 1968 and 1985 its population varied between fifty-five and ninety, and in 1985 it had a staff of thirteen; three teachers worked full time. The school charges tuition, but its per-pupil operating costs are less than those of the public schools in the surrounding area.

The Sudbury Valley School (SVS) has no curriculum and students have no schedules and are assigned to no groups. The initiative for learning is expected to come from the students. The staff teaches through informal conversation. Tutorials are organized if the students request them, and the staff initiates seminars and lectures if they can attract students. Whatever work is done, there is no institutional evaluation of it: no exams, no grades, no written or oral progress reports. However, students often seek critiques and judgments of their work from the staff. To receive a high school diploma, each student must present and defend a graduation thesis at a meeting open to all of the students, staff, parents, and trustees of the school. The thesis is that the candidate is ready to take responsibility for him- or herself in society at large. The student's support for this thesis is followed by up to two hours of questioning by anyone attending the meeting.

SVS is governed by a School Meeting composed of all students and staff. The meetings are formal and are held once a week. An agenda is distributed in advance and parliamentary procedures are observed. The entire range of administrative functions are handled in these meetings: financial management, hiring of staff, buildings and grounds, public relations, and the legislation of all rules of behavior.

The organization of SVS is about as open and flexible as one could imagine, and its governance is democratic in the most straightforward sense of the term. Its main difference from A. S. Neill's Summerhill is the fact that the latter was a boarding school.[10] The question we must ask about SVS is this: Aside from the fact that it had operated continuously for seventeen years at the time that its graduates were systematically studied, is there any evidence to suggest that its open, democratic form of organization resulted in a worthwhile education?

Of the seventy-six students who could be located from among the eighty-two who graduated between 1970 and 1981, sixty-nine (91%) participated in the study, either through the use of questionnaires, telephone interviews, face-to-face interviews, or some combination of the three. The point of the study was to discover how these people fared after high school was over. The researchers asked these former students to tell them how SVS either benefited them or handicapped them in their subsequent schooling or in their employment.

Before we look at the responses of these students, we might note just a little background information about them and their academic work at SVS. Most of the students were from the middle class, and many of them had had attitude or learning problems at the school they attended prior to entering SVS. Fourteen of the interviewees averaged ten years at SVS, and fifty-five of them averaged two and a half years. When asked to list the courses or tutorials they took at SVS, 29 percent of the former group and 56 percent of the latter group said they took none at all. Together, they estimated they spent about 8 percent of their time in school doing "academic work" of the sort done in regular school courses.

Since it lacks a curriculum and gives no tests, SVS provides no transcripts to college admissions officers and it refuses to rank its students. How many of its graduates went to college, then, and what happened when they got there? What happened when they tried to pursue careers?

As Gray and Chanoff note, "The basic premise of our graded system of education, which assumes that even a few weeks missed from the orderly progression of classroom work may leave students seriously behind, would predict that SVS graduates should not be able to handle college work."[11] It would be reasonable to expect a disaster. Instead, many SVS graduates went on to highly selective colleges and did well there.

At the time of the study, more than half of the SVS graduates had completed a college degree or were matriculating in a degree program. Only 25 percent of them had no formal schooling after they left SVS. How did they get into college without having any transcripts? Some attended a two-year institution and then transferred into a four-year college. Others were admitted on the basis of Scholastic Aptitude Test (SAT) scores and letters of recommendation. As the Eight-Year Study amply demonstrated two generations ago,[12] the belief that a sequential curriculum, regular testing, grades and class rankings and grade-point-averages are all *necessary* for college entrance is simply mistaken.

Was the program of SVS a handicap or a benefit to college work? Thirteen of the thirty-five graduates who went to college said that SVS handicapped them in some ways, but they all said that the benefits outweighed the handicaps. On the other hand, thirty-two of the thirty-five graduates said that SVS benefited them. When asked what sorts of benefits they received, many said that they communicated more easily with their professors, just as they did with their teachers at SVS. But the most frequently cited benefit was a greater motivation to continue learning and a feeling of greater responsibility for their own education. This dispositional benefit, and its relevance to doing academic work, was expressed by one of the graduates in the following way:

> A lot of the people there (in college) have had more experience in some of the substantive areas. But the attitudinal difference

> seems to allow me to catch up very quickly. The substantive things are trivial to acquire. . . . My attitude is that I'm going to college for fun and I fully intend to enjoy myself by taking full advantage of whatever it has to offer. The attitude of many people there is that they're going because they were kind of corralled. It never occurred to them that there was something else they could do.[13]

This student was an honors student, but none of the SVS graduates had trouble adjusting to the formal structure of college—required courses, assignments, exams, and so on. They were already accustomed to working on their own, without constant supervision, and they felt advantaged over the graduates of standard high schools.

The SVS graduates who went to work felt much the same as those who went to college. At SVS they pursued activities that they developed and pursued in jobs and careers: music, the visual arts, designing, cooking, mechanics, computers, physics, psychology, social service professions, and so forth. Forty-five of the graduates said that high school was a benefit to their careers; only five said it was a handicap. And while their activities at SVS were often directly related to their subsequent work, they also cited (like the college students) dispositional benefits: that they learned to be responsible, to be self-directed at work, to take initiative and to get things done, and to deal openly and directly with authority figures.

There appears to be a paradox here. At SVS, students were not required to do any academic or vocational work, yet they went on to good colleges and good jobs. Even setting aside the fact that these graduates felt good about themselves and their work, they have done well by even the most conventional standards. How can this be explained?

Gray and Chanoff offer two reasons for this. First, they claim that what's normally taught in high schools doesn't supply the knowledge and skills needed in careers or in higher education. "Rarely would an employer be concerned about a prospective employee's knowledge of ninth-grade algebra, tenth-grade biology, or eleventh-grade history. However, if the person had developed special skills and knowledge by direct involvement in the field in which employment is sought, as was the case for many of the SVS graduates, that would be of great interest to an employer."[14]

Second, Gray and Chanoff suggest that participation in the SVS community itself helped to develop attitudes and dispositions beneficial to learning. Once they were in college, SVS graduates "seem to have had little trouble catching up. . . . The graduates themselves explain this in terms of their positive attitude about learning, their feeling of responsibility for their own learning, their ability to find things out on their own, and their lack of inhibitions about communicating with professors and asking for help when needed—characteristics that they regard as having been fostered by their SVS experience."[15]

Skeptics may claim that these middle-class young people might have done just as well in college and at work had they attended a standard high school. That claim ignores the fact that many of these students went to the Sudbury Valley School *because* they were having serious trouble in standard schools. But even if the claim were true, the fact remains that the SVS students did well after high school *without* the structured curriculum, the close supervision, and the authoritarian organization of the standard high school. This means that these students were free at SVS to do things that resulted in high-quality experience for them. And because these activities involved effort and thought, it seems fair to say that the organization of the Sudbury Valley School made possible experience for its students that was genuinely aesthetic in quality. The organization of SVS was not simply anarchic. It was a democractic one, and it had beneficial consequences not only for the quality of the students' experience, but also for the quality of their relationships with others, and for the enhancement of their own futures.

2. *The First Street School*

George Dennison's *The Lives of Children: The Story of the First Street School,*[16] is unmatched in its acute observations of children, its insightful analyses of social relationships, and its creative way of showing how the activities of children can be guided by the aims of teachers. Written a generation ago, I doubt if any book written since then offers more insight into the education of low-income, ethnically diverse city kids. Dennison doesn't deal directly with what he calls the technocrat's question: How can we improve our schools? Rather, he confronts a more fundamental question, one of particular concern to scientists and philosophers: How can we educate our young?[17] In answering it, Dennison describes a school similar in spirit to the Sudbury Valley School, but institutionally as different from SVS as it is from standard public (and private) schools.

The First Street School (FSS) was small. It was located in New York's Lower East Side in classrooms, art and shop rooms, and a gymnasium rented in an old YMCA building. In its second year, the one described in Dennison's book, it enrolled twenty-three children from five to thirteen years in age. Black, Puerto Rican, and white in almost equal proportions, they all came from low-income families. Half the children were from nearby public schools and had severe learning or behavior problems.

The school had one part-time and three full-time teachers; a few others came at scheduled times for art and music. Despite this low pupil-teacher ratio, costs were no more than the annual operating costs of the surrounding public schools (for example, there were no administrative, building, or maintenance costs). The school was funded by a private (nonfoundation) grant, but since it accepted all who applied from the neighborhood, it functioned as a public school. When the grant ran out and no other donors could be found, the school closed.

FSS had no administrators, no competitive tests, and no report cards. Unlike The Sudbury Valley School (or even Summerhill), the school did not even have a deliberative body that met regularly to make decisions about policy, program, discipline, and so on. Nonetheless, I offer this school as an example of a democratic school. We noted earlier (in Chapter 2) that democracy is not to be confused with the mechanical act of voting, and in this chapter (p. 144) we noted that democratic participation implies that "all members are encouraged to express how they feel about what they have done, are doing, or are going to do, and that those feelings and points of view are taken into account when decisions about activities are made." These kinds of relationships were called "caring" by Dennison; he also discussed how forms of loving operate within them. I am calling such relations "democratic"—not to disagree with Dennison, but to call attention to *how the relations among people are organized.* These relations are often *felt* as caring or being cared for,[18] as loving or being loved. Democracy is not the sort of thing that is felt, although we might speculate that neither care nor love can flourish apart from democratic relations among people (even Aristotle declared that friendship can exist only among equals). In any case, it is enough to say here that the same relations that Dennison calls caring can be described as democratic when attention is focused on the way decisions come to be made.

The description of the First Street School has until now indicated only what it lacked: administrators, competitive tests, report cards, a preplanned curriculum. It would be reasonable to ask what educational benefits could be expected from simply eliminating certain standard features of schooling. The answer must be put in terms of what FSS *had* that standard schools usually lack. Public schools are ordinarily conceived as places of instruction, and that emphasis, along with its attendant structures (age-grading, sequential curriculum, progress reporting, etc.), puts severe constraints on the relationships among persons. Dennison writes that at FSS "we conceived of ourselves as an environment for growth, and accepted the relationships between the children and ourselves as being the very heart of the school." And at the heart of those relationships was freedom, experienced by teachers and pupils alike.

But it was not the freedom that was *experienced*; rather, it was the *activities* that were experienced. Dennison recalls a child in public school complaining, "They never let me *finish* anything." He then comments, "We might say of the child that he lacked important freedoms, but his own expression is closer to the experience: activities important to him remain unfulfilled. Our concern for freedom is our concern for fulfillment—of activities we deem important and of persons we know are unique." Thus what was of paramount importance to the teachers at FSS was very similar to what was discussed in Chapter 4 as the quality of experience.

We judge the benefits of a school in terms of what the school is trying to accomplish. FSS did succeed in raising some of its pupils' achievement scores, but that's not what it was aiming at. It aimed, as I have urged (especially in Chapter 3), at the cultivation of a range of mental and emotional dispositions. Important as these are, they cannot be assessed by paper-and-pencil tests, especially competitive tests.[19] It is well to remember that machine-scored testing became widespread when those who made decisions about the student *no longer knew the student*. In other words, decison-makers had not a clue about the dispositions (i.e., the character and personality) of the students being tested. Thus they had no idea about some of the most important of educational outcomes, and their tests offered no help in this regard. But the popularity of these tests (which are also called, curiously enough, "objective" tests) is so great that even otherwise sensible educators succumb to their authoritative aura. One such observer writes this:

> Those of us fortunate enough to have visited good English primary schools recognize almost intuitively that what we are seeing is mostly right, mostly effective, mostly sound. On the other hand, many educators have a way of asking questions that cannot be adequately answered by referring to one's per-

> sonal observations. How, in fact, do children in such schools perform on various objective measures when compared to children who have had a quite different sort of school experience?[20]

To see whether the democratic organization of FSS resulted in real benefits to the students, we will not seek the results of standard evaluative measures. We will not even seek, as we did for the Sudbury Valley School, the subsequent careers of its graduates, for FSS lasted only a short time and its teachers lost contact with their former students. Instead, we'll consult the personal observations of one of its teachers, George Dennison. Dennison articulated very clearly what FSS was trying to achieve, and by examining some of his descriptions of the interactions among students and teachers we can decide for ourselves how keen his observations were, and whether his judgments about educational outcomes ought to be trusted.

Dennison wrote, "The business of a school is not, or should not be, mere instruction, but the life of the child." We now look at some slices of the lives of children at FSS, as Dennison described and analyzed them. There is space for only a few examples. I'll summarize when it's possible, but in many cases we'll learn more by confronting Dennison's own language. To repeat, *our* question is, Did the democratic organization of FSS produce educationally valuable outcomes? That is, mental and emotional attitudes and dispositions that we would regard as desirable?

Nine-year-old Maxine had come to FSS under threat of expulsion from the public school. A typically "rebellious child," her problems were met with disciplinary action by the public school. But almost all of her disruptive behavior "was a way of asking for something she really needed. In effect, she kept saying, 'Deal with all of me! Deal with my life!'"

> The deep confusions of her life are knocking at her forehead—and who better to turn to than a teacher? She does it indirectly. She runs across the room and hugs her favorite boy, and then punches him, and then yells at the teacher, who is now yelling at her, "Do you have a boyfriend? Does he lay on top of you? Do babies really come out of the . . . out of the . . ." she wants to say the magic word . . . and she does say it—"*cunt.*" It invokes a whole world of power, heat, and confusion. Obviously it is powerful: it makes the grownups jump. But pleasure, fertility, and violence are all mixed up here, and she wants desperately to sort them out. And there is her new daddy, and something he

> has done to her mother. And there is the forthcoming rival.
>
> All these are the facts of her life. If we say that they do not belong in a classroom, we are saying that Maxine does not belong in a classroom. If we say that she must wait, then we must also say how long, for the next classroom will be just like this one, and so will the one after that.
>
> . . . Now what is so precious about a curriculum . . . , or a schedule of classes (which piles boredom upon failure and failure upon boredom) that these things should supercede the actual needs of the child?[21]

At FSS, Maxine's needs were accepted as needs, and thus diminished. Her unique powers were supported and thus allowed to grow. This was not easy to do, but it was rewarding:

> By the end of the year Maxine had changed spectacularly, especially with regard to a problem that was perhaps more important than her sexual confusion. This was the problem of relating to her peers. Here again, her own disruptive behavior often held the clue to correct action. Surely it meant something if, during a lesson, she began to fret, or shout, or tease. Perhaps she had had enough. Fine. She was free to drop the lesson, free to leave the room. . . . Often she said, "I'm going up and see [another teacher]." The answer was positive: "Go ahead."
>
> Which brings us back to the question of forming the groups. Maxine had been assigned to [the teacher of the eight- to ten-year-olds]. She reassigned herself when the need arose. Her reasons were excellent. [The other teacher] was the warmest and most motherly of the teachers. Her children were the youngest in the school. Maxine could relax among them and give rein to the infant who still lived within her. She was a different girl in this group, cooperative and affectionate. . . . Yet presently she would grow bored. What were her *real* classmates doing? What were they up to? Back she would go to [the first teacher's] room, and for several minutes, perhaps ten or fifteen, would plunge into a book or a worksheet of math. This may seem like too brief an effort—a mere fifteen minutes of concentration. But these minutes were worth hours of passive listening, and worth years of rebellious conflict. At the end of the year Maxine was reading three years beyond her age level. Which is only to say that for the first time in her life she was using the intelligence she so obviously possessed.[22]

Here is another incident which illustrates not only the educative uses of freedom for an individual, but for a group as well. It may be a little easier to see, here, how democratic forms of organization and genuine concern for children are inseparable. From another perspective, the incident exhibits the teacher's regard for the aesthetic quality of the students' experience:

> Dolores, age nine, and Elena, age ten, both Puerto Rican, begin talking to each other during the lesson in arithmetic, paying no attention to Susan, their teacher. To make matters worse, several of the children begin listening to them. Instead of calling the class to order, however, Susan also cocks an ear. Elena is talking about her older sister, who is eighteen. Their mother had bought a voodoo charm, and the charm had been stolen. Dodie, a Negro girl of nine, enters the conversation, saying in a low voice, "Voodoo! It don't mean nuthin'!" "What kind of a charm?" says Susan. "A charm against *men*!" says Elena. And now the whole class begins to discuss it. Rudella, a Negro girl of nine, says, in her broad, slow way, "Phooey! I bet she stole it herself. I know somebody I'd use that thing on." Susan agrees with Dodie that voodoo probably doesn't work, "though maybe it has a psychological effect." "Yeah," says Elena, "it makes you afraid." The discussion lasts ten or twelve minutes, and then all return to arithmetic.
>
> . . . If Susan had tried to save time by forbidding the interesting conversation about voodoo, she would first have had a stupid disciplinary problem on her hands, and second (if she succeeded in silencing the children), would have produced that smoldering, fretful resentment with which teachers are so familiar, a resentment that closes the ears and glazes the eyes. How much better it is to meander a bit—or a good bit—letting the free play of minds, adult and child, take its own very lively course! The advantages of this can hardly be overestimated. The children will feel closer to the adults, more secure, more assured of concern and individual care. Too, their own self-interest will lead them into positive relations with the natural authority of adults, and this is much to be desired, for natural authority is a far cry from authority that is merely arbitrary.[23]

Dennison's impressive discussion of helping a Puerto Rican youth to read is too extended to summarize here, so my final illustration focuses on a fight among five boys. There is, of course, no academic learning involved here; what is at issue is the quality of the personal relations among these boys. If they are full of hatred and violence, how could we *ever* hope to interest them in academic materials? Learning proceeds best in an encouraging, supportive environment, but the teacher cannot be solely responsible for this. The learners themselves constitute the group from which the support must come. But if they mistrust one another, fear one another, hate one another, there will be no support, and the teacher's academic goals will not be achieved:

> When Stanley and Willard first came to school, there was a violent fight. When Stanley came alone, there was another fight, and José pulled a knife. And for several days, with Stanley and Willard in school together, there was violence in the air, those two squared off against the Puerto Ricans. Yesterday some trivial incident occurred, and the boys decided to "fight it out." At first the fight was scheduled to take place after school, but then they decided to have it in the gym. . . .
>
> The boys shouted back and forth excitedly—insults, plans for the fight, threats, boasts, and some kind of cooperative exchange concerning vague outer limits of behavior. They cooperated, too, in getting out the mats and laying them in a great square. I [Dennison] helped them with this and then withdrew to the end of the gym, where I sat on the floor and leaned against the wall.

The teachers at FSS intervened as little as possible in the developing relations among the students. They modeled concern and respect for others, and they expected the children to develop their own forms of these traits in the belief that the children could discover for themselves their intrinsic, as well as their instrumental value. These boys had attended FSS long enough already to appreciate the value of agreed-on structures within which activities could be conducted:

> A great shout went up, a roar, and all five piled into each other . . . and stopped abruptly to let José take off his shirt. Stanley and Willard took their shirts off, too. . . . The roar went up again and they tangled, Stanley and Willard against José, Julio, and Vicente. Their fighting included both punching and wrestling.
>
> . . . There was much cursing, many shouts of pain—strange shouts, really, for each one had in it a tinge of protest

> and flattery. It was in these overtones that one could sense the fine changes in their relations. They were saying things for which they had no words, and the refinement of this communication was extraordinary and beautiful. It was apparent immediately that the boys had set some kind of limit to their violence, though they had not spoken of limits. . . . When anyone got hurt, he stepped off the mats (it was usually Julio, holding his head and complaining in a voice which paid tribute to Willard's strength); and the rule was accepted by all, without having been announced, that no one could be attacked when he stepped off the mat.

What had begun simply as a fight had become transformed into a game. This was not acknowledged, but it was apparent in the manner in which the boys fought:

> . . . Occasionally, as the boys rolled and squirmed, they also punched each other in the ribs. These blows, however, were almost formal, and were very subtly adjusted. The loser must prove that he is really struggling, and so in order to ensure himself against the contempt of the victor, he punches him in the ribs. Delivered with just the right force, these punches remain compliments ("I esteem you and want you to think well of me"). They are tributes, too, to the reality of the fight. Delivered a bit harder, they are "unfair." Delivered still harder, they precipitate a bloodletting. And so they are very nicely attuned.
>
> For about fifteen minutes the fight was a melee, a pattern of up and down, up and down, for no matter whom Stanley and Willard threw to the mats, there was always one Puerto Rican left over to tug at their feet or jump on top. Soon all the boys had lumps, and by an absolutely unspoken agreement stopped fighting to catch their breath. They wandered around enemies comparing bruises in very friendly voices and exchanging indirect flattery; e.g., José says to Vicente, in a loud voice, "Man, did you hear his head"—pointing to Julio—"hit the floor!" and Willard, who had accomplished that sound, turns away and grins.

All this time, the boys, huffing and puffing, pay no attention to Dennison and another teacher who sit at the other end of the gym. The boys resume the fight and Willard, getting the upper hand with José, is still unable to pin him to the mat. So he shouts again and again, "Give up?" and José cries, "You have to kill me!"

> . . . The decision is in Willard's hands. Soon he lets José up, but punches him on the arm so José won't think he has been let up. Willard shows great tact in his awareness of victory. . . . José is somewhat abashed by his defeat, but he squares off against Willard, bluffing to the hilt and acting tough. He takes a boxer's stance, with curled fingers and weaving shoulders, saying, "Come on, man, come on." Willard looks at him for a moment. In boxing he could demolish José, and there is no doubt about it. Nothing shows in his smile. He puts up his hands and shadowboxes with José. In fact, they are playing together, and this is the first time.[24]

Mixed with Dennison's sensitive descriptions of the children at the First Street School are his evaluations of their progress. There are other ways of evaluating, but how, on a competitive, so-called "objective" test, could one evaluate whether a child had become more courageous, or more thoughtful, or more patient? These were major aims at FSS, and it is likely that academic aims have little hope of achievement unless these are achieved. But there is one more source, beyond the teachers themselves, of evaluations of the FSS pupils: their parents. Many of them initially had strong reservations about the school's approach:

> . . . Certain of the First Street parents . . . objected to the noise, the lack of punishment, and the apparent disorder of our classes. They thought we were horsing around. But they were in contact with other of the parents, who did not share their views; and of course they noticed the changes in their own children. Before the year was well out, they had reversed their opinions.
>
> . . . The improvement in the kids had a strong effect on family life, not only because hope was revived, but because the kids were no longer sources of trouble and criticism. As the kids became happier, so did the parents. Not all changes took communal forms. Some were romantic. One mother blossomed suddenly into an off-Broadway actress. Two found new husbands. Was this an effect of the school? Who knows? A woman looks prettier when she isn't frantic with worry and depressed by the feeling of isolation. I claim it for the school. All these parental changes had further effects on the children. To some small extent, these new relations among their parents turned the neighborhood in the direction of community.[25]

There are similar stories from the Headstart schools of the 1960s, stories of mothers who became involved with Headstart, became more focused and articulate, and who subsequently became effective leaders in their neighborhood communities. Democracy has always seemed to work best in smaller groups, where people come to know one another and where changes interlock and spread out in ever-widening circles, like the ripples made by pebbles thrown into a pool. But some will say, our classes are too large for this, our schools and our school systems are too large. All we can do is use standardized tests to evaluate the children. This pessimism is misplaced. Large size and the bureaucracy that results are matters of organization and administration, and these can be changed. Our final example of democracy in schools will show this. We will discuss further the matter of institutional change in Chapter 8.

3. *The Central Park East Schools*

Our last example of the successful operation of democracy in schooling is very different from the first two. Instead of considering a particular school we'll examine a collection of schools in a school district. And instead of following the careers of graduates, or closely observing the interactions of students in a school, we'll examine the organizational arrangements that brought democratic decision-making to these schools.

Examples of exciting, innovative, democratic schools quite often turn out to be small schools, where faculty and students make up an intimate, face-to-face community. Skeptics are likely to object that in the most typical school systems at the end of the twentieth century, schools are large, bureaucratic organizations that discourage intimacy, personal responsibility, and democratic forms of control. The truth of this claim does not imply, however, that there is no alternative to this form of organization.

New York City is assuredly an example of a huge, centrally controlled, bureaucratized school system. Yet even within this system it was possible for a district superintendent (Anthony Alvarado of East Harlem's District 4) to encourage teachers to establish alternative schools of their own design. These schools made choice possible for parents in the neighborhood, and they were usually located in the same buildings in which the more traditional schools continued to operate.

These small, alternative schools were first established in 1974. They required no massive capital investment, no wide-ranging Master Plan, no detailed blueprint. They had the support of the local political establishment, there were local teachers who wanted to try out new ideas, and the superintendent was a person who "argued, cajoled, manipulated. He attracted talent, he made schooling seem an adventure. He never downplayed professionalism, didn't knock teachers, avoided looking for villains. He didn't mandate one universal top-down system for improvement."[26]

The establishment of these alternate schools began with a few model schools open to parental choice, located within existing buildings where space was available. These schools were initially quite small, with only a few classes. Having no need for their own buildings or administrative system, the programs of these schools were devised by the teachers who taught in them, in consultation with parents whose children would attend them. When people in the "regular" schools complained about favoritism, they were told by the superintendent that they, too, would receive assistance and encouragement if they had some new ideas they wanted to try out.

Some accepted this challenge. In less than ten years, fifty-one schools occupied twenty buildings, and schools in the district were no longer equated with buildings. The alternative schools remained small: some had as few as fifty students, none had more than three hundred. By 1984 the superintendent announced that no junior high would serve a specific geographic district. Provided with informatiuon about the schools from the district, parents would have to choose the schools of their new seventh graders.

Deborah Meier participated in the founding of the first of these alternate schools in 1974, and she described the establishment of these schools in 1991, when she was serving as principal of Central Park East Secondary School (how this school operated can now be seen on a remarkable videotape[27]). Her discussion clearly shows that the democratic establishment of small, autonomous schools does not guarantee that the schools will be progressive, or even particularly innovative. But it does make it *possible* for schools to operate in educationally sound ways, and in ways chosen by those who work in them and are affected by them:

> A majority of the new schools were fairly traditional, although more focused in terms of their themes (such as music, science, or journalism) and more intimate and family-oriented due to their small size. Size also meant that regardless of the formal structure, all the participants were generally informally involved in decisions about school life. Most of the schools were designed by small groups of teachers tired of compromising what they thought were their most promising ideas. As a result, there was a level of energy and esprit, a sense of co-own-

> ership that made these schools stand out. . . . A few schools used this opening to try radically different forms of teaching and learning, testing and assessment, school-family collaboration and staff self-government. In this one small district, noted only a decade earlier as one of the worst in the city, there were by 1984 dozens of schools with considerable citywide reputations and stature, alongside dozens of others that were decidedly more humane . . . A few were mediocre or worse; one or two had serious problems. The consensus from the streams of observers who came to see, and those who studied the data, was that the change was real and lasting. What was even more important, however, was that the stage was set for trying out more innovative educational ideas as professionals had the opportunity to be more directly involved in decision making.[28]

Simply to describe these schools is not to provide hard evidence that they are as good as, or better than, the larger and more traditional schools alongside which they operated. Although the additional costs of these schools were not high (equal to the cost of one additional teacher for every newly created school), a changing political climate has thus far prevented the financing of research to assess these schools and the performance of their students. But perhaps there are occasions when ideas and institutions can immediately be recognized as good ones without having to undertake extended, detailed, and costly empirical assessments. Perhaps Meier's own assessment should be taken advisedly: "Within ten years . . . District 4 totally changed the way 15,000 mostly poor Latino and African-American youngsters got educated without ever pulling the rug out from under either parents or professionals."[29] But the important thing about the schools is that they were organized democratically and that they *survived* in a climate that was often hostile. Meier is very clear about the connection between democratic organization and survival: "That the fifty-three schools have survived the past few [politically and economically threatening] years in a system that not only never officially acknowledged their existence but often worked to thwart them is a tribute to the loyalty and ingenuity that choice and co-ownership together engender."[30]

Most of what has been said thus far about learning and about democratic ideals and democratic groups has been discussed without reference to the particular conditions that obtain in existing schools and school systems. The reason for leaving current, actual situations out of account was this. The complexity of an existing situation ordinarily generates ideas intended to deal with the particular details within that complexity; *those* ideas, however, often turn out to be quite inadequate for dealing with the *next* complex situation. Problem-solving undertaken on this basis produces what are called ad hoc solutions: they are good (or pretty good, and sometimes not much good at all) for a while, and then they must be discarded in favor of new efforts. When problems are very complex and serious, as are the problems of educating the young in a modern postindustrial democracy, these ad hoc efforts to solve them are expensive, frustrating, and more often than not unsuccessful.

For the above reasons, the major part of this book has left the complex and often dismal realities of existing school settings out of account in order to avoid ad hoc solutions and to develop a theory (more accurately, a set of hypotheses) about how people learn and about the relation of learning to the kind of society we would like to live in. It is the intention of this (or any) theory to be applicable to *any* set of actual conditions, to the extent that those who use it accept the assumptions embedded in the theory. In this case, the assumptions are about democracy and what it implies for human living.

But it may be asked, what difference would this theory make if it were applied to actual conditions? To school settings and to other settings in which young people learn or fail to learn? The three examples of schools and school systems described at length in this chapter illustrate what actual learning settings might look like that are compatible with the theorizing undertaken here. But they are only examples, and there are *many* ways in which real situations can be modified on the basis of a theory.

The aim of Part III is to describe the educational settings that exist in the United States at the close of the twentieth century, and then to see what kinds of changes might be called for on the basis of what's been offered in the preceding chapters. I will try to be as "realistic" as the limitations of space and my understanding allow. Some of the changes I suggest may appear realistic to you, or they may seem fanciful or impossibly utopian. But if we have a theory, we are bound to go where the theory leads us, even if the landscape seems strange. If this landscape of new forms of education seems *too* strange, even forbidding, then we must either try to discover where the faults in the theory lie, or, failing that, overcome our disinclination to try something different.

PART III

Educational Realities: Confronting the System and Escaping the System

8 The School System: Its Purpose and Its Persistence

Part II of this book discussed ideal conditions for the effective promotion of education. As we saw at the end of the last chapter, these conditions can be found in some schools, but not often. The broad aim of Part III is to discuss the least changes in the school system that would be needed to establish the conditions of learning set forth earlier.

You will note that I speak of changes in *the school system, not* the schools. Most of the changes launched in the "reform" movements of the 1980s were aimed at schools themselves—as if each school were responsible for its own functioning, independent of the whole system of which it is a part. But evidence that these reforms have produced better education is exceedingly thin. This chapter will show why this was inevitable.

Changes in individual schools are bound to fail when they are initiated by outsiders like me or you, or Senator Smith, or BLEAT, the Bipartisan League to Eradicate Atheistic Textbooks. When we understand why these efforts must fail, we'll see why it's so important to seek change in the school system itself. But we'd better get clear about what that system includes.

The school system in countries like ours is made up of all schools, public and private, from the preschool to the graduate school. It includes their hierarchically organized personnel, the admissions systems, the testing systems, the textbook industry, the promotion and retention system, the system of teacher training, and the various school administrative bureaucracies. All of this can be called a system because its various parts work in relation to one another, and because a change in any part has the potential to induce changes in other parts. Sometimes these linkages are acknowledged: college math professors urge more effective math teaching in elementary schools so that freshmen will do better in college courses designed by the professors. Sometimes the linkages are not acknowledged: although college professors participate in the expansion of forms of assessment that exclude writing, they often complain that their students don't know how to write.

It's hard to make changes in a complex, interlocking system, mostly because people are more comfortable doing what they've *been* doing. But they seldom admit this. Instead, they resist change by showing that it's likely to have an (unwanted) effect on some other part of the system. So I'll not enter this part of the discussion lightly, or with unbridled optimism. I'll try to identify those parts of the system which, if changed, would have the most profound consequences for the rest of the system and which, because of the nature of their constituencies, might be amenable to change.

Two of these targets for change are the testing system, which permeates the entire school system, and the systems of preparing, placing, and organizing teachers. These two targets will be explored in Chapter 9. A third target for change is segregation, which pervades the school system in a variety of forms. This will be examined in Chapter 10. That chapter, and this book, will conclude with a discussion of educating the young outside formal schools altogether. The glacial pace of change might conceivably be speeded up if the school system got a little push from competing forms of education. Not the trivial and destructive competition that would result from acting on proposals for publically funded private schools,[1] but a competition between schooling and the education that could be found in the world of work.

Introduction: Paradoxes of the School System

You may recall that the democratic schools described at the end of the last chapter did not aim to fill the minds of children with large, preselected, uniform bodies of knowledge. They aimed instead at the cultivation in the young of a wide range of dispositions of the sorts that were discussed in Chapter 3: self-confidence, initiative, thoughtfulness, persistence, sensitivity, respect for others, cooperativeness, and so on. In short, apart from the particular understandings and skills that were focal in daily classroom activities, these schools aimed to cultivate traits of character that would enable the young to live productive and satisfying lives and participate in a democratic polity.

Chapters 4 through 7 discussed the conditions under which these aims could be achieved. While an education (unlike socialization) always focuses on the development of thinking, we saw in Chapter 4 that elements of the aesthetic—particularly the upsetting of expectations and the resultant search for resolution—are components of all thinking. Thus it was urged in Chapter 4 that these aesthetic elements be sought as conditions for all educative learning. The introduction of the fine arts in schools was but a special and emphatic case of the use of the aesthetic in potential learning situations.

That there be something in the environment both attractive and surprising is a condition of learning, but it's not the only one. Chapter 5 discussed the role of curiosity in the promotion of learning, and the need for the sort of leisure in schools that would be required if curiosity were ever to appear. The initiating condition of curiosity—an unfulfilled expectation—was shown to be similar in kind to the conditions of the aesthetic.

In the arts, the resolution of discrepancies from what we expect is a form of thinking, just as the pursuit of curiosity, which originates with surprise or puzzlement, is a form of intellectual problem-solving. Chapters 6 and 7 considered other kinds of problem-solving, particularly practical ones. Chapter 6 showed how the thoughtful development of plans and the pursuit of purposes both proceed by resolving situations that are discrepant from one's expectations. Thus similar conditions obtain in a wide range of learning situations, from aesthetic sensitivity to the pursuit of curiosity, to the hypothetical and ultimately tested solutions of problems. These settings may often involve learners in clarifying their purposes and in planning things, but they will always involve their encountering something they didn't expect, and finding ways of resolving those discrepancies.

We have outlined conditions that, in school classrooms, can promote thought and education. We are also committed to the development of democratic citizens. Because thought and education are often difficult to achieve, it was shown in Chapters 6 and 7 how both citizenship and intellectual goals can best be achieved when the young work with one another. Not to have students undertaking a significant part of school work cooperatively would be to waste the most important resource the schools have: their students.

So much for the conditions of learning *in theory*. When we have a look at how schools actually operate, we find things are radically different. Instead of presenting something attractive to the young, schools offer places for learning, eating, and recreation that are barren, cold, and cheerless. Instead of offering something discrepant from students' expectations, something surprising, schools offer predictable classroom routines (often recommended by experts on "method")[2] and dull, expository textbooks, selected because they didn't offend anybody. Instead of appealing to students' purposes, plans, or curiosity, schools appeal to their patience and tolerance for what is vexing, mystifying, and boring. Instead of encouraging thought, schools encourage the recollection and memorization that are needed to produce the right answers sought by the school. Instead of encouraging intellectual initiative or creativity, schools instil obedience by penalizing those who don't assiduously follow directions. Instead of fostering cooperation and sensitivity to others, schools foster insensitivity, envy, and mistrust by having children work competitively, in isolation from one another. Thus students are kept passive, seated, and silent, and the most typical dispositions produced are resentment and half-hearted acquiescence, accompanied in either case by contempt for the adults in the school. Instead of appealing to the aesthetic, which would make learning attractive and absorbing, the school functions anaesthetically, dulling the mind and the senses, putting pupils intellectually and literally to sleep.[3]

Before we can consider how to improve these sorry conditions, we must understand why they exist in the first place. Who could be responsible for schools that so steadfastly stand in the way of education? Are they designed by malevolent spirits who aim to dull the minds of the young and rot the fabric of our culture?

Alas, no one is to blame. Schools have not resulted from what anybody intended. They are complex institutions that developed in response to a few ideas and a lot of social forces that few people understood. Not that they *couldn't* understand those forces, but people tend to pay attention to what they can see and hear. Social forces operate beyond our senses and will never compete with forest fires and auto wrecks for presentation on television. The social forces that have shaped our schools can be described as *paradoxes*, for what we get is often just what we don't want.

Our first paradox concerns the relation between what we teach and how we measure the result. Tests developed to encourage study and measure achievement have in fact discouraged thought and fail to measure achievement. Why this is so will soon be explained, but first we must examine a misleading assumption that lies behind most forms of student testing.

Students take the tests individually. They are regarded as good or poor students, high or a low achievers, depending on their test results. The resources of the school—teachers, texts, the counseling office, and so forth—are *supposed* to help them learn and to improve their test performance. But sometimes those resources are flawed and inadequate, and students suffer accordingly. Yet they are judged, graded, and sent to college (or not) on the basis of their test results anyhow. Thus *it is assumed*—not for all purposes, but *for the purposes of judging students—that the resources of the school and even of the home are not reflected in the students' test performance.* This mistake enters the realm of mythology when we try to convince students that they are *totally* responsible for the quality of their work.[4]

Education is an interactive process, but testing, as noted above, implicitly denies that interaction. Imagine putting auto parts through some sort of test to see if they were fit to install on cars. A part that failed the test might simply be thrown out, but would we blame the failure *on the part itself*? Not likely. We would examine the character of the materials that went into the part, and the production and assembly processes that produced the part. We thus behave more intelligently toward auto parts than we do toward children. Not because we have anything against children, but because we haven't troubled to examine the assumptions that underlie testing.

Let's return to the paradoxical feature of testing that results in its defeating its own purpose. We will simply acknowledge it here; in Chapter 9 it will be discussed at greater length. Because the recollection of factual knowledge is the sort of performance that can be most easily and reliably tested, the widespread adoption of standardized tests of factual knowledge has pressured schools to aim more exclusively at the transmission of factual knowledge. As we saw in Chapter 3, there's no reason to suppose that this knowledge is retained for very long after the test is over. Thus the tests don't measure anything that students have learned *in any significant sense of the term.* And since repeated review of factual knowledge is the safest way to prepare for the tests, the tests discourage (and penalize) original thinking, or thinking about anything not explicitly covered in the tests. Just as teachers teach to the tests, students study for the tests, and other legitimate educational aims are sacrificed. These excluded aims include all of the dispositions and qualities of character that have been discussed throughout this book. Yet there is no reason to suppose that the exclusion of such aims was the intention of those who introduced and expanded the testing system.

The well-intentioned pursuit of justice and fairness leads to another paradox fostered by the testing system. As testing becomes more standardized and widespread, it occurs to people that it would be unfair if some students received a more appropriate preparation for the tests than others. Since so much depends on test results—retention or promotion, grades and class standing, college admission and scholarships—fairness would seem to demand that all students be similarly prepared. For all practical purposes, this means taking similar or the same courses. Standardized testing thus leads to a standardized curriculum and standardized textbooks—a prime example of the tail wagging the dog.

The paradox lies in the fact that school policy has been subject to local control ever since the founding of public schools in America. It was quite reasonably believed that within a state, different communities with different populations, different geographical characteristics, and different employment opportunities might wish to offer different educational programs. Most people even believed that individual differences among children warranted different educational programs. Thus school boards were elected locally, and were expected to shape policies appropriate for their own schools.

The policy-making power of local school boards was compromised when a greater proportion of school funding came from the state instead of the local community. But the spread of the testing movement has all but eliminated local school boards as educational policymakers (they continue to make policy about such matters as open and closed campuses, locker searches, and sex education—for which standardized tests have not yet become popular). It could be argued that there are more differences among school populations now than there were in the 1840s, when public schools were just getting started. If so, an even stronger case could be made for local control in the 1990s. Paradoxically, there is less local control of schools now. A major factor in this change has been the spread of standardized testing.[5]

Neither the testing nor the textbook industries are run as charitable institutions, and the label "nonprofit" should not obscure the fact that many jobs and some handsome salaries depend on the health and growth of these industries. Thus a peculiar combination of economic motives and good intentions have resulted in a school system whose aims have in the last several generations become increasingly narrow, and whose curriculum has become more and more standardized and thus out of joint with the concerns and interests of individual students and local communities.

This is not the sort of school system most parents or most teachers want, but its defenders will respond like this: If our textbook has been approved by a wide range of interest groups, why *shouldn't* every fourth grader in every school in the country be expected to read it? Or, if the better colleges can't accept everybody, why shouldn't all who aspire to go be expected to take the same test, and have the right to the same curriculum that prepares for the test? These are not stupid responses. They are based on arguments that have a certain validity from limited epistemological and political standpoints. The most recurrent of these standpoints are these two: (1) if an idea is a good one, there is no reason to expose students to other, competing ideas; and (2) the point of the public schools is to provide a fair basis for the competition to get into a prestigious college. But our concern is with the *educational* impact of such arrangements, and we have seen that education suffers. From an educational point of view, then, these standardizing features of the school system are fundamentally wrong.

A look at one more paradox may help us understand better how the school system came to develop the form it now has. Most people who teach in schools (and nearly all teachers at the beginning of their careers) intend to educate the young in ways that are compatible with the aims and means discussed in this book. Of course they have specific content aims: they want to help children learn to read, to calculate, to become acquainted with the past of our culture, and to understand blood circulation in mammals. But they also want to cultivate dispositions like independence (and obedience), persistence, thoughtfulness, respect for others, and so on. Very few teachers would consider themselves successful if they achieved their content aims but *failed* to achieve these dispositional aims. For of what use would good readers be, to themselves or to society, if they were selfish, lazy, and liars?

The conditions of the school system described above are in direct conflict with many of the most important aims that teachers have. Thus we confront the paradox of employing teachers to teach in a system that thwarts just what teachers are trying to do. The purposes of the school system, then, are in conflict with the purposes of teachers. But what *are* the purposes of the school system?

The Purpose of the School System

First we need to sort out a conceptual puzzle, since systems cannot literally have purposes. Purposes are uniquely possessed by people; they cannot be possessed by abstractions. The concepts "administration" and "system," for example, each connote a large number of separate units with a variety of relationships and interactions. To say that an administration or a system had a purpose would only be a way of saying that the people who make up the administration or the system had a reason for creating it, or joining it. But asking these people for their reasons would elicit many different answers, some of them conflicting. Literally, a system doesn't have a purpose, nor can we say that its purpose is the (mythical) sum or average of the purposes of the people who operate within it.

If we wished to be precise we might say that a system had consequences rather than purposes. But that way of putting it implies that the system has a direction of its own, independent of those who operate it. That's not true, either, since the consequences of the system's operation are a result of the decisions of those who run it (along with lots of other foreseen and unforeseen factors). The troublesome fact of the matter is this: we have a complex and far-flung school system the operation of which has consequences that are often different from, and even in conflict with, the purposes of the people who make the decisions that govern the system. (Of course, this is not the case for *every* decision-maker within the system. Some people—even some teachers—*want* schools to produce students who just work hard and do what they're told.)

Because purposes do govern the decisions of those who make policy for the school system, the system can't be regarded as operating blindly or automatically, as if no one were at the helm. Thus while it's technically incorrect to speak of the "purposes" of the school system, we'll speak that way anyhow, because doing so will remind us that it is different *purposes* that are in conflict, not people's purposes and the mysterious workings of a complicated bureaucratic machine. We can put the point another way. We are not asking, simply, what the *consequences* are, for society and for the young, of the operation of the school system. We are asking, what does this system *do* for society and for the young? By putting the question this way, we are reminded that the system will do something else if we make different decisions about how to organize it and how to run it.

We have seen that the familiar conditions we find in schools are not likely to promote education. What *can* they promote, then? All that's left is socialization, and the school does socialize students to its own rules, customs, and standards of behavior (as we saw in Chapter 1). To the extent that those standards and customs resemble the ones found in the wider society, the school socializes its students to the wider society.

So far, so good. Children *must* be socialized, and families are having a hard time doing it. In the late twentieth century, the capitalist economic system failed to offer individual incomes sufficient to support a family and keep it together. This has resulted in the increasing disintegration of family life, in the middle classes as well as in the lower economic classes.[6] Thus almost by default the school has been left with the task of socialization: of supplying the attitudes, skills, beliefs, and values that will enable the young to take their place in society. Socialization is, by definition, an essentially conservative enterprise. It must accept uncritically the social status quo; it does not appeal to the intelligence or the critical capacities of the young.

Even so, social mobility remains a part of the democratic ideal. So it is often said that the schools, however much they socialize their students, also make it possible for able and properly motivated children of the poor to rise in the social order to higher levels of affluence and influence. If this were true, and substantial numbers of the poor entered the middle and upper classes, the social status quo would indeed be threatened. But it is not true: only a handful of children are helped by schools to advance to a higher social class, and this is because the higher a child's family income, the better a *public* education he or she is likely to get. Thus the children of the well-to-do receive an education that prepares them for professional and executive roles, while the children of the poor and of minorities get an education appropriate for unskilled and temporary jobs. Martin Carnoy succinctly describes the way schools prepare the young to fit the society that already exists, which he calls a 'colonizing' function:

> . . . Isn't mass education one way to equalize the distribution of income? Not necessarily. There is no evidence that mass education distributed largely on the basis of parents' education and income (the way it is now in most capitalistic societies) equalizes the distribution of income and wealth. Increasing the average level of schooling in the population without altering the class distribution of schooling *maintains* the present income structure [see Barry Chiswick and Jacob Mincer, "Time Series Changes in Personal Income Inequality in the United States," *Journal of Political Economy*, 80:3, pt. 2 (May/June, 1972), S34-66]. Because wealthy children get access to the higher levels of schooling while poor children get much less schooling, there is no reason to believe that giving everybody access to a school should make much difference in who gets what in the society.[7]

Thus apart from the handful of schools committed to education (and not merely socialization), and apart from some dedicated teachers working in traditional schools, the school system socializes. That means it supports the social status quo. And because the decision-making structure of most schools is authoritarian (students seldom have much to say about what, or how, or when they will study),[8] the school system supports a largely undemocratic social status quo. The various theories of schooling as the reproduction of the social order support this conclusion,[9] although support can more readily be found simply by reviewing how the school system operates. So we ask, *how* does the school system manage to achieve its purpose of maintaining the present social order?

Many writers claim that the means for maintaining the social status quo is the "hidden curriculum."[10] This term has been a rhetorically effective one, for it focuses attention on features of schooling that have been largely ignored. These features tend to mold the young into social forms (especially privileges and prejudices) that might be rejected were they examined deliberately, out in the open. But the notion of a hidden curriculum also carries misleading connotations. It implies that somebody or some group did the hiding, so it provokes a search for the guilty parties.[11] But what isn't noticed hasn't necessarily been concealed, nor is it necessary to blame the purpose of the school system on some malevolent conspiracy. Further, the concept of "curriculum" is just too narrow to encompass *all* the features of schooling that maintain the system's purpose. As we'll see, it's not just the curriculum, but it's also the authority structures and the social climate of the classroom and school, the testing system, the promotion and retention system, and so on. All these features must be considered as means of achieving the purpose of the school system. So we'll continue to speak of the school system and its purpose rather than invoke the term "hidden curriculum."

The everyday operation of the schools helps to maintain the social status quo by fulfilling the system's primary goal: keeping as many young people in attendance as long as it can. While the educational goals of teachers are necessarily manifold, open, and flexible, a bureaucracy cannot operate well with such goals. Bureaucracies aim at efficiency, and only relatively simple, clear-cut, and easily measured goals are suited to the functioning of the bureaucracies that govern all but the smallest school systems.[12] Retaining as many students as possible for as long as possible is a simple, clear-cut, and fairly easily measured goal for the school system; it is one that the administrators of school bureaucracies can understand and work toward.

If the retention of students is understood as the school's primary day-to-day goal, we can better understand the point of many school policies and the judgments that are made about schools:

> For example, a school system is judged to be "good" if it includes a pre-school program and it sends many of its high school graduates to college. Schools are thought to be "good" if their dropout rates are low, and "poor" if they have high dropout rates. The dropout himself is regarded as morally unwholesome and urged to return to school. Guidance counselors who find him without academic talent or aspirations can then find some vocational track, or vocational or continuation school, for him to attend. Disadvantaged children and slow learners are treated to more school, either at an earlier age or in summer, and children whose test performance is high are counseled to stay in school longer. On educational and moral grounds, these policies do not always make sense. But they make perfectly good sense if we understand them as implementing the single, clear-cut goal of the educational bureaucracy: to keep children in school as long as possible.[13]

If you should wonder, why *this* particular goal, the goal of maximum retention, there are many answers. The appeal of this goal to the system's administrators has already been noted. It should also be noted that this goal gives administrators something to shoot for. A competent administrator maintains the size of the student body and staff, and a "good" one increases their size (administrators of public K to 12 schools, on the one hand, are very much at the mercy of demographic trends; university administrators, on the other hand, may have budgets to hire additional administrators and commercial agencies whose task it is to increase the size of the institution). Thus retention and expansion do not simply offer administrators a goal to aim at. They also offer a clear conception of what it means to improve one's professional standing: to become an administrator in a larger school system.

There is another reason for retention's being the system's dominant goal. The system can't fulfill its socializing role unless the students are there to be socialized. And the students *must* be there because there is, simply, nowhere else for them to go. Several generations ago most teenagers could be found at work, but one peculiar feature of our economic system is that it offers no jobs to young people.[14] Were they not required to be in school, the young would be classified as unemployed. That, in turn, would so escalate the unemployment rate that many Americans might demand serious changes in the economic system. Thus a third reason for the school system's goal of retention is directly to reduce the unemployment rate (and by so doing, to help maintain the social status quo). Schools and colleges now keep a great many young people busy whose scholarly inclinations are modest. This role used to be played by business and industry.

In the United States in the late twentieth century, only one parent, and often none at all, was to be found at home during the day. Under such conditions, *some* institution is needed to perform a custodial function. That role has fallen to the schools, and it constitutes a fourth reason that retention is the dominant goal of the school system. Whatever goes on in schools, it's important that the children be inside, because that's virtually the *only* way that adult society can maintain surveillance over its young.[15] The school system customarily distributes money to the public schools on the basis of the number of pupils in average daily attendance. Thus the youngster who cuts class is not only morally suspect, but is also endangering the school's budget.

Once it has its captive audience, the school system helps to maintain the social status quo by structuring school culture in ways that resemble the culture outside school. The more gross signs of this are the presence of soft drink and junk food machines and the use of top box office movies in schools. Educators and a great many parents know how poorly soft drinks and junk food (candy bars, chips, etc.) measure up on nutritional criteria, and they know what little aesthetic and educational value is to be found in many top box office movies. But those are the products that make the economy work outside school, and the young become accustomed to spending their money and their time on those products in school.

In the classroom, the teacher is the boss. That provides excellent socialization for what students will find later on, at work. In suburban schools the teacher-pupil relation may include giving some responsibility to some students. In low income neighborhoods the teacher is usually as authoritarian as those who manage unskilled, semiskilled, and clerical workers. And as the world of work is thought to be competitive, so classrooms are for the most part competitive. Doing better than your peers (being "number one") becomes a goal, and jealousy and envy are readily cultivated. The skills of working together are seldom learned and its advantages are not understood. Indeed, doing one's own work becomes so important an ideal that working with others seems like a morally tainted undertaking.[16]

The school system also accustoms the young to work for virtually nothing, and this too helps socialize them into the economic system. Since most school tasks are assigned to students by others, and are seldom what they would do on their own, the school system must offer rewards for performing its tasks. These rewards may for younger children be just a smile or goodwill from the teacher, or perhaps some free time to read what they like. For older children the reward is usually a recorded judgment, expressed as a letter grade. These extrinsic rewards function in the school much as the extrinsic reward of a paycheck functions outside schools. In both cases a reward, unrelated to the nature of the work, is given for work that students or workers would probably not do if they didn't want the reward.[17]

Thus similarities between the social structure in school and the social structure outside it help socialize the young. To recapitulate the above points, we find that decision-making at school, as in most places of business, is authoritarian, whether the authority is exercised harshly or in a friendly way. The nature of the work done has little intrinsic worth or significance for most students, just as work holds little meaning for many workers. Students are accustomed to accept, with little complaint, slight rewards for difficult work, as is often the case in business and industry. Finally, students are discouraged from sharing their work with peers, and they soon become disinclined even to discuss it with their peers. This, too, is found in many sectors of business and industry (but the economy would collapse altogether if typical working conditions were as isolated and competitive as typical school conditions).

In its task of maintaining the social structure in its present form, the school system has one more major goal: to sort students with promise from those who lack it, and ensure that the former are moved on to more schooling and eventually to high-status jobs. Students who lack promise are usually just forgotten. Some get a diploma from the high school, others drop out.

It would seem at first blush that the sorting and selecting function is at odds with the function of keeping as many people in school as long as possible. But there is no inconsistency here. Students who show little academic talent are still urged to stay in school—by parents, teachers, and the media. But exasperated and bored by high school classes, low and mediocre achievers tend to take two different paths, depending on their race, ethnicity, and socioeconomic class. Middle-class white youth usually stay in school until graduation, and often enter postsecondary education. Youth from low-income families, and especially those from racial and ethnic minorities, tend to drop out, or become discharged—that is, thrown out of school.

This is not contrary to the system's goal of keeping as many students in school as long as possible, because total success can't be expected. Michelle Fine has with great insight indicated the main reasons why students in low-income, minority high schools leave prior to graduation:

> Some leave with a powerful critique of schooling and/or its labor market potential [i.e., they don't believe good grades and a diploma will get them a good job and security]. Some must attend to their families' social and health needs [i.e., jobs for young men, child care for pregnant young women], making schooling irrelevant and/or disruptive. Others have internalized social ideologies about their inabilities, their uselessness, and they "opt" to leave schools. And finally many, perhaps most, are severed in their connection from schools by those schools they have a legal right to attend.[18]

The school system claims, as indeed it must, that it does its best for these students. There are enormous gaps between the rich and the poor in American society, and there are few mechanisms for redistributing income. Thus rightly or wrongly, the school system is regarded as the main vehicle for equalizing opportunities. We have already seen that it fails to do this, but the image is still maintained: dropping out is regarded as a grim last resort—something students do in spite of all the schools' best efforts.

Finally, the school system's task of sorting and selecting students has direct social utility. Whether the young have been educated or not may be of secondary importance. What matters is that *somebody* has got to sort the sheep from the goats, and ensure that employers get the recruits that they want. This is the task of schools, from kindergarten through college and graduate school. The ones who are sorted *out*, the dropouts, "come disproportionately from the underclass of our society. . . . nearly every study shows that dropping out is correlated with low socioeconomic class, minority status, low test scores and grades, and dissatisfaction with school."[19] Catterall and Cota-Robles have summarized the educational handicaps for children from poor homes and minority groups:

> School dropout rates for children from poor families are typically twice those reported as population averages; for the poorest children, dropout rates often exceed 50 percent . . . Among the adult population, about 24 percent of whites, 38 percent of blacks, and 52 percent of Hispanics never finish high school.[20]

Thus independent of its educational program and its socializing role, the sorting and selecting procedures of the school system directly help to reproduce the social structure of the wider society. Dropouts, then, don't indicate a failure of the school system. *They are the inevitable consequence of how the system works.* Michael Apple has put the point well: "The phenomenon of the dropout is not an odd aberration that randomly occurs in our school system. It is structurally generated, created out of the real and unequal relations of economic, political, and cultural resources and power that organize this society."[21]

The purpose of the school system is not readily understood, partly because of its abstract nature, and partly because it unexpectedly conflicts with purposes that people have who are concerned with schools. To recapitulate, the *system's* purpose is to support and help maintain the status quo of our dominant social institutions, which are hierarchical, authoritarian, and unequal, competitive, racist, sexist, and homophobic. It achieves this purpose by keeping the young in school under adult surveillance as long as possible; by shaping the social and academic climate of the school in ways that reflect forms of life outside school, particularly business and industrial life; by sorting students on the basis of their success at school tasks (which also sorts them by race, ethnic group, economic class, and by gender); and by selecting the winners for further education.

All the paradoxes of schooling mentioned above, and many more as well, can best be understood in terms of the ways in which the purpose of the school system conflicts with *educational* purposes of the sorts discussed in earlier chapters of this book. Education was distinguished from socialization (in Chapter 1); it was noted how the former was aimed at uniquely individual development, and how that development involved intellectual goals. It was also shown how important the quality of the learner's experience was to the achievement of those goals. But none of this is of concern to the school system, for its purpose is dominantly socialization.

It was then shown (in Chapter 2) that the ideals of democracy were a genuine part of the fabric of American life. It was argued there that the schools are obligated in their daily practice to enable the young to maintain those ideals. But in socializing the young, the school system has no room for the practice of democracy. Verbal allegiance to democratic ideals is professed, but the school system inculcates the social ideals of corporate business: hierarchy, privilege, competition, and exploitation.

It was proposed (in Chapter 3) that educational purposes could be achieved only when they were cast in terms of dispositions—in terms of the sorts of tendencies to action and traits of character that we'd like to see cultivated in the young. It was also shown that conceiving educational aims in terms of bodies of knowledge was counterproductive, since such knowledge cannot simply be implanted and then retained by the young for any significant length of time. But the tests used by the school system to sort and select children for further study demand that children recognize things they recently heard or read. Tests thus demand that teachers and children attend to conveying and receiving bodies of knowledge. This thwarts education, so that in the schools little consideration is given to the sorts of dispositions (like mutual helpfulness and intellectual risk-taking) that might be sought, and little attention is paid to the sorts of dispositions that *are* being fostered (like mutual distrust and intellectual safety-first).

The means adopted by the school system to advance its purpose are also at odds with the conditions of education that were discussed in Chapters 4 through 7. As we'll see in the next chapter, what you have to do to prepare the young to take tests is contrary to what you must do to foster aesthetic quality in their experience. Just as the single-minded pursuit of high scores on tests necessarily suppresses curiosity, the effort to retain bodies of knowledge organized by others suppresses inquiry and the generation and testing of one's own ideas. And since testing must be competitive in order to achieve the school system's sorting and selecting function, schools must underplay or eliminate cooperation among students. Thus the school system denies what is probably our greatest resource for the achievement of our purposes: the considered and considerate help of other people. The purpose of the school system keeps the young from learning virtually *anything* that might help them to survive as unique individuals or as members of a humane society.

The Poverty of Educational Reform Movements

Given the opposition between what it takes to promote education and the school system we've got, we must ask how the system could be reformed. Yet that question is seldom asked. Instead, the question that *is* asked by the media and education policymakers is, What can be done to reform the *schools*? By attending to schools and leaving the school *system* intact, reformers virtually guarantee that schools will remain unchanged. Seymour Sarason puts this point succinctly:

> It is noteworthy, indeed symptomatic, that the proponents of educational reform do not talk about changing the educational system. They will couch their reforms in terms of improving schools or the quality of education. And if there is any doubt that they have other than the most superficial conception of the educational system in mind, that doubt disappears when one examines their remedies, which add up to "we will do what we have been doing, or what we ought to be doing, only we will now do it better."[22]

I have characterized the school system in terms of its overarching purpose, while Sarason characterizes the system in terms of the power relationships among its decision makers. The two notions coalesce; one cannot sensibly be considered without the other. The most powerful shapers of educational policy and practice—who are seldom to be found in schools or even in school districts—are those whose decisions reinforce the purpose of the school system. Thus we encounter the first of three strong reasons why educational reform efforts are unlikely to work: in ignoring the system, they ignore the only means by which significant change could occur. This point is worth some elaboration.

Ideas about educational reform have typically been top-down affairs. Legislators, state department officials, and school superintendents conceive and direct reform efforts. Parents, children, and teachers are seldom consulted. They are just the objects of the plans of others. Those responsible for educational decisions have bitterly opposed the formation of teacher unions, fearing that conjoint thought and action by teachers might have an impact on educational policy. Policymakers have been committed to restricting participation in decision making. Why was this?

Sarason offers an explanation for top-down decision making in education. First, the decision makers have failed to admit the intractability of schools to past efforts at reform. And second, they have an implicit—and wholly erroneous—theory about how to achieve change:

> . . . change can come about by proclaiming new policies, or by legislation, or by new performance standards, or by creating a shape-up-or-ship-out ambience, or all of the preceding. It is a conception that in principle is similar to how you go about creating and improving an assembly line—that is, what it means to those who work on the assembly line is of secondary significance, if it has any significance at all. The workers (read: educational personnel) *will* change. It is a theory that assumes an understanding of schools as erroneous as it is laughable—not funny laughable, but grimly laughable.[23]

Thus Sarason urges that genuine reform requires widening the participation in decision making. If reform is to occur, the purpose of the school system must be altered, and the only way to do that is to include, in the policy making process, the people directly involved in teaching and learning: teachers and students. For there is no question that these people, along with parents, would consider as unduly narrow the present purpose of the school system. The fact that educational reform efforts have been imposed from above and have ignored these factors constitutes the first reason for the failure of these efforts.

The second main reason for the failure of educational reform is also a function of ignoring the systemic character of schooling. With its hierarchies, its channels of communication, and its paperwork, the school system is a classic example of a bureaucracy.[24] Bureaucracies are exceedingly slow to change. The reasons for this are many, having little to do with bad intentions, but much to do with the expectations people have about their occupational roles. Perhaps the most crucial factor in the glacial change rate of bureaucracies is the fact that those who make decisions *are expected* (by those who hired them) to keep things running smoothly and predictably. Any effort to make real changes is a threat to that smooth operation and therefore a threat to the security of all the decision makers in the bureaucracy.

Notice how the above two reasons for the failure of educational reform interact. If decision makers in a bureaucracy are institutionally reluctant to promote change, then the *only* way to promote it is to widen participation in decision making. While an extensive literature is available on the resistance of bureaucracy to change, two works of particular significance stand out. For an understanding of the bureaucratic culture of schools that must be taken into account for any reform to occur, no better source can be found than Seymour Sarason's *The Culture of the School and the Problem of Change.*[25] And for an account of the operation of bureaucracies in general, along with case studies that may stretch your credibility but will also make you smile, see Elting E. Morison, *Men, Machines, and Modern Times*[26] (especially Chapter 2: Gunfire at Sea: A Case Study of Innovation).

The third main reason for the failure of educational reform efforts lies in the particular proposals themselves. Once the purpose of the school system, as discussed above, is understood, it becomes apparent that most reform proposals are intended only to advance that purpose, and have virtually *nothing whatever to do with enhancing the conditions of education.* Theodore R. Sizer, formerly the headmaster of Phillips Academy at Andover, Massachusetts, expressed it this way:

> The degree to which the reform movement ignores the current concepts about learning is astonishing. It is doubly ironic that these educational reforms, supposedly based on a belief in the power of the mind, are in fact profoundly anti-intellectual and anti-scholarly. John Goodlad's seven-year study *A Place Called School* was published at the same time as many of these reports, but it's as if his work doesn't exist; it's as if certain common-sense notions about how schools are organized—that students, for example, can't engage their minds very well in thirty-five-minute snippets of time, or that smaller classes allow for more individual attention—play no role whatsoever in many of the state reforms.[27]

We'll look at two typical "reform" proposals to see how extravagantly they ignore the conditions under which the young might be educated. The first is the famous (or notorious) "Nation at Risk" report, produced during the Reagan administration by a blue-ribbon commission in 1983.[28] The major recommendations were these. First, students seeking a high school diploma should take, at a minimum, the following courses: four years of English, three years of math, three years of science, three years of social studies, and one-half year of computer science; for the college-bound, two years of foreign language was strongly recommended. This proposal is apparently based on the belief that you can ensure an effective education simply by listing course titles as requirements. But what shall be the content of those courses? How shall they be taught or evaluated? Who shall make those decisions? *These* are the important educational questions, but they are entirely ignored in the Report. At first glance it appears that the Commission was proposing nationwide conformity in the curriculum. That's a troubling idea. A second glance reveals that the proposals are empty. That's just as troublesome.

Second, the Report proposed "more rigorous and measurable standards" throughout the school system, and urged colleges to raise their requirements for admission. We have already seen (in Chapter 2) that raising standards can have no *educational* consequences, since it insists that people (teachers and students) who are trying as hard as they can simply try harder. But it *has* produced more student failures and more dropouts.

Third, the Report recommended a longer school day or a lengthened school year. This is a classic no-brainer proposal. *If* the schools were providing a good education, then *more* schooling might (other things being equal) make them better. But the Commission charged that the schools were *not* providing a good education (indeed, bad schooling had put "the nation at risk"). Thus *more* schooling (*without any recommended educational changes*) will produce a *worse* education. Logic was apparently not the strong suit of the Commission members.

None of the other recommendations of the Report dealt with the conditions of learning. Since that's the case, there is no reason to suppose, even if the recommendations were followed (and some of them have been, especially those about raising standards), that they would make any difference in the quality of education offered to the young.

Have the nation's leaders learned anything from the failure of empty rhetoric to produce educational reform? Ten years after "A Nation at Risk," Pete Wilson, Governor of California, offered his own plan for the reform of the state's schools.[29] First, he proposed "drug-free" and "gun-free" school zones, and he urged that juveniles of fourteen or older be prosecuted as adults for violent crimes. These proposals have no bearing on the conditions of learning that *educators* might be able to establish. Second, he proposed the expanded use of the California Learning Assessment System "to help parents judge the performance of students, teachers, schools, and administrators." More testing will certainly cost more, take more time away from teaching, and increase everybody's anxiety. It has not been shown that it bears any relation to improved conditions of learning.

Third, the Governor would free teachers from paperwork so they can devote more time to teaching—a worthy ideal, no doubt, although he didn't mention *what* paperwork could be eliminated.

Fourth, he proposed that teachers be paid according to their alleged merit—an idea tried and discarded in the 1930s, urged again in the 1980s, and again found to be unfair and impracticable.[30] He also proposed an "alternative credentialing program" that would allow aerospace and defense workers to teach. The Governor's concern over the state's unemployed notwithstanding, this idea undermines the state's credentialing program and the professional status of teaching. Finally, every classroom "should have access to the information 'superhighway' through computers and fiber-optic technology." The Governor proposed this at the very same time that his state budget has closed libraries in many California cities, towns, and schools. It is at least debatable whether the replacement of books and librarians by computers is an educational leap forward. In any event, computer hardware has no inherent educative value; it can be used to foster traditional school practices as easily as it can be used to foster innovative ones.[31]

Educational Reform: Where and Where Not to Begin

The failure of recent reform movements to enhance the conditions of education has taught us what, at least, should be avoided. First, it is widely accepted in theory but commonly ignored in practice that top-down reforms don't work. It's not that classroom teachers don't understand the orders that come from downtown. They simply don't accept them as their own. They can't act on them because they are already doing something else that makes sense to them.

Second, a complex bureaucratic institution will not be changed by an individual pursuing a bright idea, no matter how charismatic the individual or how profound the idea. Bureaucracies are designed to overcome glitches and aberrations, and that's what a new idea is. Since a bureaucracy is a system, only a systemic approach can change it; that is, an approach that takes into account the ways in which the parts of the bureaucracy interact with and support each other. To put it another way, it's the *system* that must be changed, not an isolated part of it (e.g., *just* the textbooks, or *just* the daily schedule, or *just* the way math is taught. Or even *just* the school).

Finally, if the conditions of *education* are to be changed, reform proposals must be relevant to *those* conditions. Proposals about lengthening the school day or raising standards, or about toughening admissions requirements or requiring an additional year of science, are all fundamentally irrelevant to the conditions that make it possible for people to learn. They have no bearing on the purposes of students or teachers, and they add nothing to our ability to foster curiosity, the solving of problems, the development of civilized dispositions, or the creation of high quality, aesthetic experiences for students. Teachers do not need to be told what to teach, or how to teach (or how long to teach, etc.). But they would be grateful for any changes in the school system that allowed them to create what they understood to be conditions that are needed to foster learning.

Serious change agents, unlike the members of blue-ribbon commissions, must direct their attention to areas of change that are genuinely relevant to education. Before I suggest what these areas might be, let's consider two candidates: school curriculum and the methods of teaching. We'll consider these areas only briefly because they are the wrong targets for change, despite the countless efforts of reformers. If changes were actually made in these areas, we might regret our success. But just as important, there is little likelihood that serious changes will be made in these two areas unless other, more systemic changes are made.

(1) The Curriculum

Whoever tries to change the curriculum—that is, the content of what is to be studied—must assume she has a *better* curriculum to offer. But on what grounds could anyone be so confident? The designer of a program of studies is preparing a menu for countless thousands of children whom she's never met, to be studied in the future, when conditions are far from predictable. Of course, there's no shortage of people who declare that they know what's so important that every child should study it. But these people don't agree with one another,[32] and there has never been a way of adjudicating their differences. An infinite number of good reasons can be found for defending an infinite number of reasonable curriculums,[33] and this is one reason why change efforts are easy to defeat, and why the school curriculum usually turns out to be so familiar. After all, with so many possible curriculums, a new one might be worse than the one we've got.

There's another reason why the endless search for the right curriculum ought to be abandoned. The search itself implies that teachers and students have little or no role to play in deciding what they will teach and study. We've already seen (in Chapter 3) how this passive role undermines the morale of teachers and students and wastes the considerable understandings and skills that they have.

As long as the curriculum is designed from above and given to teachers to teach, it will be treated as inert knowledge. This leads us to the reason why the curriculum has become more and more inert over the last several generations, and why it has become so difficult to change it.

The expansion of regional and national testing has quite naturally led to a concern for fairness. If students' test scores are to be compared with one another, then they ought to be equally well prepared for the tests. Thus more and more students are offered the same curriculum—that is, the same set of subjects covering the same sets of topics. The curriculum is now simply the response to whoever writes the standardized tests. By the time it reaches individual classrooms, the curriculum *has* become inert. It is somebody else's knowledge; dead information. Yet if a proposal is made to change the curriculum, one confronts this question: How *could* you change the curriculum, when parents have been convinced that the one they have is the only one that can adequately prepare their children for the tests they must take?

(2) Methods of Teaching

The most popular target of change in education has been the methods of teaching. But the attention to methods suffers from two serious misunderstandings. First, it is assumed that methods can seriously be described and detailed, independent of the content to be learned or the attitudes and dispositions to be developed. This results in the elaboration of mechanical, cookie-cutter methods that are little more than "delivery systems" for the inert knowledge chosen by others. Second, it is assumed that student learning is simply the outcome of the teacher's technique in selecting and employing this or that method of instruction. It ignores the ability and the need of students to become responsible for their own learning, to share in shaping the conditions of their own education.[34]

Four chapters of this book are partially entitled Educational Method, but the consideration of method in these chapters is in every instance equally a consideration of educational aims and content. Of course, general suggestions can be offered about how the experience of learners can be made aesthetic in quality, or about the arousal of curiosity, or about the encouragement of thinking systematically about problems. But *method*—including the choice of letting students discover their own problems—is always a matter of how particular students are to be helped with particular problems in connection with particular content. Method conceived as a set of procedures taken in the abstract, and educational research conceived simply as the expansion and fine tuning of such techniques, are little more than cosmetic changes on the same old face of the school. John Dewey, castigating a false "science" of education, put the point forcibly several generations ago:

> When, for example, psychology is employed simply to improve the existing teaching of arithmetic or spelling for pre-existing ends . . . let it not be supposed that there is really any advance in the science of education merely because there is a technical improvement in the tools of managing an educational scheme conspicuous for its formation prior to the rise of science. Such "science" only rationalizes old, customary education while improving it in minor details. [We are thus given] the specious pretensions of custom masquerading in the terminology of science.[35]

This is not to condemn every effort to improve the curriculum or the methods of teaching; it is only to suggest that we cannot expect much from it, *unless it is teachers and students themselves who are making the effort.* The chapters that follow employ two criteria for the kinds of changes that would be worth making in the school system. First, the change that is sought should not give teachers something *else* to do; it should make it more possible for them to establish in their classrooms what they think are optimum conditions for education. And second, the change should have the potential for making an impact on all the other instrumentalities of the school system. This approach is implicit when school change is conceived in terms of the school *system*, rather than as this technique, that course of study, or those schools that need to be fixed.[36]

In an effort to meet the criteria just described, our concluding discussions will suggest four kinds of changes. Chapter 9 begins by examining a change in the school system that is largely external to the schools themselves: a change in the multiple-choice and standardized testing systems and in the college admissions procedures that are closely related to them. The second part of Chapter 9 explores a set of changes internal to schools. These involve the conditions of teaching, particularly the ways in which teachers are prepared and placed in their jobs, and how teachers are organized for effective action. Another sort of change internal to schools involves the ways in which they segregate students. Chapter 10 will show

how widespread segregation is throughout the school system, and that it isn't limited simply to the separation of students by race. Finally, we'll consider teaching the young outside the school system altogether. Schools are surely not the only places where the young can learn, and one way of encouraging changes in the system is to offer alternatives outside it.

9 Targets for Change I: The Testing System and the Conditions of Teaching

Multiple-Choice Testing: The Anaesthetic in Education

Multiple-choice, machine-scored tests and standardized testing may constitute the greatest paradox in the school system. Employed to encourage and measure intellectual effort and achievement, the tests actually discourage both, and fail to measure them as well. After visiting sixty public schools around the country, one observer concluded that "standardized, multiple-choice achievement tests . . . are contributing significantly to the ill-conceived teaching and learning that they were designed to counter."[1] It was shown in previous chapters that the aesthetic is at the heart of education. This section will show why the major impact of multiple-choice testing is anaesthetic: it puts the mind to sleep and makes education virtually impossible.

To get good grades, or at least a diploma, students must do well on tests, or at least pass them. The tests that matter the most are multiple-choice tests. However idealized the aims of the school system may be, the meaning of those aims (that is, the purpose of the system) is best understood by examining the tests that students take. For what students *do* in school is governed not only by the content, but even more by the *form* of the tests. Thus tests and the way they are designed and administered dominate the everyday study of students. This has not been educationally beneficial. Milton, Pollio, and Eison questioned 4,300 college students and found that "when studying for multiple-choice tests they focus on isolated details; when studying for essay tests they focus more on general concepts and ideas."[2]

How tests make their powerful impact can best be understood by seeing how they are designed, administered, and scored. When a test has been standardized, it has been administered under controlled conditions to a presumably representative sample of test takers. After the test items have been refined, the test is readministered and then normed. When the test is used with other populations, later on, the score of any given student can be compared with the scores of other students across district and state boundaries, and then identified as average or above or below average, and by how much.

Since standardized tests are given to a great many people, reading written answers and scoring them by hand would take a very long time and would permit variations in scoring. And since the scoring, too, must be standardized, such variations cannot be permitted. For these reasons, nearly all standardized tests are scored by machines that respond to marks on answer sheets made by students in response to short questions. Students do not formulate answers to questions. They are offered four or five responses to each question and they try to recognize which one is presumably the correct one.

But not all multiple-choice tests are standardized. College and high school teachers devise and administer their own, unstandardized multiple-choice tests. The intellectual, dispositional, and educational consequences of the use of multiple-choice tests that are discussed below will occur whether the test results are scored by hand or by machine, and whether or not they are standardized.

Multiple-choice tests have a number of properties not found on other sorts of tests. They ask test takers only to recognize which answer matches the one selected by the test maker. Thus multiple-choice tests appeal mainly to memory; originality or ingenuity would jeopardize one's score. In standardized tests of achievement, memory for facts need only be approximate, since the test taker sees the fact in front of her (embedded, of course, in what examiners call "distractors"). In standardized tests of aptitude like the Scholastic Aptitude Test, one needs to recall a great many vocabulary items (especially words that are not likely to be used in conversation) and mathematical rules.[3]

Outside school settings, memory alone is seldom sufficient to handle the variety of problems that come our way, and our memories are seldom refreshed by being presented with the very thing we are trying to remember. Furthermore, while our work sometimes requires answers that someone else wants, our getting them isn't dependent on memorization. We have them with us in written form or on our computers, and we know where to look for them or we can ask someone else. As any vocational "how to" manual will tell you, success in the workplace depends on our *organization* of information, not on our memorization of it. Thus while test scores are fairly good predictors of how well the student will do in a subsequent school setting, there is little evidence that they have any predictive value outside school settings.

The form of the multiple-choice test has another peculiar characteristic. Of the five alternatives that are presented to the test taker, it is necessary that one of them be absolutely correct, and the others be unequivocally wrong. The scoring does not allow partial credit for answers that are possibly correct, or even reasonable; they must be either right or wrong. Thus nothing is debatable about the questions that are asked, and no ambiguity is tolerated.

Outside school settings we sometimes do encounter problematic situations to which there is only one unambiguously correct answer. Since the play starts at one o'clock and we don't get off work until two, we'll simply be unable to attend the matinee. But our more serious problematic situations—whether we ought to have children, whether we should accept a job offer, whether we can afford a vacation in Florida—have many answers, and none of them are unambiguously correct or incorrect. Thus again, performance on multiple-choice tests offers little predictability about performance outside school settings.

Another significant feature of testing is that all tests aim to measure individual aptitude or achievement. Thus it's quite natural for the student preparing for a test to think exclusively of herself, and to hope that she'll do better than others. Tests, then, naturally tend to discourage cooperative effort and cooperative attitudes. Outside school, much that we do on our own could be done better with a little consultation or a little help. In fact, a great deal of the world's work—not to mention its play—is done in collaboration with others. Work and play both suffer to the extent that collaboration lacks harmony. When testing is the major goal of student effort in school, some of the most useful and satisfying attitudes and abilities that could be acquired are left underdeveloped and often distorted.

The reason why testing is anaesthetic is that it destroys the conditions of learning that were described earlier (in Chapter 4). In an anaesthetic environment, students are unlikely to learn anything worthwhile. Thus it is the *form* of standardized tests, and of all unstandardized multiple-choice tests, that has the baleful consequence of anaesthetizing the educational setting.

To begin with, testing that seeks or emphasizes knowledge already acquired discourages teachers and schools from using instructional procedures that promote thinking.[4] We've already seen that, considered from the perspective of its felt quality, thinking is aesthetic—whether one's experience is dominantly aesthetic, or whether it involves the making of plans, the pursuit of curiosity, or the solving of problems. When preparation for tests emphasizes recall over thinking, the aesthetic has little role to play.

The key evaluation instruments of the educational system ask students to respond to other people's questions by identifying the answers those other people want. While we may grant that there are some things the young ought to know whether they want to or not (even though the experts disagree about *what* those things are), the exclusive focus of testing on what others require dismisses the purposes of students as irrelevant to the educational process. Preparing for a test is an arduous activity. It is unlikely to be felt as high in quality—or experienced aesthetically—if one's own purposes don't operate in it.

Since recall is important in the preparation for multiple-choice testing, the method of study focuses on repeated exposures to the knowledge that may be demanded on the test. This is the heart of what's called "cramming" for an exam. Coined by students, the term is an apt if unlovely metaphor for what is done with school knowledge. As I argued earlier, the aesthetic always involves some degree of novelty, some discrepancy from what one expected. But the activity of cramming—repetitive viewing of the same material until you think you've "got it"—directly precludes any possibilty of the aesthetic in experience.

Some students do well on multiple-choice tests after an intense period of anxious, time-pressured cramming. The announcement of a good test score is received with a kind of pleasure (and relief) that has qualities similar to the aesthetic. But those qualities are more like the feeling you get after you stop beating your head against a wall, than they are like the feeling that accompanies the resolution of a discrepant situation (which typifies the aesthetic). For the *outcome* of the test, usually announced many days or weeks after the test was taken, is separate from the activity of *taking* the test. Thus the pleasure in hearing that you scored well may be a surprise, but it is not the sort of surprise that calls for intelligent resolution. It can only be enjoyed the way a gift is enjoyed.

The aesthetic potential of the curriculum itself is also diminished by standardized testing. Since many students will take such tests and be strongly affected by how well they do compared with other test takers, schools must prepare all students for the tests in similar ways.

If schools didn't try to do this, they would be called unfair. School curriculums thus become similar, despite enormous differences in the populations they serve. Curriculum is thus largely out of the hands of local school boards, much less teachers and their students. As the curriculum becomes "test-driven," it becomes standardized itself, and separated from the purposes of those who teach and study it.[5]

The same fate has befallen the textbooks intended to transmit the curriculum. Written by committees and marketed by corporations intent on offending as few groups as possible and selling as many copies as they can, textbooks share with the curriculum an olympian distance from the lives and the concerns of schoolchildren. Subjugated to the demands of the testing system, textbooks as well as the curriculum are less likely than they ever were to foster high-quality, aesthetic experiences for those who must spend their time with them.

It is because multiple-choice tests control so many other features of the school system that the testing system must become a primary target of change. That will not be easy, given the mythology about the objectivity[6] and fairness of the tests, and the enormous number of people who make their living creating, norming, recreating, and marketing the tests. But changing the testing system would have an enormous impact on every other feature of the school system and it would have the immediate effect of freeing teachers to do what they think might effectively promote education.

How to go about changing the testing system involves more knowledge and wisdom than I can muster, but I'd suggest appealing first to the college personnel who use standardized tests in their admissions procedures. Many of these people already have doubts about the utility of the tests.[7] These doubts can be reinforced by showing how the tests are not helping to select the candidates they would like to select.[8] That is, again, a function of the form of the tests themselves.

College faculties appear distressed over what they claim is the inability of entering freshmen to write intelligible, let alone graceful English. Yet it is clear that preparation for multiple-choice tests neither encourages nor teaches students how to write. In fact, preparation for testing usurps the time students might have spent in writing.[9] So college faculties might consider the likelihood that to abandon standardized testing would be to increase the time devoted to instruction and practice in writing.

But even more important than writing skills are qualities of character inimical to scholarship that are produced by an education system driven by testing. We must remember that those who are most successful at taking tests—that is, those who are admitted to the most selective colleges—are those whose attitudes and dispositions are most likely to be shaped by the form of the tests. They become acquiescent in school, following directions and seeking and accepting the received knowledge of others. They seek academic conformity rather than initiative or originality. They conceive of academic work as dull, controlled by others, and undertaken for the sake of extrinsic rewards: grades, scholarships, or job opportunities. They tend not to see their work at school or in college as exciting, under their own control, or worth doing for its own sake. Linda Darling-Hammond and Ann Lieberman write, "Many studies have found that because of test-oriented teaching, American students . . . rarely plan or initiate anything, create their own products, read or write something substantial, or engage in analytic discussions or in projects requiring research, invention, or problem solving."[10] Good test takers are willing to work hard and compete, often brutally, with their peers; those who do this best are those with the best chance of acceptance at prestigious colleges.

It is debatable whether these students are the brightest of our young people, the most creative, the best scholars, or the ones most likely to use what they learn in the service of others. Yet *these* are the qualities that colleges and their admissions officers say they are looking for when they select their incoming students. University faculty members are deeply immersed in their own teaching, research, and professional service. They seldom have time to study education or the educational consequences of the testing system. If they were encouraged to undertake such a study, they would see that the procedures on which they depend to admit students do not reliably admit the very students they would like to work with. And they might be prompted to abandon their dependence on the testing system.

The competition among a relatively small number of students for places at a handful of prestigious colleges has resulted in a testing system that has a baneful impact on nearly all secondary school students. If you are sympathetic to abandoning the testing system and should then ask, How *shall* a fair competition be devised for the limited number of places for college freshmen? you may be disappointed. For *there cannot be a "fair" competition*. Getting an education is one thing, competing for a place in college is another. Getting an education involves risk, error, distraction, the discovery of limits, the discovery of self. Seriously to strive for an education puts one at a disadvantage in the competition for a place in college. For in order to win, you must avoid risks, keep your eye on requirements and assignments, avoid distractions, try only what you're confident you can succeed at, discover the right answers, and keep yourself out of it.

So if you're serious about education you might be a good prospect for college but you might not be in a good competitive position to get into one, or into a high-status one. Some educated young people do get into college by "playing the game" of pleasing those in authority. But many young people with recognized ability still get some low grades, some incompletes, some class cuts on their permanent record, and low SAT scores. Their chances of success in the competition for college admission will not be high. Yet there is abundant evidence (for example, the Eight-Year Study, or the graduates of Sudbury High School, both discussed in Chapter 7) that well-educated students who have not been graded or subjected to multiple-choice tests do quite well in college once they are accepted.

What can be done to correct the inequities and eliminate the waste in the competition for places in college? Mothballing multiple-choice and standardized tests was not suggested so that some *other* form of competition could be put in its place, as Crouse and Trusheim have suggested.[11] If the schools are conceived merely as places to prepare people to compete for college entrance, the schools will lose their educational function altogether. The simplest and fairest way to distribute places in college is not with a competition, but with a system of random placement, like a lottery. Random placement would save incalculable sums of money, eliminate immeasurable amounts of emotional stress, and help save the educational and intellectual life of the public school system. Space doesn't permit more detailed discussion of the issue here, but Robert Paul Wolff has offered some compelling arguments for a random system of college admissions in his challenging book, *The Ideal of the University*.[12]

The educational problems inherent in the form of multiple-choice, standardized testing have not escaped the notice of the testing industry itself. But the industry is not likely to put itself out of business simply because its product undermines education, any more than the cigarette industry would voluntarily close down simply because cigarettes cause people to die earlier than they should. Thus efforts at change need to be directed to the users, not the makers of the tests.

The group best situated to urge and organize the closing down of the testing system is the education professoriate itself. No one is more aware of the influence of tests on students and teachers than educational researchers and teacher educators. Most of them agree about the baneful impact of testing, although there are significant exceptions: professional educators whose living depends on working for and with testing agencies. These are the test writers and editors and the hordes of researchers who test the tests and keep on pronouncing them better. They are the Dr. Strangeloves of education, and if nuclear power without safe waste management really is the way to a better life for all of us, then I suppose that standardized testing is the way to a better education.

Meanwhile, it remains the task of responsible educators to help college personnel, parents, and teachers to understand why the school system must be relieved of the burden of the multiple-choice testing system. College faculties need to understand how tests limit the abilities of their students to do scholarly, original, and communicable work. Parents need to realize that the testing system does a disservice to their children, not just because the college admission system is irrational, but also because it discourages their children from using their own minds and renders the experience of school anaesthetic. And teachers, many of whom resent the intrusion of standardized testing on their own instructional aims, need to be supported if they refuse to spend time and effort preparing their students for success in the testing system.

At the very least, the education professoriate could confirm the suspicions that schoolteachers have about multiple-choice tests, by calling their attention to the kind of evidence and argument presented here. The bureaucratic weight of the school system will, of course, resist a speedy abolition of the testing system. But the road to a future free of multiple-choice testing can be paved by making clear to teachers the ill effects of such testing, and by helping them place testing and test preparation in the background of their work and their sensibilities. If they cannot be relieved of the testing system, they can at least see it as something "akin to sweeping out the garage, something that ought to be done with a decent attention to detail, but which ought never be confused with any matter of central importance."[13]

Here is an example of what it might mean to put testing into the background of teachers' work. A high school English teacher of my acquaintance makes use of her students' own purposes in her literature program. She encourages her juniors to select, with some guidance, what books they will read, and to discuss with each other, as well as with herself, what they read. One day a week she conducts—for those who wish to participate—a review of materials that are relevant to taking the SAT tests.

Since only some of her students prepare for multiple-choice tests and then spend a limited time doing it, she fulfills three objectives. First, the students who are concerned do well on the SATs. Second (and far more important, educationally speaking), a great many students develop genuine enthusiasm for literature. And third, none of her students confuse test preparation with education.

The fulfilling of this last objective has great potential for further education. Students who see test preparation for what it is are in a good position to examine the peculiar logic of multiple-choice tests, and to learn how statistics are often used and misused as a substitute for human judgment. Since it is the students who are the subjects of testing and statistical manipulation, it takes little imagination to see how they might become genuinely interested in high school mathematics—*if* math teachers were to teach statistics in a personally and socially relevant way.

There is another and more familiar meaning for the term "anaesthetic" than the one I have used here. Stemming from medical usage, it means, "to put to sleep." Everyone who has studied for an exam, everyone who has slogged through the materials used by schools to prepare for exams, has had the experience, literally, of falling asleep. Some people think this is an incidental effect of study, or is what happens to the duller students. But we should recognize falling asleep at school tasks for what it is. It isn't exceptional, nor is it a sign of personal limitation. It is the *natural* consequence of a school system driven by a testing system. It's *normal* to fall asleep when given an anaesthetic. If an anaesthetic form of schooling is to be avoided, the school system must be disengaged from the testing system. Then we can reconceive schooling in terms of its potential aesthetic dimensions, and introduce education into the school system.

The Conditions of Teaching

Like changing the testing system, our concern about changing the conditions of teaching remains largely outside the classroom. These conditions involve the education, socialization, and organization of teachers. If changes can be made here, teachers will be able to teach more effectively.

Chapters 3 through 7 explored conditions under which education can be fostered. These conditions drew attention to the quality of the experience of children in schools: to what made experience aesthetic, to what provoked curiosity, to what prompted children to make plans, and to what encouraged them to identify problems and deal with them in hypothetical, experimental ways. Now we ask, what kinds of conditions would make it possible for schoolteachers to establish these educative environments?

Put simply, the answer is to make sure that teachers understand the conditions under which education takes place. This means that those who become teachers must themselves experience the conditions they are trying to establish for their students. But this will call for some drastic changes in standard school organization. *Who* will set up these educational conditions? School boards can't be expected to do it, since their members seldom study education, and they spend very little time in schools. Administrators will not do it either, since they are hired and fired by school boards, and are expected to run schools smoothly. That, by definition, means avoiding any serious change. And education officials at the state level cannot be expected to promote changes that favor education, since they are bureaucratically far removed from school settings, and primarily concerned with such arcane matters as school finance, testing, data-gathering, and public relations.[14]

Anyone who tries to create conditions in schools favorable to education must understand teaching and care about it. They must also be in a position to act on their ideas, take responsibility for them, and make changes when their ideas don't work as they expected. The only people who meet these criteria are schoolteachers themselves. Thus if any serious changes are to be made in the conditions of teaching, it will be teachers who make them. If they don't do it, it won't be done at all.

But when we visit schools, we find that most teachers are not change agents. Few depart from traditional ways of organizing schools and classrooms. Why is this?

Young people who enter teaching are ordinarily full of enthusiasm and ideals. They sincerely want to teach well and to make schools more humane, educative places. But their ideals take a beating soon after they make a career choice. Programs for the preparation of teachers, far from encouraging students to see themselves as agents of change, train them instead to conform to the status quo of the school system.[15] And in their very first jobs, new teachers are more or less quickly and effectively socialized into conservative school customs and practices. They may have been exposed to some new ideas in their programs of teacher education, but on their first jobs they find themselves alone, a little unsure of themselves, and eager to please. They are greeted by avuncular veterans who, with the best of intentions, tell them what works and what doesn't in their school. They are told to be nice to students if they can; they are also told what they must and must not do if they expect to survive in a threatening environment. This is a subtle, usually friendly, and very powerful form of social pressure.[16] After a little while, most new teachers reflect the attitudes and behavior patterns of veteran teachers.

The few new teachers who try to initiate serious change sometimes succeed, but more often they are thwarted and even disciplined by their administrators. The latter may be reacting to negative feedback from parents. Since school administrators owe their livelihoods to public approval, they get used to bending to the public will. Yet the public can't be expected to understand very much about the conditions of education. They seldom experienced them when *they* went to school, and they are bombarded by all the instruments of culture with the message that schools should either prepare their children for a job (a futile dream) or help them beat their peers in the competition for a place in a selective college (a selfish aim that undermines education).

If teachers are to take responsibility for making planned, organized changes in their classrooms and in their schools, they must be helped to overcome these obstacles to change. Teacher preparation programs must offer conditions of learning that work as well as those we would like to establish in the schools themselves.[17] The patterns of teacher placement must be altered, so that new teachers do not become socialized into essentially conservative, traditional schools, where most experienced teachers are not sympathetic to change. And the opposition to change that comes from the public and from the school administration must be softened and overcome.

1. Undergraduate Education

Before we consider suggestions about the specific preparation of teachers (which we will call here "teacher training"), a word needs to be said about undergraduate education in general. Most of the collegiate education of teachers is handled by the arts and sciences faculty. Some changes in the instruction offered at this level will benefit all undergraduates and be especially helpful to prospective teachers.

In most colleges, the specialized demands of graduate departments become codified in extensive requirements for undergraduate majors. In consequence, many students find themselves overwhelmed by esoteric forms of specialization long before they are even sure that their major (chosen under pressure) is what they really want. Thus all undergraduates (and not just prospective teachers) need greater freedom of choice in what they study.

Future high school teachers will need to satisfy the academic criteria of their major departments, but all undergraduates should be encouraged to make choices from the college catalogue in accord with their interests—specializing where their interests deepen, and switching fields as their interests change. Greater freedom of choice in their studies will help young people discover themselves and become more mature adults; *these* are the kinds of people we should like teaching our children. It would also be advantageous if undergraduates could undertake their studies cooperatively, and it would help if they learned to judge the value of their own work. It is surely ironic that schoolteachers are expected to judge the quality of their students' work although they have neither been trained nor seriously asked to judge the quality of their *own* work in college.

These suggestions are aimed at undergraduate education in general, not just at prospective teachers. All undergraduates need to learn where their interests lie, how to be responsible for their own choices, how to judge the quality of their own work, and how to meet the standards of experts in areas where they choose to specialize. All undergraduates would also profit from a study of the role of schools in their society, and of the alternative roles that are possible and desirable. Society stands to gain from a systematic and critical study of a public institution as pervasive as schools, in which all of its citizens spend so much of their lives.[18] But the general education of prospective teachers is not to be confused with teacher training, which is practical preparation in the craft of teaching.

2. Teacher Training

There is a kind of consistency between how institutions are organized and what they can be expected to do. If we wish to maintain a democratic society, our children must learn democratic attitudes and dispositions. These traits must, in turn, be modeled on a daily basis by their teachers. But most of the nation's schoolteachers are trained in fairly large schools and colleges of education that are headed by an appointed (not an elected) dean, and schools of education tend to be organized and governed hierarchically and bureaucratically. Furthermore, the faculties of prestigious institutions are rewarded for research and publication—not for participation in the preparation of teachers.[19]

It may be too much to expect that teachers will learn democratic attitudes and dispositions when they are trained by a temporary faculty in a hierarchically organized, bureaucratic institution. Serious change in the preparation of teachers, then, depends on the democratization of teacher training institutions: on the faculty's sharing in the operation, the control, and the evaluation of their programs, and in their being rewarded for doing so.

The importance of these structural changes becomes apparent when we realize the extent of the changes needed in programs of teacher training. Traditionally, the heart of these programs has been courses in methods of teaching and student teaching in school classrooms. This is an old, desiccated heart that beats to a rhythm established in a more stable, less democratic culture. Let's consider student teaching first.

Student teaching is based on the idea that the neophyte has much to learn from experienced practitioners. In theory this makes good sense: the apprentice in the classroom watches the master, assists the master, and eventually takes over instruction in the classroom, modeling his or her teaching on that of the master. In practice, this system is usually less than perfect. In the first place, genuine "master" teachers with whom apprentices can be placed are not all that easy to find. Often, the best that can be said is that the apprentice has been placed with an "old hand." This may mean that the apprentice finds herself required to emulate tired and sometimes repressive practices aimed mainly at keeping pupils busy and relatively quiet.

But the apprenticeship model of student teaching has worse faults than this. It used to make sense to learn carpentry through apprenticeship because the techniques of journeymen and masters were generally accepted by all carpenters. That is, there wasn't much debate about what carpenters were supposed to do or how they should get it done. A similar attitude may once have been taken toward teaching, but by the close of the nineteenth century it was clear to many educators that there were real alternatives respecting educational aims and the variety of techniques that could be employed to achieve those aims.[20] This meant that the apprenticeship model had become obsolete. It was simply too narrow and confining a practice for the training of professionals in education who would be expected to determine their own aims and select methods appropriate for those aims.

Despite this, teacher training continues to be dominated by the apprenticeship model of student teaching, a hundred years after it should have been discarded. This is surely evidence that traditions die hard. But it also attests to the power of bureaucracies to maintain things as they are. Teacher training institutions are for the most part bureaucratic, and so are school systems. So it should come as no surprise that the product of the school of education is groomed to fit smoothly into her niche in the school system. The smooth fit is further guaranteed by the fact that the new teacher will not get a license unless she satisfies the criteria of the "old hand" with whom she apprentices. Student teaching, then, has little to do with helping neophytes learn to foster education in school classrooms. More commonly, student teaching passes on time-tested routines that will keep the system running as it always has. The ironic twist to all this is the fact that most teachers, however much they may have chafed when they were student teaching, regard it later on as the most valuable part of their preparation as teachers—because it was "realistic."

Courses in the methods of teaching are usually kept separate from a systematic consideration of what one might be teaching for. The methods taught can thus seem abstract and inapplicable, or they turn out to be familiar rehearsals of what's already being done in school classrooms. Either way, the divorce of methods from aims obscures for the prospective teacher some real disputes about educational aims, and it gets her accustomed to thinking of teaching methods as good or bad just as techniques, independent of aims.

Of course, there are teacher educators who do raise controversial issues in methods courses, and who examine the reasons behind opposing views. And there are institutions (usually small ones) that can justifiably be proud of their student teaching programs. But on the whole, the anachronistic old heart of teacher training is anaesthetic. It beats with the monotonous regularity of its bureaucratic home instead of offering the thought-provoking challenge of novelty or surprise. It offers a series of requirements for satisfying other people's purposes instead of helping prospective teachers find their own purposes in teaching. And it makes practical training conform to the standards of the school system, which themselves ought to be changed, instead of helping students find practical ways of pursuing their own worthwhile ideals.

These shortcomings help us to imagine what teacher training programs ought to be like. However much the details of programs may vary, the experience of students in them should be aesthetic in quality. That is, those who are learning to teach in practical settings should be enabled to experience the satisfactions that accompany the development of purposes, the making of plans, and the solving of problems that constitute their own teaching. This is the most direct way of helping teachers realize they can enjoy their work. Teachers so disposed have the best chance of achieving similar results with their own students.

At the practical level, the way to promote thoughtful activities and their accompanying satisfactions is to offer prospective teachers guidance and the freedom to teach what *they* think is worth teaching—based on their own interests, on what they have learned, and on what they understand might be worthwhile for their students. Of course, satisfaction will not appear at every step of the way. Most students will experience anxiety and frustration, too. But the down side of good practical training can itself be a learning experience. One can discover flaws in her own purposes and plans, instead of merely reacting negatively to the difficulty of following somebody else's directions, or to teaching what somebody else thinks is worth teaching.

This emphasis on freedom and on the quality of experience for the student in teacher training programs assumes some agreement about aims for the preparation of teachers. But since these aims are not universally shared, they should be made more explicit. I would hope we could agree that teachers ought to understand the alternatives for instructional aims, that they should make their own choices, and that they should have reasons for their choices. I would also expect us to agree that teachers ought to understand how to achieve their aims. Yet this approach is contrary to the many "reform" proposals that announce *what* to aim at and what to teach.[21] It is also contrary to approaches that tell teachers *how* to teach.[22] And it is contrary to approaches that tell teachers *what they must know* in order to be able to teach well.[23]

In order to see the practical import of the broad outlines just sketched, a few specific suggestions for teacher training programs can be offered. In each instance, they are designed to enhance the quality of prospective teachers' experience and thereby help them become better teachers. To begin with, processing large batches of students in a hierarchical teacher training school can be moderated if the programs in large institutions are governed by small groups of faculty working autonomously with their own students. Variety is a source of new ideas, and since there is no one best way to get the job done for everybody, small groups of faculty and students can be trusted to work out their own ideas.

For the reasons given above, student teaching and methods courses should be abolished. These traditional practices only perpetuate the ossified procedures of the school system. Prospective teachers need to have practical classroom experience, but it should be embedded in a context of critical, intellectual study, not offered simply as training in classroom routines. Critical study and the development of initiative and originality in prospective teachers is not easy to achieve in large, bureaucratic institutions; that's the reason for organizing teacher training around small, autonomous student-faculty groups. At the other end, in the public schools, students might do their student teaching in teams of three, instead of having to confront the school bureaucracy all alone as a student teacher. The student teaching team would not need the constant presence or supervision of a "master" teacher. Students could effectively do their planning together, help one another out in the classroom, and give each other criticism and support. A university supervisor could easily visit and consult with half a dozen such teams.

It is no less important for prospective teachers to work in groups than it is for children in schools. In both cases, joint efforts have a better chance of success in solving problems than do the most assiduous studies of isolated individuals. It also follows that if colleagiality among teachers is necessary for serious efforts to improve schools, then colleagiality ought to begin in the teacher preparation program. John Goodlad notes how teacher education has traditionally been headed in the opposite direction:

> Not deliberately socialized into teaching as members of cohort groups, they come through their preparation as individuals. It is a long leap in expectations to assume that they will join colleagues in schools ready and eager to effect the changes increasingly seen as necessary. Beginning teachers are likely to take responsibility only for their individual classrooms and assume that someone else will take care of everything else. To the degree that this attitude continues, the curriculum and organization of the school as a whole will continue to go unattended and our educational system will remain stagnant and in decline.[24]

Periods when prospective teachers work in schools should alternate with time spent on the university campus, where reading and discussion will contribute to the analysis of what happened in the school classroom, and facilitate planning the next session in the school. The analysis and the planning, done with the help of other students, can transform what is typically the acquisition of a set of routines into a critically informed experience. Making and carrying out their own plans and conducting inquiries into problems they have identified will enable students to experience the kinds of discrepancies and resolutions found by practicing teachers. In other words, the teacher training experience can be aesthetic in quality. Since teachers do teach as they were taught,[25] the quality of the experience of teacher training has much to do with the kind of experience the students of those new teachers will have.

3. *Teacher Placement*

An important goal in the placement of new teachers should be to preserve and enhance the attitudes and understandings they acquired during their education and training experience. New teachers are easily socialized into the customs and habits of their jobs. Entering new schools one at a time, they encounter an "old hand" when they seek advice, and they're urged to do what's "always worked." A few precautions taken by teacher training institutions, with the cooperation of schools, can help to relax the iron grip of tradition and routine.

First, new teachers should be placed in schools—even in small ones—at least two at a time. Schools that need only one new teacher should be encouraged to cover for that position until two teachers can be hired. Teacher training institutions can help their new graduates to plan a meeting with their freshly graduated new colleagues before school starts in the fall. The new teachers can plan together, support one another, keep their ideas fresh, and lay a foundation for professional relations throughout the school year.

Teacher training schools should help their students organize while they are still student teachers, and this organization should be maintained after the training experience has finished. The organization becomes "The class of _______ ,"[26] in which most of the members know one another, and to which university faculty members might sometimes be invited. Meeting from time to time, such an organization becomes a sounding board for new experiences; it can be a unique source of intellectual and emotional support for the new teachers.

The teacher training institution can also encourage the development of a correspondence network among students before they finish their training experience. This can play a supporting role for new teachers similar to that of a face-to-face organization. Things can be said in writing that are less readily said aloud, in a large group. For example, when new teachers have trouble in their jobs, the fault is usually thought to be theirs. A teacher who could have succeeded in a different school environment may leave the profession in the belief that it was she who was at fault. Of course it's important to identify the experienced teachers in a new placement who can offer support, but an organization of new teachers and correspondence with peers will help locate supportive and unsupportive school environments. It will also help new teachers make better judgments about themselves, and it can offer encouragement and strategic help in seeking a more congenial job placement.

These suggestions cannot be expected to transform traditional schools into models of educational excellence. But they can help create conditions where teachers, and particularly young teachers, can have a little more support and a little more freedom to try what they think is worth doing. If in the long run the schools themselves are affected, so much the better.

4. Teacher Organization

There is an old school myth that any teacher can close his classroom door and teach however he wishes. It is a myth for the following reasons: (1) whether the door is opened or closed, anything new or unusual that occurs in the classroom will be reported to other teachers and to parents; there are no secrets in schools; (2) if the teacher is unaware of alternatives, how he wishes to teach will be just the way most others teach in his school; and (3) even if a teacher is sympathetic to alternative ways of operating her classroom, she is unlikely to try them without encouragement, support, or help from others. What this all means is that teachers, isolated and alone in their classrooms, are not likely to try much that's new. And in fact, teachers do not innovate very much. Like anyone else, they need sources of ideas and they need support for their ideas.

The suggestions offered here are neither original nor very radical, nor are they intended to trigger immediate or wholesale changes in schools or even in classrooms. They are intended only to help create supportive conditions for those who want to try out new ideas, and perhaps to induce some more teachers to think about trying something new. Innovative ideas usually come packaged with mandates from the state or the school district, or they have the blessing of experts who demonstrated them in workshops. That hasn't worked.[27] Now, professionals are widely agreed that, if change in education is to be far-reaching and long-lived, it must be initiated and developed by teachers themselves.[28] How, then, can they manage it?

Simple things are sometimes the most important things. What teachers need before anything else is some time (and space) in the school day. Time to to meet and talk with each other about their students, their aggravations, their responsibilities. And about what's worth trying in the classroom and in the school. Because most teachers spend nearly all of their time either with students or alone, evaluating or preparing for students,[29] there's very little sense of community or collegiality in most schools, and little impetus to change. Before anything else, they need time and space to discover what they have in common.

The most direct way to get this is through the efforts of the teachers' organization: the NEA or the union. Like anything else, time and space for collegial relations can be negotiated. Unlike some things for which teachers negotiate, this item is clearly for the benefit of the whole school. If the teachers' organization is not ready to negotiate at the state or district level, then teachers who realize the value of time and space will have to try to get it in their own school building—talking it over, getting more teachers involved, and eventually presenting a broadly supported proposal to their administration.

Unfortunately, this kind of political activity will have to be done on teachers' personal time: at lunch, in the evenings, on weekends. But success in the effort means that subsequent professional planning and consultation will be done on "company time." That is, once professional interactions are a part of the school day, they will be seen as a vital part of teachers' jobs. New ideas, new struggles, and new crises will no longer be occasions for teachers' giving up their evenings or their weekends.

You may ask, how much time and space do teachers need, and how many teachers should be meeting with each other at once? But these are not questions for others to answer. What matters is that teachers *get* the time and space. When they do, they can decide, in terms of their own circumstances, how much they need, and for whom. If you worry that children might be left unsupervised while teachers are meeting, recall that a major aim of education is to enable children to work without adult supervision.

Teachers' organizations (like all labor organizations) are often treated by the media as a threat to the public. This negative image obscures the fact that the real public hazard is underfunded schools that are autocratically controlled. In such schools, neither teachers nor students can engage in the democratic practices for the sake of which they are supposed to be teaching and learning.

The point of teachers' organizing themselves is to become better at what they do; it is not to create adversarial relations so they can bargain for higher salaries.[30] When they are organized, teachers can communicate with each other, work cooperatively, and support each other. But organizations must operate at a local level in order for this to happen; it doesn't work at centralized state or national levels.

When teachers become accustomed to more contact with each other, more communication, and more cooperation, their attitudes will change, their teaching will improve, and they will become more articulate about what they're doing and why they're doing it. Finding this new voice will become a major factor in teachers' relations with the public.[31] It can replace the planned and mutually destructive conflict of the bargaining table, and it can substitute mutual respect and understanding for the mistrust that now attends confrontations between teachers and the public.

5. Teachers and Parents

In an ideal world, parents might actively support the efforts of teachers and actually help them in their work. But in our world, most parents are caught up in their own affairs. They remain concerned about the education of their children, but they are willing to turn the schools over to the professionals.

Occasionally, however, parents and the local public will oppose what teachers are trying to do. When this happens, the first concern of teachers should be to help parents better understand the situation; this can sometimes be done by inviting a concerned parent to visit in class. But since a single teacher is no match for a single, complaining parent (let alone an organized segment of the community), the most important factor in making the views of teachers understood is the organization of teachers that speaks for them. If a teacher who has taken a risk by trying something new is subsequently questioned by the administration or by parents, prior consultation with her peers will either support and sustain her efforts, or it will prompt her to reconsider what she is doing.

Sometimes it's not just a few parents objecting to a particular teacher. Parents and others in the community can get stirred up by a politically or a religiously inspired group that opposes a method or a text or a whole curriculum because it is "Godless," "immoral," or "un-American." In these cases it's not just teachers who are under attack. Children, too, are threatened, and so is the very idea of free inquiry and a democratic education.

Teachers acting alone and administrators whose jobs depend on the goodwill of the public easily succumb to organized pressure groups. A community's best protection against intemperate attacks on school programs made by pressure groups is an organized body of teachers. Speaking for the profession in their community, it can get a serious hearing. And it also has the resources to go to court.

The targets for change discussed in this chapter, testing and the conditions of teaching, have very little to do with the curriculum of the schools. They have nothing directly to do with teaching techniques, with new leadership structures, with school finance, or with raising "standards." In short, they are not the sorts of "reforms" that have captured the attention of the public and that are dear to the hearts of politicians.

Changing the testing system and changing the training, the placement, and the organization of teachers is not intended to tell teachers how to do their jobs. It is certainly not aimed at getting teachers to work harder and take their jobs more seriously. It *is* aimed at removing obstacles (e.g., the multiple-choice testing system) that stand in the way of what teachers would like to do, and at providing experiences (training and placement) and support (teacher organizations) so that teachers will be able to think more productively about what's *worth* doing, in a setting that supports such thought and action.

If you have been thinking about these suggestions, you will have noticed that they all enrich the experience and extend the freedom of teachers. This implies that teachers should be treated as learners, too: that *their* experience as professionals should be high in quality and permeated with a democratic spirit. It also implies that we must *trust* the teachers to whom we entrust our children. If that makes you uncomfortable, consider this. The popular reforms of recent decades—more required academics, a national curriculum, more homework, higher standards, and more testing—all imply that teachers *cannot* be trusted. (After all, why didn't *they* come up with these ideas?) But that is the fundamental flaw in all of the popular reforms. *If we cannot trust teachers to do what they think makes educational sense, then we certainly can't trust them to do what the experts tell them to do.* If there is no trust, there cannot be any education. Changing the testing system and the conditions of teaching are first steps in the reconstruction of the school system. They would make it possible for teachers to consider ideas of the sort offered earlier in this book, and to act on the ideas they have adopted as their own.

10 Targets for Change II: Segregated Schools and Education through Work

The Desegregation of Schools and Classrooms: Moral versus Educational Issues

Desegregation has been one of the great moral issues in America in the twentieth century. It is a moral issue in any society in which there is a heterogeneous population, and it is also a controversial political issue. Segregation in schools occurs whenever people are kept apart from others for no defensible reason other than their membership in a group into which they were born or were arbitrarily assigned.

To put it more simply, segregation occurs when people are arbitrarily kept apart from others. Those who do the segregating always claim that it is advantageous to both groups when they are kept apart. The evidence suggests that the benefits accrue to the segregating group, while the costs are usually borne by those who are segregated. All this is true of any segregated group, whether it be Cambodian-born citizens, Jews, African Americans, women, lower-class children, all the children born in 1985, or the handicapped.

That segregation is morally wrong will not be elaborated any further here. It should be clear from what's already been said (especially in the second section of Chapter 2) that segregation is a clear violation of the respect for persons that is an integral part of the American ideal. Contemporary discussions of desegregating schools tend to focus on the political or economic feasibility of various strategies, and on its popularity or unpopularity. That these discussions are often acrimonious and often reveal tolerance of segregated programs suggests that the moral issue is easily forgotten—especially by those responsible for the segregation. But it is morally wrong, and it should be abolished on those grounds.

Segregation in schools will be examined here not so much as a moral but as an educational issue. We seek to understand the bearing of segregation and desegregation on *learning*, independent of moral issues, of considerations of popularity, or of how economically or politically difficult desegregation may be. We need to understand this because many educators, parents, and school boards firmly believe that keeping students apart (for example, the high from the low achievers, or the six-year-olds from the seven-year-olds) has positive educational value. But the consequence of maintaining these apparently benign forms of keeping people apart has often been to promote other, morally repugnant, forms of segregation: for example, black from white students, low-income from high-income students, less experienced from more experienced students.

Some educators and parents are willing to tolerate, reluctantly or with barely concealed enthusiasm, the moral evil of segregation for the sake of what they believe are educational benefits. Since education is itself held to be a moral good, we might ask whether anything could be educationally good and morally bad at the same time. But rather than explore this conceptual issue, we'll simply ask whether there is any reason to believe that segregation in any form has positive educational value. We'll find that the evidence points to no educational benefits whatever—with a few exceptions which will be noted.

While segregation is morally wrong, it is not morally wrong to keep people apart who have communicable diseases. That's because it's a greater moral wrong knowingly to spread a disease (moreover, when the patient's health is restored, she rejoins the community). The case is similar in schooling. While segregation is without educational benefit, there are some cases in which a defensible reason for setting people apart (for a period of time) can be found. Here are two such cases. If there are others, they will have to be defended with reasons as strong as the ones below.

The Severely Handicapped

A child may be blind, paraplegic, or emotionally disturbed. There are skills and dispositions such a child needs to learn that aren't needed in the same ways by children not similarly handicapped. This learning is sometimes best acquired working alone with a tutor, sometimes in the company of other handicapped persons. But these children should not be kept apart all of the time from children who lack such handicaps. For reasons that will be indicated below, it's important that handicapped children spend a significant part of their day in the company of their less handicapped peers.

The Development of Special Interests

A child has pursued introductory studies in, say, creative writing or chemistry. Unlike her peers, she can now benefit from more specialized studies in these fields, from the application of more rigorous standards, and from spontaneous but critical discourse about these topics. These activities are best fostered alone, with a tutor, or with a small group of similarly interested and experienced peers. Again, this doesn't imply keeping these students apart from others all of the time. It's important that children with developed interests spend a significant part of their time in school in the company of peers who don't share those interests or that expertise. The reason for this is the same as the reason why handicapped children shouldn't be placed permanently with other handicapped children.

Reasons for establishing heterogeneous groups were discussed in Chapter 7 under the heading of the inclusiveness criterion for learning groups. Now we will explore in a different way the moral demand generated by heterogeneity: the demand to respect other persons. We usually choose our friends and our social contacts, but we have much less choice about our family of origin, our community, or even most of our working associates. People with whom we choose to associate are usually similar to us in important respects. The others—those with whom we find ourselves simply because of circumstances—may be quite unlike us. We don't have to be told to respect the people we've chosen because, after all, we *like* each other. But we don't ordinarily have a liking for people who are different from us, and in fact we may mistrust or even dislike others simply *because* they are different.

Respect for persons, then, has a very practical connotation: if we have it, we interact in mutually beneficial ways with others who may be different from us. But we can't do this if we don't understand those others, and we won't understand them if we're kept apart from them. Moral regard and moral action are not simply matters of putting on a happy face and being nice, for *we don't know how to be nice to people who are different* and, because of that difference, may generate mistrust or dislike. Of course, if we don't know them there's no reason to dislike them, but such dislike isn't based on reasons. It's probably a matter of the instinct for survival to be a bit leery about what seems strange and unfamiliar. In some people this leeriness turns into prejudice and downright hatred.

Apart from the moral issues, an interdependent society simply cannot survive these irrational and destructive attitudes. Our natural antipathy to strangers, to those who are different from us, often leads to our trying to dominate them. But if we are to live together productively with them, we must try to understand them, instead. Reading about others is helpful, especially if the reader is a scholar, or the writing is artistic. But understanding others ordinarily demands knowing those others: being with them, interacting, doing things with them. Those with advantages conferred by birth or circumstance will remain contemptuous of those who lack them as long as they are kept separate. As long as they are kept separate, the handicapped will be manipulated and treated as less than persons.

Technology has made new forms of segregation convenient and easy: prisons, schools, nurseries, hospitals, asylums, retirement villages, museums, sports arenas, a multitude of specialized workplaces; and freeways, ghettos, slums, and suburbs. People who are different can be assigned to places where we are not. We will not have to see them or think about them except briefly, when television shows us a ghetto burning, a school vandalized, a prison rioting, or soccer fans murdering each other. In a segregated world, people with power organize the conditions of living for the powerless, whom they neither know nor understand. But no one except a powerful minority is satisfied with the result. Compared to the more hardened forms of segregation to be found outside of schools, the segregation in schools can be relatively easy to overcome so that the young can get to know one another. Attitudes and dispositions developed in the schools are the only weapons we have with which to confront the more intractable segregations of the adult world.

Thus while there are good reasons for keeping some students apart from others, some of the time, in schools, it is in the long run socially destructive to keep them apart all of the time. This is the general reason for maintaining a substantial amount of heterogeneous grouping among students. It is grounded in a common morality and in widely shared democratic ideals. The *educational* reasons for that heterogeneity are practical: the morality and the ideals are not given at birth; they have to be learned. And the only way to learn them is through sharing activities with people who are different from us—a sharing that will be enhanced by the guidance of responsible adults.

Now we can consider more specifically some corrective measures for three particularly virulent forms of school segregation: segregation by age, by ability, and by school. I will not directly consider segregation by race, ethnic group, gender, or sexual inclination. These forms of segregation remain widely practiced, but they are acknowledged to be wrong, and there is a great deal of literature available making it clear why they are wrong. I wish to deal here with forms of segregation that are not widely understood to be wrong, but that *are* wrong anyhow—either because they interfere with education directly, or because they promote the more obviously wrong forms of minority group segregation.

1. Segregation by Age

The most common form of segregation in schools occurs in terms of children's age. It is now accepted automatically as standard practice to put children together in classrooms whose birth dates fall within a given time period. It's called an administrative convenience, not segregation. But imagine a child whose abilities, interests, health, and maturity are so similar to those of other children that you would assume they could all study together profitably. If this child is kept separate from the others just because her skin is a different color, we'd object and call it segregation. But when we keep the child separate because her age is different, we call it a convenience. But for whom is it convenient? Certainly not the child!

Any time a child is arbitrarily kept separate from others in circumstances where that separation can have socially, emotionally, or educationally damaging consequences, it is a form of segregation—no matter what we call it. It may be convenient to place all six-year-olds in the first grade *even though we know not all six-year-olds are alike*, but the practice is a form of personally and socially damaging segregation if it's not modified by new placements based on the particular characteristics of particular children. This is why the administrative convenience of age-grading is not worth the damaging placements to which it often leads.

That children are similar in age is no reason to suppose that they'll be equally similar in background, interests, maturity, or abilities. Since the latter are all relevant grounds for having children do things together, placing them in classrooms independent of those grounds risks doing them harm. For example, sixteen-year-olds taking a class in physics and a twelve-year-old for whom experimentation in physics has been a hobby would benefit from studying together instead of being kept separate. Similarly, a ten-year-old who reads well and a group of teenagers whose reading is weak might all learn better by reading with (and to) each other rather than being kept apart. If you fear that the age differences might result in jealousy, resentment, or teasing, recall that an important part of education is learning to interact sensitively and intelligently with others who are different. The common practice of age-grading *teaches* school pupils to be contemptuous of those who are younger. It is an important responsibility of schools to modify rather than promote that sort of attitude.

There are enormous educational advantages in having young people of different ages work and study together. Despite our (ordinarily conservative) *social* inclination to seek out people similar to us, our greatest opportunities for learning come from interacting with people who are different—whose experience includes things to which we've not been exposed. Other people remain the richest source of variety we can find, and variety *is* the spice of life. It brings richness to experience and enhances its aesthetic quality, which together are the reasons why younger and older people can learn from each other. The younger get help, guidance, and encouragement from the older, while the latter acquire confidence, responsibility, polish, and a sense of self-worth by helping the younger. In schools that have provided opportunities for children of different ages to work together, isolation and mutual distrust have been replaced by a sense of community. And everyone's achievement has improved.[1]

Another reason for the adoption of mixed-age grading in school classrooms is the resulting transformation in the relationships between children and teachers. American schoolchildren typically enter their class in the fall and leave in the spring; they enter a new class with a new teacher the following fall. The nine months thus made available to child and adult are not conducive to the development of a stable, enduring relationship.

Children may occasionally be grateful at not having to bear certain teachers for more than a year, but every year they also have to terminate relationships with adults who provide care and security. The situation is worse during the turbulent adolescent years, where secondary schools offer a half dozen teachers a day with whom children can have only temporary relations. Just when a child's personal, social, sexual, and intellectual identity is undergoing dislocation and transformation, the pattern of switching classes with one's age mates every hour and every year seems almost diabolically calculated to remove all hope of having any stable, long-term relationships with adults.

The failure of the educational system to create conditions for the developement of stable relationships between children and adults is in part responsible for the development of children's peer groups (sometimes called gangs), loyalty to which further erodes child-adult relations. But while the peer group provides security and a significant focus for schoolchildren,[2] teachers themselves are left with even less emotional and social stability. Responsible for a child for less than a year at the elementary level, and for only a few hours a week of that year at the secondary level, the teacher has two distasteful choices. He can try to develop a relationship with the child and then see it arbitrarily terminated in spring. Or he can distance himself from the child on the grounds that the emotional investment in a relationship is too costly for the disruption that will come. Most new teachers don't make these choices in a calculated way. Experienced teachers feel the choices in their bones, for they know that, whatever their technique, the heart of their role as teachers lies in the quality of the relations they have with their students.

The educational worth of a teacher to her students is a function of the extent to which she cares about, and cares for her students.[3] An education system that ensures that relations between teachers and students will be short-lived makes it very difficult for teachers to develop these caring relationships. Absent the care, we are left only with authority relations. They may be warm or cold, kind or harsh, casual or calculated. But they will not be stable, human relations, and their educative value will be minimal. Thus age-grading in classrooms not only deprives children of stable, adult emotional support. It also deprives teachers of the structural conditions that would encourage the development of genuine care for their students.

Students and teachers all need an environment in which emotional support and caring can flourish. This means, before all else, a stable environment not threatened by imminent dissolution. The practice of shuffling new batches of students in and out every year should be discontinued, and that means the termination of the age-grading system. There are many alternative ways of organizing classrooms, and it's best if these are independently determined at each school site. But here is a suggestion that could serve as a model for an alternative. Not the only or necessarily the best model, but one which will illustrate the classroom conditions that are being sought.

Imagine that each classroom in a school contains about thirty children whose ages span at least three years. Imagine that in the spring the oldest third of these pupils moves on to another teacher and another classroom, while ten new pupils enter in the fall. By this means the entering pupils can be socialized by last year's holdovers, many of the more experienced pupils can assist in the instruction of the less experienced, and teacher and pupils will all have a full three years to spend with one another. Enough time to develop a sense of community, and enough time not only to develop stable personal relationships, but for the teacher to guide and actually see educative changes occurring in students.

Other sorts of flexibilities must be built into such a model. If the teacher, a student, or both, are convinced that the student is in the wrong group, it should be possible to locate her in a new classroom. The reasons may be academic or intellectual, social or emotional. There may also be reasons for a student to leave the classroom group temporarily: for example, if the emotional climate has become too strained, and a "vacation" is in order; or if a student's interests and skills are called on to help with instruction in another, perhaps younger group of children.

These adjustments are made in the classroom not only to help individuals but also to develop a community: a group of people who will be together for a significant period of time so they can come to know one another, care about one another, and help one another with what they do together. Of course, providing organizational conditions doesn't by itself guarantee that a community will be produced. That takes planning and goodwill and hard work, which is what we hope teachers will provide. But it *is* virtually guaranteed that a new batch of students turning over every year in a bureaucratically organized classroom is not likely to become a stable community. Without a community, and without the personal and social traits that community implies, the educative potential of the classroom is drastically diminished.

2. *Segregation by Ability*

After age-grading, the most common form of segregation in schools is done according to ability or achievement. Called "ability grouping" or "homogeneous grouping," it is thought by many to be a benign way of organizing classrooms. The basic premise of segregation by ability is that if you put the bright children in one class and the dull ones in another, then each group will reap educational benefits. The quick ones can move forward without being slowed down by the ones who don't get it. The slow ones can be offered simplified lessons, over and over again, until they get it right. Everybody wins.

Aside from the moral questions that could be raised about separating human sheep from human goats, the trouble with this comic book conception of learning and schooling is that it doesn't work. That's because it's based on a faulty conception of achievement and a discredited conception of ability. Homogeneous grouping in schools has failed to enhance achievement, but it has developed socially divisive attitudes. So everybody loses.

If children were to be segregated ("grouped") by ability, it would be important to decide *which* abilities to use as the basis for grouping. Musical abilities? Artistic or physical abilities? Since school is regarded as an academic institution (even if most of its students happen not to be academically inclined), efforts to group children are often based on the presumed presence of academic abilities. Thus we imply to children that their artistic, physical, or social abilities are not important, since what they learn in school is strictly academic. But what sorts of abilities are academic ones?

Academic abilities are sooner or later boiled down to mathematical and verbal skills—the heart of the SAT tests as well as the college curriculum. How does a child acquire these skills? On the one hand, by learning math and solving problems that deal with quantity. And on the other hand, by talking with people. Reading helps, too. No mystery here.

But why is it that some youngsters get high scores on tests of mathematical and verbal ability, and others don't? People who have more experience doing math and playing certain kinds of games get higher scores on mathematical tests than other people. And tests of verbal ability are based on a style of language found in certain ethnic and economic classes. If you grow up in the right kind of home, your conversation will involve the style of language found on the tests. Thus children raised in white, middle class homes get higher scores on tests of mathematical and verbal ability than children with other kinds of racial, ethnic, and economic backgrounds. There's no mystery about this, either. Schools that practice ability grouping put white, middle-class children in the high groups, and low-income, minority children in the low groups.[4] The abilities that are tested are *learned*, and are not anybody's genetic endowment. Thus homogeneous grouping in schools based on these abilities turns out to be another way of imposing economic, racial, and ethnic segregation. This is morally repugnant.

But does ability grouping enhance achievement, despite its moral and social warts? Before answering this question, we must examine another form of grouping, this time based on achievement. Since the abilities used as a basis for classroom segregation are so dependent on home learnings, schools may instead segregate students on the basis of their achievement—the grades they get in school subjects. Of course, school grades also correlate with home background, so this move fails in its attempt to neutralize the home factor in learning. But it does add a new form of irrationality to grouping procedures.

Grades in school subjects are strongly dependent on tests, and tests most typically ask students to remember material for a short amount of time and then recognize it on a given day. Most of the material is forgotten shortly afterward (see the first section of Chapter 3). Thus the "achievement" on which grouping is based is a trivial, short-lived sort of achievement that has little to do with the sorts of thinking involved when experience is aesthetic, when planning is undertaken, when curiosity is pursued, or when problems are solved. It seems quite arbitrary, if not just foolish, to group students for purposes of learning on the basis of such trivial and transient skills.

What are the consequences of segregating students by ability or achievement? Those who do not investigate the issue easily assume that students *must* learn more effectively when they are segregated with others of similar ability. But those who have investigated the issue have found otherwise. Overwhelmingly, the research shows again and again that grouping students produces no academic benefits at all. The following statement by a leading researcher summarizes a generation of careful investigation:

> . . . "Common sense" would argue that, at least in certain subjects, ability grouping is imperative in secondary schools. How can an eighth grade math teacher teach a class composed of students who are fully ready for algebra and students who are still not firm in subtraction and multiplication? How does an English teacher teach literature and writing to a class in which reading levels range from third to twelfth grade? Yet study after study, including randomized experiments of a quality rarely seen in educational research, finds no positive effect of ability grouping in any subject or at any grade level, even for the high achievers most widely assumed to benefit from grouping.[5]

There *are* consequences of segregating students by ability, but they tend to be social rather than academic. To begin with, once students are placed in a group or a track, they tend to stay there. Official rules notwithstanding, once you get onto the low track, you stay on the low track. That's partly because you acquire a reputation, and partly because being on the low track means you aren't able to take the courses that are required for you to get into the high track. That's the catch-22 of high school.

One's reputation as a member of an ability group has social and personal consequences. Years of segregation in an ability group develops in children a corresponding sense of personal identity. Children in the high groups see themselves as brighter and more deserving than the other students. Children in the low groups see themselves as inferior, their futures as beyond their own control. And since no one can live comfortably with such self-perceptions, students in the lower groups tend to reject the school as a significant institution. They become mental and emotional dropouts whether they officially drop out or not.

The development of these personal and social attitudes in students who are ability grouped would be deplorable in any case. But it's made worse by the fact that neighborhood and family membership has more to do with placing children in groups than does any genuine intellectual ability. Thus ability grouping in schools makes more permanent the disadvantages already accumulated by children of low-income, ethnic, and minority status. The practice not only makes a travesty of intellectual values, but it subverts the development of democratic values and behaviors. These are reasons enough to terminate the practice of segregation by ability or achievement in American schools.

3. *Segregation by School*

Of all of the forms of educational segregation, the most consequential and the most difficult to deal with is the segregation of entire schools and school districts by race, ethnic group, and economic class. Entire populations are excluded not just from classrooms, but from schools themselves. The United States Supreme Court declared the practice unconstitutional in 1954. Its reasoning was straightforward: to separate students solely because of their race "generates a feeling of inferiority as to their status in the community that may affect their hearts and minds in a way unlikely ever to be undone."[6]

The Court's argument was apparently not convincing to a sufficient number of white Americans. Orders to desegregate, even with "all deliberate speed," were circumvented in many cities.[7]

Even when schools were desegregated, their newly mixed populations were often resegregated by the devices of ability grouping and tracking. As this is written, public schools in America are more segregated than they were in the late 1960s. In 1991-92, two out of every three African-American children attended schools that were predominantly African American or Latino, while the proportion of Latinos in minority-dominated schools rose from 54 percent in 1968 to 73 percent in 1991-92.[8] The Harvard study from which these figures were drawn claimed that the trend toward greater segregation was fed by the federal courts' abandonment of mandatory school desegregation orders and by local school officials who believe that integration is no longer viewed or enforced as an important national goal.[9]

The difficulties of desegregating schools have been made worse by growing patterns of neighborhood segregation in America. Low income and minority children no longer live close to schools that are predominantly white and middle class. Integration is thwarted because appropriate schools are too far away for minority children to walk, cars are not available, and public transportation is inconvenient or nonexistent. This led to the provision of special buses to bring children to school from distant neighborhoods. But this provoked concerted resistance on the part of many white majorities; they claimed that the expense was too great and that it took too much time away from children's studies. They did not wish to defend segregation itself; they only claimed that desegregation was too costly and too time-consuming.[10]

The arguments against busing were transparently self-serving and drew the thinnest of veils over American racism. The same people who railed against the costs and the inconvenience of busing for purposes of desegregation fairly leapt at the chance to send their children from rural and village homes to consolidated rural schools, where the curriculum and other activities were thought to be richer. Spending a couple of hours a day on a school bus was considered a small price to pay. But transportation for purposes of school desegregation was called (even by the newspapers) "forced busing." The connotation was that people shouldn't be forced to desegregate; that it's the right of all Americans to keep their kids away from groups of other Americans they don't like.

Showing that the opposition to busing is hypocritical doesn't get us much closer to seeing how desegregation can be achieved. In what follows I'll try to show why desegregation *must* be achieved, by offering reasons that may be more compelling than those offered by the Supreme Court. There is, of course, no easy way to integrate American schools or American society, which is why Gunnar Myrdal's characterization of racism as "an American dilemma" is as poignantly accurate today as it was when he wrote his pathbreaking book in 1944. But there is little chance of a serious effort to desegregate unless people have a sense of the urgent need for it. Here is why the need is so urgent.

We have seen that the school's task is both to educate its students and to socialize them into democratic forms of community life. But success is dependent on the sort of socialization to which children have already been exposed. By the time they enter kindergarten, children have already adopted the customs, attitudes, and beliefs of their homes and neighborhoods. If these attitudes and beliefs support education and democracy, the school's job seems easy. But if they are inimical to values that support education and democratic relationships, the school will have difficulty, and may fail to achieve its task.

Here are some simple examples to illustrate this. In some homes and neighborhoods, typical responses to conflict are to shout, to withdraw, or to become violent. In some places where children grow up, people are relegated to an inferior status simply because of their gender. The socialization that results from these behavior patterns will interfere with education, which focuses on dialogue as a first step in resolving conflict, and which cannot succeed if those to be educated are the objects of discrimination. That kind of socialization is also resistant to fostering democratic attitudes. On the other hand, the use of language in dealing with conflicts is encouraged in some homes, and in some homes, rights and responsibilities are distributed equally, independent of gender. The socialization that results in such homes will enhance the efforts of the school.

Attitudes and values like those just mentioned are sometimes called middle-class or lower-class values. This is a form of stereotyping and can become prejudicial, for no economic class is the exclusive owner of any particular patterns of action or sets of values. But people don't ordinarily *choose* their customs or their values. The latter typically *result* from traditions and, most especially, from the conditions under which people grow up. Let's carry our examples a little further.

Imagine a child growing up under crowded conditions: a large family in a physically limited living space. Imagine that child also experiencing insecurity: her parents working sporadically and for low wages, sickness spreading rapidly through the family and inadequate medical care, high crime rates and hostility from the police. Under these crowded and insecure living conditions, children might find it normal to shout, act violently, and act prejudicially as a means of securing their own privileges. On the other hand, imagine a child reared in a small family with plenty of living space and the security afforded by parents who are high-salaried and who can afford health care, police protection, and ballet lessons. Here, there is ordinarily no need to shout; because there is enough for everybody, violence and discrimination serve no useful purpose.

These examples are oversimplified; homes and the processes of socialization are more complex than that, and people's attitudes are always more than *just* the consequences of conditions over which they have no control. But the point remains: how people get socialized at home depends a great deal on their conditions of living. And another point needs to be made: the conditions under which they live are crucially affected by how much money they have to spend.

It will be objected that if you give poor people money they are likely to spend it unwisely and all at once, and then they'll be poor again. But that avoids the issue. Poor people have *already learned* sets of attitudes and values that will not go away simply because money becomes available. The conditions of living in a family that lacks the things that money can buy (especially space, privacy, adequate nutrition and health care) create forms of socialization that are often inhospitable to education or democracy, and that may persist when a person's financial situation changes.

Now let's see what happens to children—not just poor children, but all children—when they attend segregated schools. Consider first the children of the poor. If we bear in mind the fact that most members of minorities in America are poor, our consideration of low-income children will also apply to most African Americans, Latinos, and recent immigrants from Central and South America, Africa, and Asia. In a segregated school, these children will constitute the dominant majority. They will find few peers whose socialization has been markedly different, and from whom they might learn different attitudes and customary ways of behaving. And their teacher, as was shown in Chapter 1, cannot single-handedly socialize a large group of children in ways that are contrary to what they have already learned. The teacher may get support from the school itself, but we have also seen that the school's norms and values are typically (although not invariably) those of the education system. And those values do not support either education or democracy.

For poor and minority children, there is little hope that a segregated school can either educate or provide democratic socialization. It cannot be a good school. Yet this is often vigorously denied, even by those who should know better. The president of a large city Urban League was recently quoted as saying, "I'm more concerned about the quality of education than I am about the color of the classroom"[11]—as if education *could* be high in quality in a segregated school. And a sociologist, writing about the valiant and often ingenious efforts of faculty and staff in segregated high schools, concluded that these schools were "good schools."[12] That was a mistake, and a very misleading one at that. For the reasons given here, a segregated school cannot be a good school—even if it makes the best of what it's got (and it hasn't got much, as Jonathon Kozol makes clear in discussing the resources of schools for the poor[13]). The consequences of requiring poor and minority children to attend segregated schools are disastrous for them personally. And because these children will be our fellow citizens, the consequences of their attending segregated schools are a growing calamity for society as a whole.

If schools for minorities and the poor are mostly segregated, then by definition the other schools—the ones for middle-class and predominantly white children—are also segregated. Can *these* segregated schools be good schools? Can a democratic society survive and prosper if the children of its middle classes get an education in these schools? Suppose the suffocating grip of the education system were relaxed, and teachers were free to establish environments in these schools where the quality of children's experience became important, and where thinking and intelligent planning were encouraged. Could these schools then be good ones, schools that maintained and advanced the ideals that are distinctive to this nation?

Segregated schools for the middle classes will, of course, exclude many classes and kinds of other children. Lacking contact with such children, students in these schools are unlikely to understand them. Of course, they can read and pass tests about people of other classes, colors, and ethnic backgrounds. But lacking face-to-face contact, they will not understand them, in the sense of understanding their living conditions and the way those conditions affect their opportunities, their thinking, their emotional lives, and their aspirations. If you're not sure about this, consider an example from contemporary political life.

We all learned in school about our "good neighbors" to the south: the peoples of Central and South America. Yet we helped plan and support the overthrow of a democratically elected president (Allende, in Chile), we placed a crippling embargo on a government (in Cuba) that had overthrown a ruthless dictator, we illegally armed and supported mercenaries (Contras) who tried forcibly to dislodge a legitimate government (in Nicaragua), we made war on countries (Grenada, Panama) in order to pursue our own domestic agendas, and for years we cooperated with a military junta (in Haiti) that expelled a democratically elected president (Aristide) and then broke its promise to reinstate him. Despite this clear and persistent pattern of actions, we who have learned about our good neighbors to the south made only sporadic protests and then reelected the people responsible for these actions.

Now, hundreds of thousands of these good neighbors live in the United States, and more are coming. Many were driven here by the turmoil at home that our foreign policies helped to create. Most of the children of these people attend schools in which few North American white children can be found. Will white Anglos, in *their* segregated schools, understand these children or their situations, as they study their lessons about our good neighbors to the south? Or will our segregated schools help produce forms of violence within our own borders, on the model of the violence we have practiced south of the border?

Conflict and domination often result from failing to understand or care about other people, and this kind of understanding and care is very hard to acquire from school books. A segregated school for the white middle classes is not likely to foster this kind of understanding. Yet if the teaching conditions are ideal, it may be thought that such a school will at least itself be a democratic community. But it will be an exclusive democracy—one that excludes the children of poor and minority groups. America, however, is not an exclusive nation. It encompasses all kinds of people from all conditions of life, and they are affected by the same economic policies, the same technologies, the same weather—although they are not affected in the same ways. We cannot have democracy for middle-class schoolchildren, any more than we can have a political democracy that is limited to the middle classes. If we are not *all* members of the democratic community, then none of us are.

Segregated schools, even the placid, industrious, college-oriented schools of the middle class, cannot provide an adequate education. Nor can they in the long run contribute to the maintenance and survival of a democratic society. Desegregation, then, is not just for the sake of minorities and the economically depressed classes; it is not, as some school officials are accustomed to saying, just for "those" people.[14]

Here and there, handfuls of dedicated teachers will swim against the tide and make a heroic contribution to democracy and education. This inevitably drains their spirit and their physical energies. We should be proud of such men and women, but we can't expect to survive hoping that these few will supply the education that's needed for all our children.

Segregated schools are bad schools, but how do we get rid of them? Educators can't do it by themselves because it's a social problem, a part of the American Dilemma, not just an educational problem. De jure segregation—segregation by law—could be ameliorated with new laws. But de facto segregation, which is *not* decreed by law, is much harder to defeat. Most of today's segregated schools are a result of segregation in neighborhoods. The latter are the result of many interacting social forces: a real estate industry that divides cities into homogeneous economic and racial districts; banks that discriminate among those who apply for loans; businesses and industries that situate their shops, offices, and plants solely on the basis of maximizing investors' profits; and parents themselves who, if they can afford it, choose to live near schools that are academically strong, safe, and attended by children similar to their own.

Since segregation is a social problem, it calls for a political solution. Ironically, school reform is a favorite issue among politicians, yet they seldom have anything to say about school segregation. Their commitment to "better schools" is a commitment to a "better" curriculum, "better" teachers, and "more rigorous" academic standards. Such reforms are easy to embrace, cost little, and usually win some votes. But they are vague and empty and they avoid the major problems of American schools and American society. The school reforms of politicians of both parties in the late twentieth century are without any redeeming educational or social value.

The educational programs of schools are beyond the competence of politicians, but the segregation of schools *is* a political issue demanding a clear public policy. The style of political "leadership" for several generations in America has been to tell the public what it wants (on the basis of polls), and then to promise to get it for them. This pandering to public fantasies and public fears only makes worse our social ills. But it is possible to conceive of leaders who know something about the conditions and the consequences of social policies, and who have the courage and intelligence to inform the public about those policies. A serious political movement will use the media to enlighten the public about the educational and social costs of school segregation and the need to discontinue the practice. Constituencies must be developed who will demand desegregation, and who will vote for leaders who promise to desegregate.

Realistically speaking, the integration of housing and of neighborhoods now seems like a very long-range social goal. Until that is achieved, redrawing school district lines and moving students by bus seem to be the only ways of desegregating schools. But they are not easy ways, as the Wausau, Wisconsin school board recently discovered. There, in America's heartland, the voters ousted a school board that had approved a busing plan to integrate central-city Hmong students into suburban schools attended mostly by white, middle-class students. The complexity and the particular conditions of school segregation cannot hide an enduring fact about America: it is a racist society. And racism is in fundamental conflict with America's chosen identity as a democratic society.

There is another option for overcoming segregated schools and breaking down the barriers that isolate young people from one another. It is to look beyond schools altogether. We might consider sending the young somewhere else for their education. That is the topic of the next section.

Alternatives to School: Education through Work

Children in the United States are required to attend school until they are sixteen. Most are urged to stay longer. If it is suggested that they be sent to places other than schools for their education, the idea may go against the grain.

Yet it is reasonable to ask why *all* of the nation's children should go to school *for so long*. Why should so many people who are so different from one another in so many respects spend so much of their lives in an institution that is dominantly academic? When school's over, people confront an enormous range of occupations. They seek jobs that match the variety in their personalities and skills. Why then, should all this rich human diversity be funneled into a single-purpose institution for ten or twelve years? Isn't it personally and socially wasteful, and sometimes downright cruel?

The justification for universal elementary schooling in a modern postindustrial democracy seems straightforward. We assume a need for reading and writing and calculating, and for a commitment to the values, dispositions, and habits that are agreed on in society.

But the values and dispositions learned in schools as they operate now are not always the ones we are proud to associate with American culture. (Our misgivings could be dispelled if the system were changed so that teachers could actually educate their students.)

The justification for universal secondary schooling is much weaker. It usually has two parts. The first refers to the important facts and ideas that all youth should be expected to know. This justification collapses as soon as we realize that people can't acquire and remember knowledge just because other people think it's important. The explanation for this was detailed in the first section of Chapter 3.

The second part of the justification for universal secondary schooling refers to the different sorts of educational experiences that are said to be available for youth who have different personalities and skills. Thus high schools that are called "comprehensive" channel people into different tracks: the academic, the vocational, and the general. Typically, the academic track is composed of rigidly sequenced college preparatory courses; the vocational track prepares for a limited number of vocations using equipment that is often out of date; and the general track, lacking any identifiable aim, is often intended for youth who are thought to have no identifiable interests. These three tracks are said to match the different personalities, skills, and interests of high school youth. But placement in the tracks ordinarily matches students' scores on tests of achievement or ability. As shown above, the tracks are ordinarily segregated on the basis of race, ethnic background, and income level. So the tracks have little to do with differences in students' personalities, abilities, or interests.

Despite the tracking in high school, instruction is dominantly academic; that is, it focuses on books, lectures,[15] and exams. Thus high schools offer a handful of Procrustean beds to which students can be fitted only by ignoring the variety of their differences. If what people do when they get out of school is any indication, academic activities are suitable for only a small proportion of the population. It seems odd, then, to compel *all* of the youth of a nation to pursue these rather specialized activities until they are sixteen or older.

In sum, the justification for universal secondary schooling *as it is conducted now* is very weak. It would be far more honest to justify sending young people to high school on the grounds that the economy simply can't provide jobs for them, and we need to put them someplace where they can be supervised by adults. The weakness of the official justifications for high schools, coupled with the more honest one just noted, makes it reasonable to raise this question:

until the school system is changed in ways that encourage learning, why not put young people who don't thrive on the schools' current offerings someplace else, where they *could* learn? After all, we know we can learn a great deal outside school.

What we are after is some form of productive activity young people could undertake with the help and supervision of adults. This productive activity can be found in the world of work: in adult occupations and professions. Most high school students could learn something valuable out of school, on the job. Not in whatever job they were lucky enough to get, but under the supervision of teachers and their fellow workers in a selected sampling of the occupations that can be found in the nation.

The aim is not just to learn job skills and acquire appropriate work attitudes, although this would surely occur. But more important, the young could discover what sorts of work suited their temperaments, and what sorts didn't.[16] The young could also learn in the world of work how particular jobs are related to entire industries and to the wider economy. They could learn what sorts of problems face various industries and the economy as a whole. And as they learned about the world of work, they would make a contribution to the economy and would be paid for it, although on a scale lower than that of full-time adult workers.

The important learnings of an education through work should probably be expected of all students for a semester or a year, near the beginning of the high school program. Traditional vocational education is usually undertaken only by the children of the poor and minorities, and has become another means of segregation in schools. This will be avoided if all students participate in a program of education through work, regardless of their income level, background or gender. The students could decide whether to pursue the program longer or return to academic studies.

The idea that productive work should contribute to the education of youth has merit on general grounds and has been suggested by many writers.[17] Some of the more important features of such a program can be brought to light in the form of answers to several of the stronger objections to it.

1. Working people have enough to do just fulfilling the demands of their job. How can they be expected to to take additional time needed to train and supervise youth?

But the jobs initially made available to youth would be relatively simple; they will learn much by simply watching and imitating other workers. Even in jobs that require more training, the additional help provided by the young will more than offset the time lost in training them.

2. Young people have traditionally been overworked and underpaid. Child labor laws were passed in this country to end that exploitation. But if millions of youth entered the workplace, what would prevent the resumption of exploitative labor practices?

Violations of labor laws became widespread in the late twentieth century. As a means of "reducing government expenses," staffs were drastically cut back in the federal agencies charged with monitoring business and industry. As a result, violations of health and safety laws in America's commercial and industrial workplaces became as common as crime in the streets of America's ghettos.[18] But since in private work spaces it was shielded from public view, industrial and commercial crime was a lot less noticeable.

But even adequately funded regulatory agencies wouldn't be needed to monitor all the places where young people might be working because that monitoring ought to be the responsibility of the schools. For the educative value of working is not to be gained simply by placing young people in jobs and then forgetting about them. The job itself may not *be* particularly educative. What can make it so is the opportunity the young worker has to examine it critically in a disciplined way. Teachers would continue to work with youth, but in a new way. Instead of preparing them to take academic exams, teachers could help them find educative value in their work. To do this, teachers will have to visit job sites. While their aim would primarily be educational, teachers may find themselves witnessing dangerous, mentally stupefying, and other kinds of exploitative conditions. When the secrecy that shrouds most worker exploitation is removed, exploitation itself will diminish.

3. Work is for adults. Putting children into job settings would only place unreasonable demands on them and distract the adults. Keep the kids in school where they belong.

No one would have made this objection even a century ago, when youths were expected to go to work to support themselves and, in the process, learn to become an adult. But what was offered on the job in those days was largely socialization—not education of the sort discussed here. There are always certain benefits when young people work productively in association with responsible adults. But the emphasis here is on creating genuinely educational conditions that were not available in the past.

4. The economy in late twentieth-century America has been unable to employ all the adults who need jobs. How would it be

possible to create jobs for literally millions of young people?

A program of education through work is not intended to compete with the adult labor market. The aim is educational; as such, adults' jobs would not be threatened. First, the pay for such work would be minimal and without fringe benefits. Insurance would be paid by the state, as it is for children in school. Employers who added youth to their work force would be prohibited by law from laying off higher-paid workers.

Second, there are areas of social need that private enterprise has been reluctant to enter. In the past, government took up the slack. Some of our best looking and most functional post offices and schools, not to mention bridges and dams, attest to the past role of active government participation in the economy. If the private sector will not provide desperately needed goods and services (e.g., low-income housing, public infrastructure), then the government must, if society is not to deteriorate. But public services also offer vast educational potential. A few examples will make this clear. As you examine them, consider the condition of these services in your own community, and consider what would happen if hundreds of new workers were made available for each of them.

Young children are in need of tutors, and hospitals and hospices are in need of more nurses and other workers. Additional help is needed for the care of the aged, the physically handicapped, the mentally ill. Public agencies could use additional help, from libraries to post offices, the police, public parks, and so on. There is a desperate need for help in the maintenance and repair of infrastructure: pavement, roads, bridges, buildings, sewers, street lights, and so forth, not to mention public arts projects, national parks, forests, and wildlife preserves. Not only could American youth learn a great deal in the performance of these jobs, but the jobs themselves are vitally needed.

Opponents of such programs will still claim that we can't afford it—as if libraries and hospitals were luxuries that we could just as well do without. Answers to this objection can be put in economic as well as educational terms. First, the wages of these young people would be low, and their services would contribute to a healthier economy. Safer streets and better health care are not only public goods, but they also expand investment opportunities in the long run. Thus they enhance the operation of the economy.

Second, the range of occupations like those just mentioned is so great that a vast number of interests and skills among the young could be accommodated. This not only helps their efforts to match themselves with a career, but it also means that jobs might be performed by people who are suited for them. The skills and dispositions learned in these jobs can offer unexcelled occupational preparation, as well as cultivate a wide range of dispositions important for the development of democratic citizenship.

New Roles for Teachers: Education, Work, and the Aesthetic Quality of Life

When we examine one more objection to the idea of educating the young through work, we'll see the connections between working, learning, and the aesthetic quality of experience. We'll also see that a serious reconsideration of how people learn and where they can do it helps us discover some new roles for teachers.

This last objection to education through work can be put something like this. Most of the jobs that would be available to young people will require little knowledge, skill or special preparation. Since such jobs would be relatively simple, what could kids learn from them?

The objection is sound. Most jobs available to the young have little to teach after the first week or so of working, and I am suggesting that seventeen- or eighteen-year-olds work at such jobs for several months. But I am also suggesting that the resultant thinning of school classrooms will enable the school to provide time, space, and teachers for regular discussions of jobs with young workers. These discussions would cover such things as the wider personal and social responsibilities of the job; the relations among and between workers, supervisors, and employers; the relation of the service given or product made to the economy and to social needs and values; and the value to the worker of the work done and the payment received. Although these discussions cannot adequately be undertaken on the job, school sponsorship of them away from the workplace can transform the job into a genuinely educational experience.

At school, teachers could conduct discussions once or twice a week with as many as a dozen students who had similar jobs. These discussions could be extended by written work which would focus on students' expectations, observations, analyses, judgments, and complaints. The economic and the social function of the job could be the subject of extensive writing. When students are writing about things that matter to them, their writing is likely to improve.

The same teachers who meet regularly with young workers in schools might also visit their workplaces. Since an education through work program demands considerable cooperation between school and workplace, site visits by teachers can enhance that cooperation. These visits will also provide teachers firsthand experience that can serve as a check on what the students, back at school, are talking and writing about.

Vocational education programs ordinarily have two features that distinguish them from the education through work program suggested here. First, they often simply place students in a job and leave them there, with little or no supervision or opportunity for intellectual exploration. The work becomes routine and what students get out of it is a form of socialization, not education.

The other typical feature of vocational education programs is their dominant aim of preparing students for specific jobs. However reasonable this may seem, a stronger case can be made for helping the young to explore a wide range of job possibilities, and to explore their own interests and abilities as they learn about jobs. Some will discover what kind of work suits them; others will find that they want further education. Specific-job training closes off these possibilities; it narrows their learning, reduces their adaptability, and withholds the promise of a democratic society.

This rigidity and narrowness can be overcome by a school-supervised education through work program like the one described here, which has much in common with the vocational education proposed generations ago by John Dewey.[19] When he urged that the school program be based on the experience of learners, he didn't conceive experience as the passive ingestion of other people's wisdom, but rather as active participation in occupations. The term "occupation" meant for Dewey much more than a job. He defined it formally as "a continuous activity having a purpose." It denoted the play, games, and constructive activities in which children naturally engage. As an occupation, work was to be understood in terms of what was being done, rather than simply as a source of income. Of course, that's the *only* way we can understand "women's work." "Unemployed" women are not paid for raising children and maintaining their families, yet society can't survive unless they carry on this work. If we are to understand how work can foster learning, we must understand it as an occupation, an activity, and not simply as employment—a way to get paid.

After noting similarities and differences between play and work, Dewey observed that "work which remains permeated with the play attitude is art—in quality if not in conventional designation."[20] Play is undertaken for its own sake; for the player, it has intrinsic value. Work produces a tangible result: a pot, an automobile, a quarterly report. But there is no reason, apart from external industrial conditions, why work cannot be undertaken with the same sense of intrinsic value found in play. To say that such work "permeated with the play attitude" is art is not to make a claim about its aesthetic value for others. Rather, it is to emphasize its intrinsic value for the worker.

Work is felt to be intrinsically valuable when workers believe they are effectively managing whatever had become problematic for them. In other words, they are resolving the discrepancy between what they expected and what they ran into. Work may have various aims, but it is *experienced* as monotony (when it's a routine), as frustration (when it's not succeeding), or as satisfaction (when discrepancies are being resolved). What makes work attractive is the promise that discrepancies will appear that *can* be resolved. Insofar as it deals with novelty or difficulties to be overcome, the pattern of work is not different from artistic creativity. And it is similar to the pattern our feelings take when we are deeply absorbed in the arts. In work or play or art, that pattern enables experience to become aesthetic in quality, for it involves the operation of thought and the arousal and resolution of feeling.

When work is merely routine, it cannot have aesthetic quality, any more than routine studies can. Dewey was well aware of the mind-numbing effects of work throughout most of human history:

> When one bears in mind the social environment of the Greeks and the people of the Middle Ages, where such practical activities as could be successfully carried on were mostly of a routine and external sort and even servile in nature, one is not surprised that educators turned their back upon them as unfitted to cultivate intelligence. But now that even the occupations of the household, agriculture, and manufacturing as well as transportation and intercourse are instinct with [i.e., permeated by] applied science, the case stands otherwise. It is true that many of those who now engage in them are not aware of the intellectual content upon which their personal actions depend. But this fact only gives an added reason why schooling should use these pursuits so as to enable the coming generation to acquire a comprehension now too generally lacking.[21]

Earlier, I tried to show that school is without educative value for many older students. The school system has, on the whole, ignored Dewey's advice in the above passage: to use occupations in school settings. Now I am suggesting that an alternative to further incarceration in school can be found: utilizing the world of work itself for the purpose of education.

Dewey believed, in 1915, that education could "acknowledge the full intellectual and social meaning of a vocation." But schools may have retrogressed since he wrote about them. They are typically bigger, more bureaucratized, and less subject to local control than they were in 1915. It's harder to be experimental and to make changes in them. For these reasons, I am suggesting that the education Dewey urged, an education through occupations, be seriously tried in the world of work itself, and not just in the schools.

Putting young people in workplaces and affording them teachers who will help them examine the consequences and the worth of what they are doing may not appeal to those who control the nation's workplaces. When workers are helped to examine and judge the nature of their work, they are bound to think of ways of making it better. In the long run this will be good for business and for society as a whole. In the short run it may be seen as an interference in the prerogatives of ownership and management: a threat to the right of privacy itself. But an effort to make the world of work serve educational ends is bound to provoke opposition from those who would control business autocratically for their own private ends. Dewey wrote:

> This ideal [of the vocational aspects of education] has to contend not only with the inertia of existing educational traditions, but also with the oppostion of those who are intrenched in command of the industrial machinery, and who realize that such an educational system if made general would threaten their ability to use others for their own ends.[22]

American ideals fall far short of realization. They can remain vital only if they are constantly recalled in the course of our everyday activities. A thoughtful and critical examination of our daily work will help in the transformation of our bureaucratized and privatized society into one in which participation in work and in citizenship is widespread, free, and fulfilling. It is fitting that leadership in this examination be taken by those who are nearly ready to enter society.[23]

For teachers willing to risk participation in such a program, it will be a revitalizing learning experience. It will transform the nature of their work and make them the connecting links between a rather aloof, academic school and the real world in which people not only make their living, but are shaped by the nature of the work they do.

There is another benefit to be gained by having teachers supervise a program of education through work. Teachers have become concerned with texts and exams, bureaucratic constraints, and a mountain of forms to fill out. Students have been socialized to care about money, sex, drugs, what to do for a living, and how to get a new pair of Nikes.[24] Without much in common, teachers and students often mistrust and even fear one another.[25] This makes for a poor emotional climate in the classroom; for no one is experience high in quality.

When teachers learn about the same workplace in which their students are learning, they will have something in common with them. When they explore together the impact on the wider society of the work that's done, they'll have more in common. When they explore together the ways in which the organization of production both facilitates their work and constrains them—as teachers, students, workers, and citizens—they'll discover that they have a great deal in common. A program of education through work can transform the relationships between teachers and students by closing the chasm that divides them. It can foster experience that is genuinely aesthetic in quality—that is mutually satisfying because it provokes thought and contributes to personal growth.

Living in the School System and Teaching Well

1. Living in the School System

Large-scale efforts to foster education through work are a long way off. Only a few teachers would be ready to provide the needed supervision; only a few employers are ready to have youth in their workplaces; only a few schools are ready to temper their academic bias. In the immediate future, most teachers will continue to work in their classrooms.

What we need to know, then, is this: How serious are the obstacles to education that have been discussed in this and in the previous chapter? Do they actually prevent education from going on? Is there a way to overcome them, or somehow get around them? Or should we just ignore them and carry on business as usual?

The short answer is that we'd better not ignore the multiple-choice testing system, the ways in which prospective teachers are trained and placed, and our segregated schools. They really do constitute obstacles to the promotion of education, and ignoring them will make it increasingly less likely for schools to foster education. But we *can* get around them.

An obstacle is not the same thing as a prohibition. Having a stone in your shoe doesn't keep you from running. But it can keep you from running as fast as you'd like, or as far as you might. Teachers and children will have to live with systemic obstacles to education for some time to come. But in the meantime, conditions of education *can* be established in the schools, despite these obstacles.

Once you understand the systemic nature of the obstacles—the fact that they are embedded within the structure and operation of a complex system—then you understand that you can't overcome them by yourself. In the same way, a teacher or a citizen, acting alone, can't make up for the insufficient funding of schools. But this understanding itself helps to demystify[26] the school system. To understand what you cannot achieve right now makes it possible to direct your attention to what you *can* achieve now. Understanding empowers people.

We can see what this sort of empowerment means by reviewing some of the things that have been said or implied in earlier chapters. First we'll see that some of the obstacles to education that are fretted over by contemporary reformers are not really obstacles at all. Then we'll review some of the things teachers can effectively do, in spite of systemic obstacles, to establish genuinely educative conditions in their classrooms.

Teachers, administrators, and parents expend a great deal of worry and effort over what they take to be serious obstacles to a high-quality education. But not all of these are really obstacles. They may just be the consequences of the systemic obstacles already noted: the testing system, the training of teachers, and the segregation of schools. If this is so, then they don't need to be addressed at all. They can simply be ignored, or put on the back burner. Freed from dealing with pseudoproblems, the pressures on teachers will be reduced so that they can turn their attention to more productive matters. Here are a few examples of these pseudoproblems.

(a) Low scores on achievement tests. When test scores are publically compared, teachers and children, parents and administrators are

in perpetual fear of being outdone by other kids, other schools, other districts. Enormous energies are expended to raise the scores. Cheating (by school personnel as well as children) is tried and sometimes discovered. Teachers consider teaching to the tests, and their judgments about what's *worth* teaching are given second priority. Administrators realize they can raise the scores of their schools by encouraging their weaker students to drop out.

But low achievement scores are an *inevitable* consequence of a standardized, competitive testing system. *They cannot be eliminated.* Half the students will always be below the norm, and any improvement by some groups entails a decline by other groups. So one of the consequences of the testing system is that the pressures will *never* go away.

(b) Insufficient time to cover the curriculum. This is mainly a worry for teachers, although it easily infects students as well. When a great deal of material needs to be examined (just place any high school student's biology textbook on your bathroom scale) in order to cover other people's curriculum guidelines and prepare for other people's tests, time is always a problem. There never seems to be enough. Not only does this increase the pressure on teachers, but it also ensures that nothing else of significance will find its way into the curriculum; there certainy wouldn't be time for *that.* Yet having more time would be no more of a help than more homework would be for low-achieving students. Additional time is only helpful when you spend it in worthwhile ways.

(c) Diversity in the classroom. Segregated schools reduce diversity in classrooms, but the differences among students that remain are still seen as problems by many teachers. They are rightly concerned about how difficult it is to teach the same thing to a room full of young people whose backgrounds and interests and abilities are different. The difficulty, of course, is simply a consequence of having to herd different kinds of students through the same curriculum and the same tests in the same amount of time. When that rigid regimen is seen for what it is—as a socializing process with little potential for education—then the problem disappears. Diversity is a help, not an obstacle, in a setting where education is sought.

The consequences of systemic obstacles to education can be dealt with in various ways, and need not inexorably lead to stress for teachers and resentment for students.[27] And the obstacles themselves *can* to a significant extent be overcome in the classroom. Teachers can devise their own ways of judging the work of their students, and avoid the use of multiple-choice tests in their own classrooms. Teachers can meet with their colleagues for purposes of mutual support and professional growth and development (which receive little attention in teacher training programs). And even in segregated schools, teachers can try to desegregate their own classrooms; that is, they can ensure that students with different backgrounds have opportunities to work with each other.

Even if teachers act on the above suggestions, the larger, systemic obstacles to education will remain in place. *You cannot truthfully say that a school is a "good" school as long as it is segregated, and as long as the experience of its students is shaped by standardized, multiple-choice tests. But you can say that in your classroom you have created genuinely educative conditions despite the obstacles presented by the school system.* These obstacles are serious enough to distract teachers from doing their job as educators, but they don't prevent them from promoting high-quality, educative experiences in their classrooms—especially if teachers maintain the ideals that led them to their careers in the first place. This brings us to our final consideration.

2. Teaching Well

Very early in this book I discussed the uses of standards and ideals in education. Standards ordinarily have a regulatory function, and are applied to products and to professional people. We expect our automobiles and our airline pilots to meet certain standards. With ordinary citizens, including children, the case is different. Moral standards are the only ones we can expect them to meet. Failure to meet an educational "standard," whatever that might mean, is not a reason to accord a child any less respect, nor is it a reason to make that child a failure and thereby encourage her to lose her self-respect. Education that works is directed not by other people's standards, but by ideals that teachers have adopted as their own.

Of course, teachers will teach in different ways because they work in different settings with different children, they have different temperaments, and they hold different sorts of ideals. Uniformity of approach would be quite impossible—as well as being a bad idea. Yet because we are fellow citizens, we do share some ideals, and as teachers we share still more ideals.

The aims and values of a democratic society constitute a set of ideals that most of us share. Only the possession of these ideals can leave us disappointed when actual social conditions fall short of them. If a democratic society doesn't live up to its ideals in all its institutions, that's not an excuse to keep these ideals from functioning in its schools.

We expect our children to be educated for democratic citizenship: to respect others as moral equals and regard them as equal before the law; to expect and to extend to others equality of opportunity and the freedoms guaranteed by the Constitution; and to participate in their own governance. These are ideals we expect all teachers to hold. To the extent that they are free to act in their own classrooms, they can establish conditions that will both socialize and educate their students to act on these ideals. This is the first consideration for any conception of education in a democratic society. Only action that accords with democratic ideals will make possible the achievement of our other educational ideals, not to mention the maintenance of democracy itself.

When we examined the acquisition of dispositions (in Chapter 3), we focused on another set of ideals that most teachers share. When we realize that vast amounts of academic knowledge simply cannot be imprinted on people's minds, it becomes obligatory to look for something else to aim for. It's been suggested that this "something else" is a set of dispositions, of tendencies to act, that are particularly germane to the solving of problems and to working with other people. Attention was called to the dispositions to be sensitive to problems, to be hypothetical and experimental, to be respectful of evidence, to take risks, to be persistent, to be self-critical and to take pride in one's work, to be sensitive to other people and act responsibly toward them, to be open to criticism, and to work cooperatively with others.

Most teachers have a high regard for these dispositions and consider them to be educational ideals. But it may be hard to see how you would *act* on these ideals in the light of the curriculum expectations and the multiple-choice tests of the school system. Because teachers are led to believe that getting students to ingest knowledge is their first priority, they are distracted from the effort to cultivate educationally worthwhile dispositions. What's important, then, is to make the cultivation of dispositions a first priority. What beginning teachers bring with them as serious ideals, and what most experienced teachers have always known made sense, is just what should be *acted* on. The ideals teachers have about dispositions worth cultivating should not be treated as "mere" ideals. They should be translated into classroom goals that guide daily practice. These ideals should also be treated as practical criteria for judging the worth of the activities that go on in the classroom.

What students do in school, and the impact it has on them, determines the character and the quality of the education they get. Any test worth taking should have reference to what the students have been doing, although the school system turns that relation upside-down: the test is designed first, and then activities are planned with that test in mind. Sadly, the designers of the test are not the people who teach children like the ones who will be taking the test. If the *conception* of testing is turned right-side-up, we will see that *tests should help us judge what people have done, not determine what people shall do*. Because people learn from what they do, students' activities are of primary importance.

Our discussion has repeatedly emphasized that if the key to what students learn is what they *do*, then what they do must have a positive impact on the quality of their experience. The emphasis on testing and on student behaviors (or "behavioral objectives") tended to separate those behaviors (and their consequences) from the students themselves. This is something like caring for the test score more than caring for the student—as if all that mattered about Tom or Nancy was the score they produced. But the main theme of this book has been to remind you that we'd like our schools to produce well-educated students: *people of a certain character*, not just high test scores or college admissions rates. Trainers, socializers, and educators all are properly concerned about what students *do*, but only educators—who care about the kinds of people children become—must be concerned about the quality of their students' experience. The emphasis of the central chapters of this book (4 through 7) has been to show that this quality must be aesthetic in character, because the conditions for the appearance of aesthetic quality in experience are also the conditions that foster learning.

Earlier I discussed some of the ways in which classroom teachers could circumvent some of the obstacles to learning that have been created by the school system. These are, in a way, defensive actions—ways that teachers can keep from being overwhelmed by the countereducational excesses of the school system. But when teachers take conscious account of the aesthetic quality of their students' experience, and when they try to arrange conditions for the appearance of that quality, they are actively fostering the conditions of learning. They are educating their students.

There is no foolproof method by which the quality of every student's experience can be rendered aesthetic. To the contrary, a concern for the aesthetic is a commitment to recognize the individuality of students and, just as important, the individuality of teachers. Common interests and similar abilities ensure that some activities will appeal to more than one student, just as some classroom techniques will be effective for more than one teacher. But all learning is experimental (the learner has to *try* something), and so is teaching. Teachers must plan, and they must try out their plans. If it isn't working, they must—like all experimenters—be ready to change the plan or get rid of it altogether. What's crucial is unflagging attention to the students because it is *their* experience that's focal to education.

Many teachers, and most of those who are beginning their careers, have at least an intuitive understanding of this. That's why their (usually unspoken) ideal is to create a classroom setting in which the experience of students is high in quality. When it's not, there are a thousand ways students will let you know about it. And quite often their experience is not high in quality—partly because of the obstacles to education we've already discussed, and partly because teachers aren't always clear about what constitutes high-quality experience, or how to arrange for it. We'll recapitulate some of the conditions that can be established that can foster aesthetic quality in the experience of students and that will, therefore, be genuinely educative.

In Western culture, the fine arts have traditionally served as sources of the aesthetic. In response to the arts, people's minds are engaged and their feelings are aroused, agitated, and resolved. Those who have learned to immerse themselves in a book or a play, a sonata or a movie, have had experiences of exceptionally high quality. While such experience is properly called aesthetic, I have tried to show (in Chapter 4) that the arts are not the only sources of the aesthetic. In fact, the aesthetic characterizes any experience in which a form of thinking has been successfully undertaken to resolve the feelings aroused by discrepancies from what we expected.

So the aesthetic is much broader than the arts. It can appear in virtually any sort of activity, and it is regarded as being so valuable (whether or not we *name* it as "aesthetic") that we often plan for it deliberately. Aesthetic satisfaction can be experienced at work. Some of us plan for it, seeking challenge, novelty, and surprise—all situations that offer discrepancies: difficulties to be overcome. We seek discrepancies and the satisfaction that attends their resolution when we play: if we knew what the score of the game would be before it started, we might want to bet on it, but we might not want to watch it. And we seek discrepancies and the satisfactions they make possible in our meals, in our recreations, our friendships, and our courtships ("For me? You really shouldn't have! But what can I give you in return?").

We seek the aesthetic in our own lives even if that's not what we call it. Pianists and poets *know* that's what they're after, and the people who hear them experience it, too. All of us seek the aesthetic if we are not overburdened with routine or frustration. In fact, we long for it, because we know how it feels and how it helps us grow, and we know there are no material substitutes for it. Of course, the aesthetic is a worthy aim for teachers to have for their students, although it cannot be *given* to them, or bestowed on them. What teachers *can* do is try to establish the conditions for the appearance of the aesthetic—which is what Shakespeare did when he put his words on paper. The crucial feature of these conditions is a discrepancy: something that takes us by surprise. The surprise must then be followed by an effort to make sense of it, to resolve it.

Even infants, a short while after they are born, begin to have expectations about the world. Kindergarteners have vast and complex expectations about what the world is like, and what will happen when they act on it. A teacher who knows her students knows what they expect of things, and she can find this out by paying attention to how they react. If a teacher is successfully to offer discrepancies from what her students expect, then she must have an idea, first, of what it is that they expect.

The discrepancies can be of many kinds. Works of art can offer discrepancies in what's seen or heard, although it must be remembered that the discrepancy is not inherently *in* the art itself. Since the discrepancy is a function of the relationship between the art and the observer, the observer must have some familiarity with the style or genre of which the presented work is an example. He must have some expectations, if his expectations are to be thwarted!

In a classroom where routines don't demand that students be constantly busy, teachers can allow students to follow up their curiosity about things that puzzle them, that present them with a discrepancy. Teachers can also set up situations, within any field of study, that provoke curiosity: not problems that call for solution, but puzzles, anomalies, things that pique one's interest; situations that are seductive, not demanding. Of course, not all students will be attracted by the same puzzles. Only a fool or a martinet would think that every student could become curious about algebraic functions, or about Egypt.

The experience of a problem is related to curiosity, because it, too, is a felt response to a discrepancy from what was expected. But a problem, unlike a curious situation, demands to be solved. It makes this demand because it interferes with our purposes, with what we actively seek to achieve. Teachers can utilize some of the purposes that students have to initiate activities that are likely to encounter problems. These are the conditions for problem-solving. But if students' own purposes are not operating, they cannot solve problems; they can only seek the answers to someone else's puzzles. As noted above, puzzles, unlike problems, do not demand solutions. That's why the school system encourages the use of rewards and punishments, which *do* demand that students do *something*. But to leave the students' purposes out of the classroom is to leave education out as well.

It is often easier to give up, or to turn to something else, than it is to act intelligently when we're confronted by something discrepant. White Americans once dismissed jazz, believing it was simple and crude. A child may be too confounded to try to explain how a bumblebee could possibly fly. A teacher may discipline his class because its enthusiasm for an activity led to spontaneous talking. Because, from an educational point of view, a discrepancy is wasted if it's not followed up and resolved, students need all the help they can get. The teacher can supply some of the help, but the greatest source of help is other students. It would be unbearable if we had to face all our problems in the world all by ourselves. The objective difficulties and the feeling of isolation are no different when they appear in the classroom. It is no defense of isolated study to say that students are used to it. Humans are capable of getting used to nearly anything. Even slavery.

But it is democracy that we're concerned to maintain in our society, and it's democracy that we need to establish in our schools. There's nothing new about the need for many people to work together to solve difficult problems. It took more than a small group to build the pyramids. But *that* form of organization, and the religious beliefs that supported a dominating social hierarchy, is not what's wanted in a democratic society.

A community that is good to live in is one in which people have interests and hold values in common, and in which they voluntarily cooperate to achieve common goals. When such a community also cherishes the freedoms that are promised in the Constitution, the warmth of brotherhood and sisterhood is enlivened by the satisfactions of the aesthetic. The school is the place to establish such communities, because that's how people learn. And the school can be a far more receptive place for the establishment of such communities than the world outside the school. It begins with freedom for teachers and it is nurtured when teachers become one another's colleagues. It comes to fruition when the aesthetic becomes characteristic of teaching and learning. Its consequence in the long run is freedom for all of us.

Notes

Introduction

1. This may not be a good example, but there was one recorded in South Dakota, in 1978.

Chapter 1

1. Albert Shanker, in Mark Danner (ed.), "How Not to Fix the Schools," *Harper's* (February 1986), 48.

2. Emile Durkheim, *Moral Education* (New York: The Free Press, 1961), 37.

3. A thorough analysis that indicates the contradictions of values implicit in contemporary Western attitudes toward work can be found in Daniel Bell, *The Cultural Contradictions of Capitalism* (New York: Basic Books, 1976).

4. For a discussion of the close connection between education and the development of critical thought, see Harvey Siegel, *Educating Reason* (New York: Routledge, 1988).

5. See J. S. Brown et al., "Situated Cognition and the Culture of Learning," *Educational Researcher*, 18:1 (1989), 34, who write, "contrary to the aim of schooling, success within this [school] culture often has little bearing on performance elsewhere."

6. John Dewey argues forcibly for this point in the opening chapters of *Democracy and Education* (New York: Macmillan, 1916), especially in Chapter 1, "Education as a Necessity of Life."

7. Durkheim, op. cit., 52.

8. See Siegel's discussion of a rational person as one who is "appropriately moved by reasons." See *Educating Reason*, op. cit., 23.

9. The artistic quality of experience independent of the artistic value of the product is discussed at length by Seymour B. Sarason in *The Challenge of Art to Psychology* (New Haven: Yale University Press, 1990), especially in Chapter 3.

Chapter 2

1. Children who are held back a year or more (i.e., who "fail" in school) learn less than peers of similar ability who are promoted. Research also shows that neither socialization nor learning readiness are increased by nonpromotion. In these areas, pupils who are retained actually show regression. Nonpromotion also tends to foster discipline problems, negative self-concepts, and personal maladjustment. See M. Scott Norton, "Student Promotion and Retention: What the Research Says," *Contemporary Education*, LIV (Summer, 1983), 283-286.

2. Education for national preparedness is discussed in James B. Conant, *The Comprehensive High School* (McGraw-Hill, 1967). A more blatant form of such an education is discussed in Hyman G. Rickover, *Education and Freedom* (New York: E. P. Dutton, 1959).

3. National Commission on Excellence in Education, *A Nation at Risk* (Washington, D.C.: United States Government Printing Office, 1983).

4. Horace Mann, a key figure in the establishment of a public school system in Massachusetts, wrote, "If education be equably diffused, it will draw property after it, by the strongest of all attractions; for such a thing never did happen, and never can happen, as that an intelligent and practical body of men should be permanently poor. . . . Education, then, beyond all other devices of human origin, is the great equalizer of the conditions of men—the balance-wheel of the social machinery." See Horace Mann, "Twelfth Annual Report to the Board of Education of the State of Massachusetts (1848)," in Lawrence A. Cremin (ed.), *The Republic and the School: Horace Mann and the Education of Free Men* (New York: Teachers College, Columbia University, 1957), 86, 87.

5. In American secondary schools, the low income, non-college-bound youth get the most crowded classes, the least experienced teachers, and the dullest curriculum materials. See Barbara Benham Tye, *Multiple Realities: A Study of Thirteen American High Schools* (Lanham, Md.: University Press of America, 1985), p. 308.

6. Cognitive development in children, conceived as proceeding through a succession of invariant stages, is discussed at length in the work of the psychologist Jean Piaget. For a thoughtful discussion of his work, see John H. Flavell, *The Developmental Psychology of Jean Piaget* (New York: D. Van Nostrand, 1963), especially pp. 19ff.

7. It makes sense to remain neutral on issues about which we have insufficient information, and we can maintain neutrality about issues that have no impact on us or our students. The former might be called a sort of temporary neutrality; the latter, a neutrality of unconcern. But for a teacher to maintain neutrality about consequential issues that she does understand would be morally irresponsible, pedagogically indefensible, and a dereliction of citizenship. For another view, see Robert Ennis's provocative essay, "Is It Impossible for the Schools to be Neutral?" in B. Othanel Smith and Robert H. Ennis (eds.), *Language and Concepts in Education* (Chicago: Rand McNally, 1961), 102-111.

8. Joseph Schumpeter, *Capitalism, Socialism, and Democracy* (New York: Harper & Row, 1962), 269.

9. An editorial in *The New Republic* (November 15, 1982) observed that, "Across the country, the average expenditure for House [of Representatives] candidates was $54,000 in 1974 and $ 157,000 in 1980. For Senate finalists, it was $437,500 in 1974 and $1,075,000 in 1980." In 1992 the average price of election for a House seat was $543,000; for a Senate seat it was $3,900,000. And in the elections, the top money-getter wins nine times out of ten (see Jamin B. Raskin, "Challenging the 'Wealth Primary,'" *The Nation*, November 21, 1994, 610). In the 1994 campaign for the U.S. Senate in California, candidate Michael Huffington had already spent *$20,000,000, prior* to the final week of the campaign, on television ads alone (see the Sacramento *Bee*, November 4, 1994).

John Larson, Chair of California's Fair Political Practices Commission, was deeply impressed by the role of money in politics by the time his five-year term expired. He said that the legislative process is more dominated by monied special interests than he ever imagined when he got the job: "I think that the special interests get the consideration and the votes. . . . Most of the people [in the Capitol] think that a member of the public—an individual with an individual problem—is a sort of nuisance." See James Richardson, "Chairman looks forward to FPPC job running out," Sacramento *Bee*, December 10, 1990. Former U.S. Senate majority leader George Mitchell characterized contemporary politics in America thus: "It stinks! Money *is* the system (see Raskin, op. cit., 609)."

10. An early and original account of democracy as a way of living, and its implications for education, may be found in Boyd H. Bode, *Democracy as a Way of LIfe* (New York: Macmillan, 1937).

11. A readable account of curriculum differentiation in the history of American schools can be found in Herbert M. Kliebard, *The Struggle for the American Curriculum, 1893-1958* (Boston: Routledge & Kegan Paul, 1986), especially chapters 4 and 5.

12. A statistically precise account of the advantages of tracking in secondary schools that are conferred on middle- and upper-class youth can be

found in Beth E. Vanfossen, James D. Jones, and Joan Z. Spade, "Curriculum tracking and status maintenance," *Sociology of Education*, 60 (April, 1987), 104-122. A more comprehensive treatment of socioeconomic and ethnic inequalities built into tracking systems appears in Jeannie Oakes, *Keeping Track: How High Schools Structure Inequality* (New Haven: Yale University Press, 1985).

13. Professor James McClellan has called my attention to the fact that when the U.S. Constitution forbid Congress from issuing patents of nobility, it established an equality among citizens tempered only by differences in property. Thus it established a sort of bourgeois equality that permits serious economic inequalities. The Thirteenth Amendment extended equality by abolishing slavery. The Fourteenth Amendment extended the full protection of the law to all—even to private corporations and *their* ownership of property, which generated new forms of economic inequality. As is the case with other ideals, equality can generate its own opposite.

14. A. S. Neill, a very serious educator, answered the question unequivocally: he argued that children should have a choice about all their activities, with only a few, explicitly noted exceptions. Few schools have followed his advice. See Neill, *Summerhill* (New York: Hart, 1960).

15. This point was argued effectively by Paul Goodman in *Growing Up Absurd* (New York: Vintage, 1960). It was argued more directly although in a less scholarly way by Jerry Farber in *The Student as Nigger* (New York: Contact, 1969). And it has been documented widely on the basis of careful and extended school classroom observations. For example, see Philip A. Cusick, "Adolescent Groups and the School Organization," *School Review*, 82:1 (November, 1973), 116-126; or Barbara Benham Tye, *Multiple Realities* (op. cit., 1985), who wrote that "classroom decisions in virtually all areas were made by the teacher, although in some classes, students were allowed to decide where they would sit" (p. 200). Tye concluded from her study of thirteen high schools that the young are kept "in a dependent and subordinate position until they are seventeen or eighteen" (259).

16. A strong argument can be made against the view that a representative government can be democratic. See Robert Paul Wolff, *In Defense of Anarchism* (New York: Harper & Row, 1970).

17. Many psychological and even anthropological studies are available that deal with the emotional effects of endless striving and competing, and the resultant insecurities. A recent and excellent study is Paul L. Wachtel, *The Poverty of Affluence* (Philadelphia: New Society Publishers, 1989).

18. Edward A. Wynne and Kevin Ryan, *Reclaiming Our Schools: A Handbook in Teaching Character, Academics, and Discipline* (New York: Macmillan, 1993), 58.

19. It was a major theme in all of John Dewey's writings about education that the first obligation of schools in a democracy is to instill democratic ideals in the next generation. See Dewey, *Democracy and Education* (New York: Macmillan, 1916). This idea continues to find expression in thoughtful contemporary studies of education, such as Richard Pratte, *The Civic Imperative* (New York: Teachers College Press, 1988); Robert D. Heslep, *Education in Democracy* (Ames, Iowa: Iowa State University Press, 1989); or Amy Gutmann, *Democratic Education* (Princeton, N.J.: Princeton University Press, 1987), who writes, "The main problem with primary schooling today is . . . that it does not prepare students for democratic citizenship. If they were educated to exercise the rights and to fulfill the responsibilities of democratic citizenship, these future citizens collectively could decide whether to change the way that social institutions (including schools) structure their life chances" (148).

In *The Morality of Democratic Citizenship* (Calabasas, Calif.: Center for Civic Education, 1988), R. Freeman Butts writes, "The common core of the curriculum throughout school . . . should be the morality of citizenship. For this goal to be realized, scholarly study of civic morality should be the first priority in the liberal and professional education of the teaching profession" (184). And although they entertain a very different ideal of morality and citizenship, Wynne and Ryan (in *Reclaiming Our Schools*, op. cit.) are unambiguous about the importance of these matters as educational goals.

Chapter 3

1. The educational work of Comenius is described in John Edward Sadler, *J. A. Comenius and the Concept of Universal Education* (New York: Barnes & Noble, 1966). A briefer account can be found in Jerome Clausen, "The Pansophist: Comenius," in P. Nash, A. M. Kazamias, and H. J. Perkinson (eds.), *The Educated Man* (New York: Wiley, 1965).

2. See *History-Social Science Framework* (Sacramento, Calif.: California State Department of Education, June 10, 1987).

3. The following works express the sentiments of the academicians who favor the transmission of organized bodies of knowledge to children in schools: Mortimer Adler, *The Paideia Proposal: An Educational Manifesto* (New York: Macmillan, 1982); Allan Bloom, *The Closing of the American Mind* (New York: Simon & Schuster, 1987); E. D. Hirsch, Jr., *Cultural Literacy: What Every American Should Know* (Boston: Houghton Mifflin, 1987). Not to be confused with the above are the more philosophically sophisticated arguments of scholars who join the acquisition of knowledge to the understanding of how knowledge is acquired and to the criteria by which it is evaluated. See, for example, Harry S. Broudy, *Building a Philosophy of Education* (Englewood Cliffs, N.J.: 1961), Chapter 13; Paul H. Hirst,

"Education and the Nature of Knowledge," in R. D. Archambault (ed.), *Philosophical Analysis and Education* (London: Routledge and Kegan Paul, 1965), 113-138; and R. S. Peters, *Ethics and Education* (London: George Allen & Unwin, 1966), Chapter 4.

4. Robert M. Hutchins, *The Higher Learning in America* (New Haven: Yale University Press, 1936), p. 60.

5. For differences in retention in two different approaches to mathematics instruction, see Jane M. Watson, "The Keller Plan, final examinations, and long-term retention," *Journal for Research in Math Education,* 17:1 (January 1986), 60-68.

6. To see how, for purposes of facilitating retention, a hierarchical sequence of learning units is superior to a discontinuous array of discrete courses, see Hanna J. Arzi et al., "Proactive and retroactive facilitation of long-term retention by curriculum continuity," *American Educational Research Journal,* 22:3 (Fall, 1985), 369-388.

7. To consider particuar instructional techniques for the facilitation of retention, see, for example, Ellen E. Peters and Joel R. Levin, "Effects of a mnemonic imagery strategy on good and poor readers' prose recall," *Reading Research Quarterly,* 21:12 (Spring, 1986), 179-192; or David Berliner and Ursula Casanova, "Are you teaching students the right skills for retention?" *Instructor,* 96:6 (February 1987), 18-19.

8. John P. Houston, *Fundamentals of Learning and Memory* (New York: Harcourt, Brace, Jovanovich, 1986).

9. Jack A. Adams, *Learning and Memory: An Introduction* (Homewood, Illinois: The Dorsey Press, 1976).

10. Lee J. Cronbach, *Educational Psychology,* 3rd ed. (New York: Harcourt, Brace, Jovanovich, 1977), 60.

11. Kjell Harnqvist, "Enduring Effects of Schooling—A Neglected Area in Educational Research," *Educational Researcher,* 6:10 (November 1977), 5-11.

12. In looking for research that dealt with the retention of school subjects, the following journals were consulted for the years 1986-1990 inclusive: *American Educational Research Journal*; *American Journal of Education*; *Educational Researcher*; *Harvard Educational Review*; and *Teachers College Record.*

13. George B. Semb and John A. Ellis, "Knowledge Taught in School: What Is Remembered?" *Review of Educational Research,* 64:2 (Summer, 1994), 279, 254. I am indebted to Professor Carl Spring for calling my attention to this article.

14. Ulric Neisser, "Memory: What Are the Important Questions?" in M. M. Gruneberg, P. E. Morris, and H. N. Sykes (eds.), *Practical Aspects of Memory* (London: Academic Press, 1978), 5.

15. Harry S. Broudy (*The Uses of Schooling*, New York: Routledge, 1988) also sees little hope for what he calls the replicative and the applicative uses of schooling. But in defense of the school's effort to transmit knowledge, he claims that it can profitably be put to associative and interpretive uses, even though its details have been forgotten. It is difficult to imagine concrete examples of associative and interpretive uses of forgotten knowledge.

16. Many cognitive scientists liken the human mind to an information-processing system. They usually claim that information once acquired remains in memory, awaiting retrieval. Marvin Minsky puts it this way: "Suppose that one part P of your mind has just experienced a mental event E which led to achieving some goal—call it G. Suppose another part of your mind declares this to be 'memorable.' We postulate that two things happen: . . . A new agent, called a *K-node,* is created and somehow linked with G. . . . [and] every K-node comes with a wire, called its *K-line,* that has potential connections to every agent in the P-pyramid [a hierarchical collection of abilities]. The act of 'memorizing' causes this K-line to make an excitatory attachment to every currently active P-agent. Consequently, when KE is activated at some later time, this will make P 'reenact' that partial state—by arousing those P-agents that were active when E was 'memorized.' Thus, activation of KE causes the P-net to become 'disposed' to behave the way it was working when the original goal G was achieved." See Marvin Minsky, "K-Lines: A Theory of Memory," in D. A. Norman (ed.) *Perspectives on Cognitive Science* (Norwood, N.J.: Ablex, 1981), 92.

As Minsky's discussion shows, cognitive scientists tend to invent legions of new mental entities, along with a lexicon for identifying them. What's most striking is the way in which these mechanisms appear to operate all on their own, as if a person were little more than their passive container. For example, Roger C. Schank posits four types, or levels, of memory: one for events (an Event Memory), a General Event Memory, a Situational Memory, and an Intentional Memory. Without discussing why it is that people sometimes do and sometimes don't remember certain things, Schank claims that parts of our experience get sorted out into one or more of these different types of memory. "The main point," he says, "is that memory breaks down its new information into appropriately interesting pieces and stores those pieces in the context to which they are relevant, i.e., the context which originally recognized them and explained them." See Schank, "Language and Memory," in Norman, op. cit., 121-123, 126. Having thus invented a smoothly operating system, Schank must now account for the fact that we imperfect humans don't always seem to operate so efficiently.

Not all cognitive psychologists describe mental functioning as information-processing. For example, Jerome Bruner borrows from constructivism to claim that, through the use of language, we recreate the (constructed) world that was "given" to us (see Bruner, *Actual Minds, Possible Worlds*; Cambridge, Mass.: Harvard University Press, 1986, especially chapters 3 and 7). This suggests, however, that the term 'cognitive psychology' covers so great a variety of opinions that it is worthless as a term of classification.

17. Under consideration here are ordinary cases of forgetting, not cases that can be explained by special psychologicl reasons. We may forget the name of an acquaintance because she resembles our dominating mother, but that explanation (and its psychoanalytic relatives) won't explain why we forgot our history lessons.

18. The importance of dispositions as educational aims has begun to appear in the literature on teaching. See, for example, Shari Tishman, David N. Perkins, and Eileen Jay, *The Thinking Classroom* (Boston: Allyn and Bacon, 1995), especially Chapter 4, "Thinking Dispositions." While the account of dispositions that is offered is sensible, there is no discussion of the relation of a person's dispositions to the purposes she might be pursuing, nor is there any intelligible account of what thinking might involve, or be *for* (despite the book's title). For example, a lesson on "thinking" is described that focuses on curiosity (pp. 56 and 57), but the curiosity is not followed up in a thoughtful way. What is encouraged, then, is *only* the asking of lots of questions—which may or may not be pleasant for the children, but which certainly pleases the teacher. The writers have not considered the fact that, if one's curiosity and one's questions don't generate any purposes, then there will be nothing to think *about*. These issues will receive extended treatment here in chapters 5 (on curiosity) and 6 (on thinking as problem-solving).

19. High IQs no longer command the respect that they did when IQ tests were thought to measure people's intelligence accurately. At the time of this writing it is widely believed that environmental factors have more to do with people's intelligent performances (including performances on paper-and-pencil tests) than hereditary factors. It follows that when people's environments are changed, the quality of their performances can be expected to change, too. See Leon J. Kamin, *The Science and Politics of IQ* (New York: Wiley, 1974), or Stephen Jay Gould, *The Mismeasure of Man* (New York: Norton, 1981).

There is an even more fundamental criticism of the concept of intelligence as expressed as an IQ score. This criticism conceives intelligence as a way of acting that calls for judgment rather than a possession that calls for measurement. It can be found in John Dewey, *Democracy and Education* (New York: Macmillan, 1916):

> . . . Mind is not a name for something complete by itself; it is a name for a course of action in so far as that is intelligently directed; in

> so far, that is to say, as aims, ends, enter into it, with selection of means to further the attainment of aims. Intelligence is not a peculiar possession which a person owns; but a person is intelligent in so far as the activities in which he plays a part have the qualities mentioned. Nor are the activities in which a person engages, whether intelligently or not, exclusive properties of himself; they are something in which he *engages or partakes*. (155)

This conception of mind and intelligence is developed more fully in Dewey, *Experience and Nature*, 2nd ed. (New York: W. W. Norton, 1929), especially in chapters 5-8. A similar action-based conception of mind and intelligence can be found in Gilbert Ryle, *The Concept of Mind* (New York: Barnes & Noble, 1949).

Despite the conceptual clarification that is available, writers continue to treat intelligence as a number, claiming that some groups have "more of it"; see R. J. Herrnstein and C. Murray, *The Bell Curve* (New York: Free Press, 1994). S. J. Gould effectively exposes the book's conceptual muddles, statistical chicanery, and social Darwinism in "Curveball," *The New Yorker*, November, 1994.

20. For all the apparent change it has undergone, the curriculum of the American high school has remained remarkably stable. See Edward A. Krug, *The Shaping of the American High School, Vol. I, 1880-1920*, and *Vol. II, 1920-1941* (Madison: University of Wisconsin Press, 1969 and 1972).

21. I'm indebted to Professor Henry Alexander of the University of Judaism for this trenchant observation.

22. Israel Scheffler is an influential philosopher of education who has devoted much of his career to arguing that rationality should be the dominant focus of schooling. See Scheffler, *Conditions of Knowledge* (Chicago: Scott, Foresman, 1965), and *Reason and Teaching* (Indianapolis: Bobbs-Merrill, 1973).

23. Sensitivity to others, and caring for them, are sometimes thought to be the idiosyncratic concerns of certain psychologists and therapists. To the contrary, these are dispositions the absence of which would leave society harsh and intolerable. For a detailed discussion and argument of this point in an educational context, see Nel Noddings, *Caring: A Feminine Approach to Ethics and Moral Education* (Berkeley: University of California Press, 1984).

24. The disposition to be thoughtful and the disposition to care for others are not alternative—let alone conflicting—educational aims. Barbara Arnstine effectively argues that thoughtfulness and caring are aims that support one another; see "Rational and Caring Teachers: Reconstructing Teacher Preparation," *Teachers College Record*, 92:2 (Winter, 1990), 230-247.

25. Classic examples of the humiliation to which students can be subjected during recitation in class are reported by Jules Henry, "Attitude Organization in the Elementary Classroom," *American Journal of Orthopsychiatry* 27 (1957), 117-133.

26. There are other ways of characterizing what are being called here dispositions. When John Dewey discussed "traits of individual method," he was talking about much the same thing; see Dewey, *Democracy and Education* (New York: Macmillan, 1916), 203 ff. More broadly speaking, Dewey's entire discussion of intelligence, thinking, and problem-solving was an elaboration of a set of interrelated dispositions; see *Democracy and Education*, 146-192.

Chapter 4

1. Abraham Maslow employed the concept of "peak experience" in a way very similar to what is here called "aesthetic quality." But his peak experience was reserved for very special occasions, and it was denied to persons who had certain deficiencies of character. Maslow also failed to make clear how conditions could be established to foster peak experiences. See Maslow, *Motivation and Personality* (New York: Harper, 1954).

A clearer and more useful discussion of experience closely related to what is here called "aesthetic" can be found in the concept of "flow," discussed by Mihaly Csikszentmihalyi in *Beyond Boredom and Anxiety* (San Francisco: Jossey-Bass, 1975), and in *Flow: The Psychology of Optimal Experience* (New York: Harper & Row, 1990).

2. A recent effort to broaden our traditional conceptions of mind and thinking can be found in Howard Gardner, *Frames of Mind: The Theory of Multiple Intelligences* (New York: Basic Books, 1983). Even this comes only part of the distance needed to reach the breadth implicit in Gilbert Ryles's formulation of mind and thinking in *The Concept of Mind* (New York: Barnes and Noble, 1949).

3. John Dewey referred to these kinds of thinking as "qualitative thought." See "Qualitative Thought," in Dewey (ed.), *Philosophy and Civilization* (New York: Capricorn, 1931).

4. John Dewey put this point as succinctly as it could be put: "When the parent or teacher has provided the conditions which stimulate thinking and has taken a sympathetic attitude toward the activities of the learner by entering into a common or conjoint experience, all has been done which a second party can do to instigate learning. The rest lies with the one directly concerned." See Dewey, *Democracy and Education* (New York: Macmillan, 1916), 188.

5. The role of discrepancies in attracting and holding attention has been discussed by psychologists under the heading of "affective arousal." Some landmark works in this field which support the present discussion about the role of discrepancies are: David C. McClelland et al., *The Achievement Motive* (New York: Appleton-Century-Crofts, 1953), especially 43, 60-62; D. O. Hebb, "Drives and the C.N.S.," *Psychological Review,* LXII (1955), 243-254; and Leon Festinger, *A Theory of Cognitive Dissonance* (Evanston, Ill.: Row, Peterson, 1957).

6. There are many different levels at which games are played, and the character of the thinking changes markedly as the experience and sophistication of the player increases. A useful discussion of these distinctions can be found in Hubert L. Dreyfus and Stuart E. Dreyfus, *Mind over Machine* (New York: The Free Press, 1986), Chapter 1.

7. The relevance of discrepancy theories of affective arousal to the experience of art is discussed in D. E. Berlyne, *Conflict, Arousal, and Curiosity* (New York: McGraw-Hill, 1960), and its incorporation into a theory of music appears in Leonard B. Meyer, *Emotion and Meaning in Music* (Chicago: Univesity of Chicago Press, 1956). The relation of affective arousal, experience in the arts, and the phenomenon of learning is discussed in Donald Arnstine, *Philosophy of Education: Learning and Schooling* (New York: Harper & Row, 1967), Chapters VI and VII. All these ideas were anticipated much earlier by John Dewey when he wrote about the literally dramatic nature of consciousness in *Experience and Nature* (LaSalle, Ill.: Open Court, 1929), 249, 250.

8. It is the writer's view that the appeal of works of art is fundamentally based on the way in which their designed patterns are perceived by viewers with particular backgrounds. But other theories of art and aesthetics reject a view that makes the impact of art relative to its interaction with particular viewers. In the hope of finding some permanent, if not eternal value in works of art, they claim that "the reason we contemplate works of art or aesthetic objects (such as sunsets) is simply that we derive pleasure from their inherent properties."

In contrast to this, the view offered here holds that all properties can be understood as *relations* (e.g., weight is not a "property" of the lead, but a relation between the lead and the earth; the color blue is not a property of the sky, but a relation between sunlight, our atmosphere, and our eyes). Therefore, there *are* no "inherent properties." It follows, then, that beauty is not "in" the sculpture (much less in the eye of the beholder); it is, rather, a function of the relations between the sculpture and beholders who are cognizant of certain traditions.

This philosophical dispute can be pursued in aesthetic theory, although it is at base an epistemological and metaphysical issue. Useful summaries of varying views on the issue can be found in Marcia Muelder Eaton, *Basic Issue in Aesthetics* (Belmont, CA: Wadsworth, 1988), especially chapters 3 and 7.

9. Susanne Langer's most extended discussion of nondiscursive thinking can be found in *Philosophy in a New Key* (Cambridge, MA: Harvard University Press, 1942). Also see John Dewey, "Qualitative Thought," op. cit. Nathaniel Champlin and Francis Villemain elaborated the idea of qualitative thinking with reference to education in "Frontiers for an Experimentalist Philosophy of Education," *Antioch Review*, XIX (1959), 345-359. More recently, Elliot W. Eisner wrote that "any conception of intelligence that omits the ordering of qualities through direct experience is neglecting a central feature of intellectual functioning." See Eisner, "The role of the arts in cognition and curriculum," *Phi Delta Kappan*, 63:1 (1981), 52.

10. See Jules Henry, "Attitude Organization in the Elementary Classroom," *American Journal of Orthopsychiatry*, 27 (1957), 117-133.

11. The way in which the appreciation of art can enhance one's appreciation of nature was called the "subjectification of nature" by Susanne K. Langer. She wrote of "the education of vision that we receive in seeing, hearing, reading works of art—the development of the artist's eye, that assimilates ordinary sights (or sounds, motions, or events) to inward vision, and lends expressiveness and emotional import to the world." See Langer, *Problems of Art* (New York: Charles Scribner's Sons, 1957), 72, 73.

12. John Dewey, *Art as Experience* (New York: Minton, Balch, 1934), 346.

13. An insight into the relation between aesthetic and commercial values can be found in Joan Kron's satirical essay, "The serious collector's guide to 'doing' SoHo," *Avenue* (February, 1989), 111-113.

14. The therapeutic values of art and art education were stated in their classic form by Victor Lowenfeld; see Lowenfeld and W. L. Brittain, *Creative and Mental Growth*, 7th ed. (New York: Macmillan, 1982). The role of the arts in the cultivation of taste has systematically been discussed in Harry S. Broudy, *Enlightened Cherishing: An Essay on Aesthetic Education* (Urbana, IL: University of Illinois Press, 1972), and in Broudy, *The Uses of Schooling* (New York: Routledge, 1988), Chapter 5.

The contribution of art education to the development of creativity and perceptual acuity is discussed in June King McFee, *Preparation for Art* (San Francisco: Wadsworth, 1961). The role of the arts in the education of the emotions has been developed by Susanne K. Langer in *Problems of Art* (New York: Charles Scribner's Sons, 1957). The indispensable contribution of the arts to the development of a healthy emotional and psychic life was argued by Herbert Read in *Education Through Art* (London: Faber and Faber, 1943).

A recent, broad-gauged approach to education in the arts is described by Gilbert A. Clark, et al., in "Discipline-based art education: becoming students of art," *Journal of Aesthetic Education*, 21:2 (Summer, 1987), 129-193. While it considers the arts in all of their dimensions, this approach fails to consider the relations between the arts and other aesthetic dimensions of experience, and it largely ignores political, social, and economic ties to the arts. This criticism is elaborated in Donald Arnstine, "Art, Aesthetics, and the Pitfalls of Discipline-based Art Education," *Educational Theory*, 40:4 (Fall, 1990), 415-422. Elliot W. Eisner responds to the criticism in "Discipline-based Art Education: Conceptions and Misconceptions," *Educational Theory*, 40:4 (Fall, 1990), 423-430.

15. The rich literature in art education would include but not be limited to the following: H. S. Broudy, *Enlightened Cherishing: An Essay on Aesthetic Education* (op. cit.); Laura Chapman, *Approaches to Art Education* (New York: Harcourt, Brace, Jovanovich, 1978); Elliot W. Eisner, *Educating Artistic Vision* (New York: Macmillan, 1972); Edward B. Feldman, *Becoming Human Through Art* (Englewood Cliffs, N.J.: Prentice-Hall, 1970); Howard Gardner and David Perkins (eds.), *Art, Mind, and Education: Research from Project Zero* (Urbana, Ill.: University of Illinois Press, 1988); J. E. Grigsby, *Art and Ethnics: Background for Teaching Youth in a Pluralistic Society* (Dubuque, Iowa: William C. Brown, 1977); J. Paul Getty Trust, *Beyond Creating: The Place of Art in America's Schools* (Los Angeles: The Getty Center for Education in the Arts, 1985); Vincent Lanier, *The Visual Arts and the Elementary Child* (New York: Teachers College Press, 1983); Viktor Lowenfeld and W. L. Brittain, *Creative and Mental Growth* (op. cit.); June K. McFee and R. M. Degge, *Art, Culture, and Environment: A Catalyst for Teaching* (Belmont, Calif.: Wadsworth, 1977); and Ralph A. Smith (ed.), *Aesthetic Concepts and Education* (Urbana, Ill.: University of Illinois Press, 1970).

16. This idea is not a new one. It was put very clearly at midcentury by Thomas Munro in *Art Education: Its Philosophy and Psychology* (New York: Liberal Arts Press, 1956):

> Art is broad enough and powerful enough, if set free, to illuminate every branch of human thought and experience. In a school where the artistic point of view is ably championed, integration might well result in bringing out the aesthetic aspects and artistic possibilities of every other activity, including the physical and social sciences, history, literature, athletics, dances, and personal relations. In such an integrated school, art would be the dominating subject. (284)

17. Herbert Read, (op. cit.), 216, 217.

18. Dewey's discussion of the natural impulses and instincts of the young can be found in "The school and the life of the child," in *School and Society* (Chicago: University of Chicago Press, 1899).

19. Read is explicit about the importance of the aesthetic to education. Dewey's sympathies are usually implicit, although he occasionally confronts the educational value of the aesthetic directly. See, for example, Dewey, *Democracy and Education* (op. cit.), 242, 279.

20. Seymour Sarason argues persuasively that artistic activity is both natural and psychologically important for all people (and not just a minority of "talented" people) in *The Challenge of Art to Psychology* (New Haven: Yale University Press, 1990). He finds empirical support for this view in the teaching of poetry as described by Kenneth Koch in *Wishes, Lies, and Dreams* (New York: Chelsea House, 1970), and in the teaching of the graphic arts as described by Henry W. Schaefer-Simmern in *The Unfolding of Artistic Activity* (Berkeley: University of California Press, 1970).

21. Anita Silvers discusses the educational value of the inherent ambiguity of the arts in "Show and Tell: The Arts, Cognition, and Basic Modes of Referring," in Stanley S. Madeja (ed.), *The Arts, Cognition, and Basic Skills* (St. Louis: CEMREL, Inc., 1978), 31-50.

22. Dewey, *Art as Experience* (op. cit.), 334.

23. Vincent Lanier, "The teaching of art as social revolution," *Phi Delta Kappan*, 50:6 (February, 1969), 315. Thomas Munro admitted that the popular arts did treat things of interest to the young. Despite his low regard for popular art, Munro wrote, somewhat reluctantly, "One must consider the possibility of some slight concession to adolescent interest . . ." See Munro, "The Interrelation of the Arts in Secondary Education," in Munro and Herbert Read, *The Creative Arts in American Education* (Cambridge, Mass.: Harvard University Press, 1960), 30.

Chapter 5

1. I am claiming that in cases of natural beauty, like a sunset, it is a discrepancy that attracts our attention. Yet it may be objected that it's not a discrepancy, but rather the beauty of color and form that attracts attention. In fact, both amount to pretty much the same thing. Not all sunsets are the same, but most of the time the sun becomes more orange as it begins to set, and the sky gradually darkens. Most people take little notice of this rather standard sort of sunset. But colorful sunsets attract attention because they are not what we expect; they're a little out of the ordinary. That is, they offer a discrepancy from our expectation. There's very little for us to resolve in this discrepancy; the sun eventually disappears, as it always does, and it gradually gets dark. Thus the experience of the sunset is perhaps more sensuous than it is aesthetic in character; it pleases our eye the way a warm bath pleases our body.

2. The independence of curiosity from strong goals or drives is established on empirical grounds in Harry F. Harlow, "Mice, Monkeys, Men and Motives," *Psychological Review*, 60 (1953).

3. For discussion of the role of the nervous system in behavior that is not goal-driven, see D. O. Hebb, *The Organization of Behavior* (New York:

Wiley, 1949), and K. H. Pribram, "A Review of Theory in Physiological Psychology," in P. R. Farnsworth and Q. McNemar (eds.), *Annual Review of Psychology*, 11 (Palo Alto, Calif.: Annual Reviews, Inc., 1960). For the peculiar physiology of boredom, see Woodburn Heron, "The pathology of boredom," *Scientific American*, 196 (1957), and D. E. Berlyne, *Conflict, Arousal, and Curiosity* (New York: McGraw-Hill, 1960).

4. The classic discussion of exploratory behavior is found in Robert W. White, "Motivation reconsidered," *Psychological Review*, 65 (1959).

5. For discussions of empirical research touching on discrepancies from expectation, people's adaptation levels, and curiosity, see Berlyne, op. cit., and D. C. McClelland, *The Achievement Motive* (New York: Appleton-Century-Crofts, 1953), and Harry Helson, *Adaptation Level Theory* (New York: Harper & Row, 1964).

6. Marie Curie, *Pierre Curie* (trans. Charlotte and Vernon Kellogg; New York: Macmillan, 1923), 97, 98.

7. Why are culturally respectable places like museums and fire stations considered the only legitimate sites for classroom field trips? Why not a flea market? For those studying history, what better resource is there for collecting artifacts that reveal our past? The discarded treasures of flea markets are relevant to virtually everything that is studied in school.

8. The classic works on the relation of the Protestant work ethic to the development of capitalism are R. H. Tawney, *Religion and the Rise of Capitalism* (London: Murray, 1947), and Max Weber, *The Protestant Ethic and the Spirit of Capitalism* (trans. Talcott Parsons; London: Allen and Unwin, 1930).

9. By the turn of the century and thereafter, according to Button and Provenzo, "the development of an increasingly sophisticated technological culture . . . had the effect of making the services of the youth population more nearly superfluous . . . [and] protective legislation in the field of child labor, while preventing children from being abused, also made it increasingly difficult for youths to enter the job market . . ." At the same time, "there was a corresponding increase in compulsory schooling." See H. Warren Button and Eugene F. Provenzo, Jr., *History of Education and Culture in America* (Englewood Cliffs, N.J.: Prentice-Hall, 1983), 210-211.

10. The increasing specificity of school curriculums and school goals, from the turn of the century forward, can be traced in Herbert M. Kliebard, *The Struggle for the American Curriculum, 1893-1958* (Boston: Routledge and Kegan Paul, 1986).

11. Parallels between the organization of schools and the organization of industrial institutions first came to my attention in an unpublished paper by Joseph C. Grannis, "The School as Model of Society." These par-

allels have since been convincingly drawn, with different sorts of emphases, by various writers, for example, Raymond E. Callahan, *Education and the Cult of Efficiency: A Study of the Social Forces That Have Shaped the Administration of the Public Schools* (Chicago: University of Chicago Press, 1962); Donald Arnstine, "Freedom and Bureaucracy in the Schools," in Vernon F. Haubrich (ed.), *Freedom, Bureaucracy, and Schooling* (Washington, D.C.: ASCD, 1971); Herbert Kliebard, "Bureaucracy and Curriculum Theory," in Haubrich (op. cit.); and Michael B. Katz, *Class, Bureaucracy, and Schools* (expanded ed.; New York: Praeger, 1975).

12. There is another side to this Great Paradox, in which the genius of technological productivity was to have increased the leisure of those who work. The development of machine industry, of the assembly line, of automation, and of computerization have all been heralded as promoters of efficiency and as labor-saving devices. Yet it is not clear that people have achieved more leisure since the invention and utilization of these devices. Many more women work outside the home (yet still do most of the housework), and many men need to work two jobs. Those who worked less in the last decade of the twentieth century were simply laid off.

For purposes of comparison we might note the work week of modern Bushmen living on the edge of the Kalihari Desert. According to the research of Richard Lee, "less than three hours per day per adult is all that is needed for the Bushmen to obtain a diet rich in proteins and other essential nutrients." See Marvin Harris, *Cannibals and Kings* (New York: Vintage, 1977), 13. Harris goes on to say that "Lee found that in one day a woman could gather enough food to feed her family for three days and that she spent the rest of her time resting, entertaining visitors, doing embroidery, or visiting other camps" (p. 14). The duration of this labor is similar to the time needed for hunting by our stone age ancestors from the upper-paleolithic period (30,000-10,000 B.C.). Without putting too fine a point on it, we might say there's very little evidence that industrial civilization has brought greater leisure to humankind. I'm grateful to Professor James McClellan for the reference to Harris's work.

13. The disastrously damaging effects on the environment of unlimited productivity and industrial growth are discussed in Barry Comnoner, *The Closing Circle* (New York: Bantam, 1972), and in Robert M. Heilbroner, *An Inquiry into the Human Prospect* (New York: Norton, 1975). The disastrous effects of unlimited productivity and growth on the human psyche are discussed in Paul L. Wachtel, *The Poverty of Affluence* (Philadelphia: New Society Publishers, 1989).

14. This and other examples of promoting inquiry among students are described in J. Richard Suchman, "Inquiry Training: Building Skills for Autonomous Discovery," *Merrill-Palmer Quarterly*, 7 (1961). It may seem unusual to cite research in teaching methods from a generation ago, but the date of research in education doesn't seem relevant to its significance for

current policy or practice. The latter is the worse for its dependence on contemporary ("up-to-date") inquiries and suggestions that ignore what was learned in the past.

15. Nel Noddings (a philosopher of education and a former math teacher) has, for a number of reasons "come to suspect that teaching everyone algebra and geometry is both wasteful and inconsiderate." See Noddings, "Excellence as a Guide to Educational Conversation," in H. A. Alexander (ed.), *Philosophy of Education 1992: Proceedings of the 48th Annual Meeting of the Philosophy of Education Society* (Urbana, Ill.: Philosophy of Education Society, 1993), 11, 12.

16. The problem of teaching history when school materials do not reveal the falsification and mythologizing of the past is discussed by Bill Bigelow in "Columbus in the Classroom," in Hans Koning, *Columbus: His Enterprise* (New York: Monthly Review Press, 1991).

Chapter 6

1. Of course, most students, even in math classes, do have a purpose: to pass the course. The teacher's assignment then becomes for them an obstacle to *that* purpose. But when the purpose is to pass the course rather than to learn math, an effective solution may not include the exercise of any mathematical understanding. (For example, one could do the assignment by copying the work of a friend.)

2. John Dewey, *Democracy and Education* (New York: Macmillan, 1916), 181.

3. Dewey, *How We Think* (Boston: D. C. Heath, 1933), 106.

4. Some recent research on learning has concluded that what one learns and knows is a function of what one is doing in a particular situation. The resulting "situated cognition" is discussed at length in John Seely Brown, Allen Collins, and Paul Duguid, "Situated Cognition and the Culture of Learning," *Educational Researcher*, 18:1 (1989), 32-42.

Claiming that activity is necessary for learning, Brown and his associates correctly note that "classroom activity very much takes place within the culture of schools, although it is attributed to [yet very *unlike*] the culture of readers, writers, mathematicians, historians . . . [etc.]" (p. 34). Therefore, what students do in classrooms is called "ersatz activity." The authors recommend that students instead be enabled to engage in "cognitive apprenticeship," wherein students will "acquire, develop, and use cognitive tools in authentic domain activity" (p. 39)—that is, in the kinds of activities undertaken by readers, writers, mathematicians, historians, and so on.

Aside from what appears to be a precipitous plunge into academic specialization that pays no heed to the purposes that students might have, Brown and his associates have focused on an important aspect of learning. Yet they are quite mistaken when they write about "the unheralded importance of activity and enculturation to learning" (p. 41). The importance of activity and enculturation to learning was made eminently clear in 1915 in John Dewey's *Democracy and Education* (op. cit.). Brown et al. might have achieved greater clarity in their own views, and made better pedagogical sense, if they had consulted the epistemological or educational writings of Dewey, William James, George Herbert Mead, or other theorists who wrote in the pragmatic tradition over the past century.

5. This example is described in Carl G. Hempel, *Philosophy of Natural Science* (Englewood Cliffs, N.J.: Prentice-Hall, 1966), 3-6. I'm grateful to Professor Harvey Siegel for suggesting the example.

6. To accept a hypothesis as true because its prediction is experimentally confirmed would be to commit the fallacy of affirming the consequent. For further discussion of this logical point, see Hempel, op. cit., 6ff.

7. Although people can be placed together in a group on the basis of some measured similarity, they are likely to differ markedly from one another on a great many other measures. This rather pedestrian fact has significant consequences for the efforts of schools to group their students homogeneously. Walter W. Cook made this clear two generations ago when he wrote: "The harm resulting from homogeneous grouping is inherent in the assumption that the group *is* homogeneous and that instructional materials and procedures can be adjusted to the needs of the group as a whole . . ." See Cook, *Grouping and Promotion in the Elementary Schools* (Minneapolis: University of Minnesota Press, 1941), 33.

A generation later, Cook and Theodore Clymer were unequivocal about the impossibility of achieving homogeneity by any means of grouping: "One of the invariable characteristics of measures of achievement is the wide range of ability found whenever any group of individuals is tested. This range exists for all types of measurement, whether personality, mental, or achievement characteristics are being studied. Individuals do vary, and all attempts by educational institutions from the kindergarten to the Ph.D. seminar have failed to produce groups of individuals who are alike." See Cook and Clymer, Chapter 11, in Nelson B. Henry (ed.), *Individualizing Instruction,* The Sixty-first Yearbook of the National Society for the Study of Education (Chicago: University of Chicago Press, 1962), 185.

8. Aristotle, "Nicomachean Ethics," trans. W. D. Ross, in *The Basic Works of Aristotle* (Richard McKeon, ed., New York: Random House, 1941), 952.

9. Bruno Bettelheim offered support for the view that we should be aiming to develop dispositions already present, rather than creating dispo-

sitions previously absent. He discussed desirable dispositions that are developed during play, when children pursue their own interests: "Play teaches the child, without his being aware of it, the habits most needed for intellectual growth, such as stick-to-it-iveness, which is so important in all learning. Perseverence is easily acquired around enjoyable activities such as play. But if it has not become a habit through what is enjoyable, it is not likely to become one through an endeavor like schoolwork. . . . A child at play begins to realize that he need not give up in despair if a block doesn't balance neatly on another block the first time around. Fascinated by the challenge of building a tower, he gradually learns that even if he doesn't succeed immediately, success can be his if he perseveres." See Bettelheim, "The Importance of Play," *The Atlantic Monthly*, March, 1987, 36.

10. There is an answer to this question: "To prepare them for life, since life is hard (i.e., difficult, monotonous, distasteful)." This gloomy response is less a description of the world than it is a paradigm case of the self-fulfilling prophecy. After having studied progressive education for a month, a group of Boston junior high school teachers chose to continue using the more traditional approach of lesson-assignment-test. When asked why, they told the writer that they did consider a progressive approach more educationally defensible. But the high school was taught in the traditional way; therefore, traditional forms of teaching would be the best preparation in the junior high. Thus pessimism posing as realism maintains the status quo with all of its faults.

11. While emphasizing the importance of children's purposes for learning, John Dewey also allowed that many young children don't *have* purposes, although they may have wishes and desires. In a remarkably insightful passage, he discusses the nature of these concepts and the conditions that are needed to transform desires into purposes. See Dewey, *Experience and Education* (New York: Collier, 1963), 67-72.

12. Exploitation is most simply defined as "a situation in which the individual is induced, by his relative lack of economic power, to work for less return than the economy generally pays for such effort"; see John Kenneth Galbraith, *Economics and the Public Purpose* (Boston: Houghton Mifflin, 1973), 73. The William T. Grant Foundation Commission on Work, Family, and Citizenship reported the following: in 1985, only 43.7 percent of twenty- to twenty-four-year-old males earned enough to support a family of three above the poverty line. Fewer than 25 percent of African-American males in this age group could support a family. See *Education Letter*, IV:4 (1988), 6. That this exploitation is not accidental, but a requirement of the system itself, is clearly explained by Galbraith, ibid., especially in Chapter 8.

Understanding the economic system is indispensable if the young are to acquire any understanding of the circumstances of their own lives. Support for the present discussion, as well as a resource for secondary school teachers, can be found in Richard C. Edwards, Michael Reich, and Thomas E. Weisskopf (eds.), *The Capitalist System* (Englewood Cliffs, N.J.: Prentice-Hall, 1972).

13. One of the classic studies of differences in language which, by transmission to the young, perpetuate differences in the cultures of social and economic classes, can be found in Basil Bernstein, *Class, Codes and Control* (New York: Schocken, 1975). A more pointed focus on language differences among racial and ethnic subcultures can be found in Charles A. Ferguson and Shirley Brice Heath (eds.), *Language in the USA* (Cambridge, Mass.: Cambridge University Press, 1981).

14. Plenty of research supports this, but the point is obvious to anyone who finished high school and gave it a moment's thought. Readers might begin by considering themselves and their friends, most of whom "took" a foreign language for a couple of years. How many of them could *ever* carry on a conversation in that language?

15. The more general reasons why segregation in schools diminishes the value of education for all are discussed in Chapter 10.

16. If I have understood her correctly, Lisa D. Delpit makes a similar point about the learning of white, middle-class English—not because it's either the "correct" or the "better" form of speech, but because only through its selective use can members of language minorities attain economic success. She writes, "I suggest that students must be *taught* the codes needed to participate fully in the mainstream of American life, not by being forced to attend to hollow, inane, decontextualized subskills, but rather within the context of meaningful communicative endeavors; that . . . they must also be helped to learn about the arbitrariness of those codes and about the power relationships they represent." She puts the matter more simply when citing a Native Alaskan teacher speaking to her students: "'We're going to learn two ways to say things. Isn't that better? One way will be our Heritage way. The other will be Formal English. Then, when we go to get jobs, we'll be able to talk like those people who only know and can only really listen to one way.'" See Delpit, "The Silenced Dialogue: Power and Pedagogy in Educating Other People's Children," *Harvard Educational Review* (58:3), August, 1988, pp. 296, 293. I'm grateful to Professor Carl Spring for calling my attention to this essay.

17. Catherine Camp Mayhew and Anna Camp Edwards, *The Dewey School: The Laboratory School of the University of Chicago 1896-1903* (New York: D. Appleton-Century, 1936), 228-229.

18. The relation between wishes and desires, and plans and purposes, is elaborated by Dewey in *Experience and Education*, op. cit., Chapter 6.

19. Mayhew and Edwards, ibid., 229.

20. Ibid., 232, 233.

Chapter 7

1. College professors may do this more often than other people, since their profession demands it. But when some of them generalize about the nature of thinking on the basis of their own experience, we can see why college professors are easily misled.

2. The evidence for the counterproductive consequences of homogeneous grouping is vast. One might consult Walter E. Schafer and Carol Olexa, *Tracking and Opportunity* (Scranton, Pa.: Chandler, 1971); James E. Rosenbaum, *Making Inequality: The Hidden Curriculum of High School Tracking* (New York: Wiley, 1976); Charles Baily and David Bridges, *Mixed Ability Grouping: A Philosophical Perspective* (London: George Allen & Unwin, 1983); and Jeannie Oakes, *Keeping Track: How Schools Structure Inequality* (New Haven: Yale University Press, 1985). Recent summaries of research on homogeneous grouping can be found in R. E. Slavin, "Ability Grouping and Student Achievement in Elementary Schools: A Best-Evidence Synthesis," *Review of Educational Research* (1987), 293-336; and in Slavin, "Achievement effects of ability grouping in secondary scools: a best-evidence synthesis," *Review of Educational Research* (1990), 471-500.

As is often the case in much educational research, earlier studies that reached essentially the same conclusions have largely been forgotten. A classic study showing the failure of ability grouping to increase achievement is reported in Miriam L. Goldberg and A. Harry Passow, "The Effects of Ability Grouping," *Education*, 82:8 (April, 1962), 482-487.

3. Empirical evidence supports the third part of this complex statement. One of the earliest but most convincing sources of this evidence can be found in Gordon Allport, *The Nature of Prejudice* (Cambridge, Mass.: Addison-Wesley, 1954).

4. It's reasonable to ask, How *can* a loquacious person learn from a person who is shy and quiet? The nature of their dissimilar personalities will reduce the likelihood of such learning, and it might not occur at all if such people are left to their own devices as members of a group. Problems associated with specific character traits like these can sometimes be confronted in smaller (e.g., dyadic) groups, or with individual help from teachers or specialists. I'm grateful to Professor Gerald M. Phillips for calling my attention to these sorts of problems, which are beyond the scope of the present discussion and beyond the competence of the writer. Those wishing to investigate further may consult Phillips, *Communication Incompetencies* (Carbondale, Ill.: Southern Illinois University Press, 1991), and Phillips, *Teaching How to Work in Groups* (Norwood, N.J.: Ablex, 1991).

5. See, for example, Steven M. Cahn, *The Eclipse of Excellence: A Critique of American Higher Education* (Washington, D.C.: Public Affairs Press, 1973), who writes, "Majority rule is a sound decision procedure only

when no one can reasonably claim special competence in the matter being decided. . . . If the faculty had no such competence, what would qualify them to be teachers? And if the students had nothing to learn, why would they be students? Furthermore, what sense would there be in certifying a student's competence if the student himself chose the criteria of competence? The academic expertise of the faculty provides the *raison d'etre* for a college, and so at Utopia U. [Cahn's model university] all decisions of educational policy are made in accord with the expert judgment of faculty" (39).

When Cahn speaks of a faculty's "academic expertise," he does not distinguish among (1) what a teacher knows about the subject she teaches from (2) what she knows about teaching and learning, (3) what she knows about the particular students in her charge, and (4) what she knows about the value—if any—of her subject to the development of her society or the course of human civilization. Since college faculty are *not* distinguished for their expertise in the latter three areas, Cahn's claim about their academic expertise is misleading if not false.

6. See Jerry Farber, "The Student and Society," in *The Student as Nigger* (New York: Contact Books, 1969), pp. 14-55.

7. The American posture toward gun control is a prime example of the growth of legalism, litigation, and police force in lieu of public participation in governance. At the time of this writing, nearly anyone in the United States could buy a handgun—even a rapid fire automatic weapon—with little or no delay. Tens of thousands of Americans have been killed each year by these handguns—sometimes deliberately, sometimes when children pulled the triggers of guns they thought weren't loaded, sometimes in the course of the commission of other crimes, sometimes inadvertently by people under the influence of alcohol or other drugs, and sometimes in "drive-by" shootings, when guns are fired from moving vehicles at pedestrians or homes.

One looks in vain for laws that might terminate this deadly violence. Instead, police forces have expanded and have been more heavily armed. But to little avail: in the year 1980, 11,522 people were killed in the United States with handguns. For purposes of comparison, in the same year four people were killed with handguns in Australia, eight were killed in Great Britain, eight in Canada, eighteen in Sweden, twenty-four in Switzerland, and in Japan, 77 people were killed by all types of guns (data reported by Handgun Control, Inc., 810 18th Street, Washington, D.C.). These astonishing figures indicate an enduring trend. In 1988, 1,849 people were murdered in New York City alone (reported in the Manchester *Guardian*, January 1, 1989).

The flavor of armed violence in America is conveyed by an incident that occurred in Sacramento, California, in 1991. Gunwielding thieves tried to hold up a man delivering a pizza to an apartment house. But the delivery man was armed himself, and he fired back at the thieves, who then fled. Later, the city council discussed whether or not to prohibit people who deliver pizzas from carrying guns, on the grounds that innocent people might be shot.

What is so bizarre about the persistence of this carnage is the fact that in surveys made of public opinion (Harris Surveys, Gallup Polls, and polls taken by various newspapers and press associations), from two-thirds to 90 percent of Americans favor some form of delay or control of the purchase of handguns. Yet the elected representatives of the people, in state and federal legislatures, have rejected, year in and year out, every effort to substantially control the sale of guns. Fearful of well-armed criminals on one side and well-armed police on the other, many citizens have chosen to arm themselves. The moral of this story is hardly a secret. When the government in a democracy fails to respond to the will of the people, the result may be lawlessness or a police state. The campaigns of congesssional and even presidential candidates in both U.S. political parties make no issue of this massive life-threatening state of affairs.

8. The redistribution of America's resources from civilian to military purposes, independent of democratic procedures, was recently discussed by Seymour Melman. He describes the U.S. economic system as military state capitalism, wherein military activity—building and operating armed forces and their industrial base—is the primary activity of government. What this has *cost* the American people is summarized by Melman:

> The United States has been operating under military state capitalism almost since the beginning of the long cold war. Consider that from 1949 to 1989, the total budget of the Defense Department (in 1982 dollars) was $8.2 trillion. That was greater than the monetary value of civilian industry's plant and equipment *and* of the nation's infrastructure in 1982, a total of $7.3 trillion. In other words, the government has invested more capital in its military account than would be required to replace most of the human-made machines and structures in the country.
>
> In every year from 1951 to 1990, the Defense Department budget has exceeded the combined net profits of all American corporations. The Pentagon uses 75 percent of the federal government's research and development funds, has more employees than the rest of the government put together and has machinery assets that dwarf those of many corporations. . . .
>
> When the nation's largest capital fund is used for products [i.e., military hardware] that lack use-value for consumption or further production, then decay of infrastructure and industry is to be expected. This has happened in the United States, and can be seen in the catastrophic breakdown of production in the [former] Soviet Union. In the United States the burden of this plundering—a virtual war against our

> own people—falls most heavily on working people, minorities, children and all who have been made into a castoff population of homeless, hungry and untended sick.

See Seymour Melman, "The Juggernaut: Military State Capitalism," *The Nation*, 252:19 (May 20, 1991), 666, 667.

9. For a fuller description of the Sudbury Valley School and a report of a follow-up study of its graduates, see Peter Gray and David Chanoff, "Democratic Schooling: What Happens to Young People Who Have Charge of Their Own Education?" *American Journal of Education*, 94:2 (February, 1986), 182-213. Further discussion of SVS can be found in Daniel Greenberg, *Outline of a New Philosophy* (1974), and *The Sudbury Valley School Experience* (1985), both published by the Sudbury Valley School Press in Framingham, Massachusetts. Greenberg is described by Gray and Chanoff as "the principal philosopher among the group of parents and others who founded SVS."

10. See A. S. Neill, *Summerhill* (New York: Hart, 1960).

11. Ibid., 195.

12. See Wilford M. Aiken, *The Story of the Eight-Year Study* (New York: Harper & Row, 1942).

13. Gray and Chanoff, op. cit., 195.

14. Ibid., 210, 211.

15. Ibid., 211.

16. George Dennison, *The Lives of Children: The Strory of the First Street School* (New York: Vintage, 1969).

17. Ibid., 250.

18. Nel Noddings has written extensively and with great insight about caring relationships and their place in schooling. See her *Caring: A Feminine Approach to Ethics and Moral Education* (Berkeley: University of California Press, 1984), and *The Challenge to Care in Schools: An Alternative Approach to Education* (New York: Teachers College Press, 1992).

19. But a competitive test will, ironically, measure the extent to which a student is or is not disposed to be competitive. The irony lies in the fact that the student's score is usually misunderstood as indicating the level of the student's understanding or, what is even more egregious, the degree of her mental ability.

20. Vincent R. Rogers, "English and American Primary Schools," *Phi Delta Kappan*, 51:2 (October, 1969), 74.

21. Dennison, op. cit., 16, 17.

22. Ibid., 18, 19.

23. Ibid., 22, 23, 24.

24. Ibid., 132, 33, 34, 35, 36, 37.

25. Ibid., 267, 269.

26. Deborah Meier, "Good Schools Are Still Possible," *Dissent* (Fall 1987), 545.

27. Without actually visiting this school, we can now observe the character of the personal interactions between and among its teachers, administrators, students, and parents. One of America's finest documentary filmmakers, Frederick Wiseman, has made a videotape of what goes on in the classrooms, the offices, and the halls of the Central Park East Secondary School. The video lasts three and a half hours and has no titles or voiceovers. Viewers can watch and listen and make their own judgments about the operation of democracy in the school, and about the quality of students' experience. The video was released in 1994 by Zipporah Films.

28. Deborah Meier, "Choice Can *Save* Public Education," *The Nation,* March 4, 1991, 268.

29. Ibid., 266.

30. Ibid., 268.

Chapter 8

1. See John E. Chubb and Terry M. Moe, *Politics, Markets, and America's Schools* (Washington, D.C.: The Brookings Institution, 1990). It is not surprising that the authors favor taxing the public to finance private schools, since they declare a profound mistrust of democracy (which they mistakenly or disingenuously confound with bureaucracy). The authors claim that public bureaucracies produce poor education, and that privatization of schools will remedy the situation because bureaucracies in the private sector are more efficient. One can only wonder what they had in mind. The steel industry? The automobile industry? The banking and savings and loan industries? One shudders to think of what would happen to the education of the young if it were managed the way these notoriously inefficient giants of the private sector go about their business.

2. See Madeline Hunter, "Knowing, Teaching, and Supervising," in Philip L. Hosford (Ed.), *Using What We Know about Teaching* (Alexandria, Va.: Association for Supervision and Curriculum Development, 1984, 169-192.

3. It will be protested that not all schools answer to this dismal description, and there *are* exceptions, some of which were noted in the previous chapter. But this description does apply to *most* schools (especially at the secondary level), and the simplest corroboration of this is to consult your own experience and that of your friends. But if you are convinced that this description is inaccurate and unfair, or if you have come from another planet, you might consult some extended and scholarly accounts of conditions in schools, based on controlled observation. See, for example, Jules Henry, "In Suburban Classrooms," in Beatrice and Ronald Gross (eds.), *Radical School Reform* (New York: Simon and Schuster, 1969); John I. Goodlad, *A Place Called School: Prospects for the Future* (New York: McGraw-Hill, 1984); Philip A. Cusick, *The Egalitarian Ideal and the American High School: Studies of Three Schools* (New York: Longman, 1983); or Edwin Farrell, *Hanging In and Dropping Out: Voices of At-Risk High School Students* (New York: Teachers College Press, 1990). An examination of Jonathon Kozol's *Savage Inequalities: Children in America's Schools* (New York: Crown, 1991) might suggest that I've painted too rosy a picture of schooling.

4. Glen Smith, "Schools and the American Dilemma Over Social Class," in Glen Smith and Charles R. Kniker (eds.), *Myth and Reality: A Reader in Educational Foundations* (Boston: Allyn and Bacon, 1972), 204-213.

5. The negative effects of statewide testing on local school systems have been thoroughly documented in H. Dickson Corbett and Bruce L. Wilson, *Testing, Reform and Rebellion* (Norwood, N.J.: Ablex, 1991).

6. Conservative politicians (regardless of political party) are fond of attributing the disintegration of family life to a failure to honor something called "family values." As a previous administration urged Americans to "just say no" as a means of solving America's drug problems, conservatives now claim that honoring "family values" (whatever that might mean) will repair our disintegrating families. This rhetoric relieves them from examining the real economic conditions that place severe strains on American families.

7. Martin Carnoy, *Education as Cultural Imperialism* (New York: David McKay, 1974), 9.

8. Summarizing the extensive observations made by teams of researchers in thirteen high schools, Barbara Benham Tye concludes: "Evidently our society values obedience and passivity very highly . . . For regardless of what we *say* about the importance of originality, independence, and responsible self-direction, we do not provide our young people with a schooling environment which allows them to develop such behaviors." See Tye, *Multiple Realities: A Study of Thirteen American High Schools* (New York: University Press of America, 1985), 335.

9. Probably the clearest early formulation of schooling as the reproduction of the social order can be found in Samuel Bowles and Herbert Gintis, *Schooling in Capitalist America* (New York: Basic Books, 1976. Other formulations can be found in Paolo Friere, *Pedagogy of the Oppressed* (trans. M. B. Rames. New York: Seabury, 1970); Pierre Bourdieu and Jean Claude Passeron, *Reproduction in Education, Society, and Culture* (Beverly Hills, Calif.: Sage, 1977); and Henry A. Giroux, *Theory and Resistance in Education* (South Hadley, Mass.: Bergin and Garvey, 1983).

10. One of the earliest identifications of the hidden curriculum can be found in Ivan Illich, *Deschooling Society* (New York: Harper & Row, 1970).

11. See Elizabeth Vallance, "Hiding the Hidden Curriculum," *Curriculum Theory Network*, 4:1 (1973-74), 5-21.

12. That the school system is governed by bureaucracies is no longer a debatable issue; an early exposition of this point can be found in Donald Arnstine, "Freedom and Bureaucracy in the Schools," in Vernon F. Haubrich (ed.), *Freedom, Bureaucracy, and Schooling* (Washington, D.C.: Association for Supervision and Curriculum Development, 1971), 3-28. The need for bureaucracies to have relatively simple and clear-cut goals is made clear in Peter M. Blau, *Bureaucracy in Modern Society* (New York: Random House, 1956), 22-23.

13. Donald Arnstine, "The Use of Coercion in Changing the Schools," *Educational Theory*, 23:4 (Fall, 1973), 282. The extension of schooling downward, the extension of the compulsory attendance age upward, and the expansion of college education have resulted in what Ivan Illich called a virtual monopolization of education by schools. Other institutions—the family, the church, political life, work, and leisure—which in the past performed many important educational functions, are now discouraged from doing so. See Illich, *Deschooling Society* (New York: Harrow Books, 1972), 11.

14. It could be said that the unemployment of youth was the expected and even the desired result of child-labor legislation, which aimed to reduce the exploitation of the young by ruthless employers and afford the young an opportunity for formal schooling. Thus there are (legitimate) educational reasons for youth unemployment, not (deplorable) economic reasons.

This, however, would be a very fanciful view of history. Has there ever been a society that deliberately withheld needed workers from the labor market? A more likely explanation of the unemployment of young workers aged sixteen to twenty-one would cite the growth of technology, typically overestimated demands for products, and a desire to reduce costs. This probably led to agreement in practice between management and labor, the former wishing to avoid an unseemly large and unruly pool of unemployed, and the latter disinclined to compete for jobs with those who had no families to support. Nowhere was this more clear than in American cities, late in the nineteenth and early in the twentieth century:

> The city child, especially the child of the newcomers, had generated both compassion and fear. He was unkempt, uncared for, and untutored. He was in need of help. But he was also a threat, a threat to the workingman, a threat to social customs, mores, and institutions, a threat to the future of American democracy. Partly from fear and partly from compassion, thirty-one states enacted some form of compulsory education law by 1900. [Henry J. Perkinson, *The Imperfect Panacea: American Faith in Education, 1865-1965* (New York: Random House, 1968), 70]

15. Albert Shanker, president of the American Federation of Teachers, put the matter this way: "The need to control children, to harbor them for a certain amount of time away from their working or otherwise engaged parents, tends to become the most important function schools perform. And this custodial function often conflicts with, even dominates, the others." See Mark D. Danner (ed.), "How Not to Fix the Schools," *Harper's* (February, 1986), 44.

16. Michelle Fine summarizes these points nicely, referring to Goodlad's analysis in *A Place Called School* (op. cit.) of many observation reports of schools: "For the most part, . . . schooling is structured so that student opinions, voices, and critical thoughts remain silenced . . . Classrooms are organized more around control than conversation, more around the authority of teacher than autonomy of students, and more around competition than collaboration. When students talk to each other or cooperate it often provokes accusations of cheating from their teachers." See Fine, "Why Urban Adolescents Drop into and out of Public High School," *Teachers College Record*, 87:3 (Spring, 1986), 403.

17. The school must convince its students that grades are valuable. In fact, they are quite worthless, except to a minority that competes for acceptance in highly selective colleges—where they'll continue to compete for grades, thus postponing the discovery that nobody really cares what grades they got, and that high grades, even in college, have an approximately zero correlation with success in a wide variety of occupations and professions. See Ivar Berg, *Education and Jobs: The Great Training Robbery* (New York: Praeger, 1970), and Ohmer Milton, Howard R. Pollio, and James A. Eison, *Making Sense of College Grades* (San Francisco: Jossey-Bass, 1986).

18. Michelle Fine, op. cit., 397.

19. Gary G. Wehlage, "Dropping Out: Can Schools Be Expected to Prevent It?" in Lois Weis, Eleanor Farrar, and Hugh G. Petrie (eds.), *Dropouts from School* (New York: State University of New York Press, 1989), 1.

20. James Catterall and Eugene Cota-Robles, "The Educationally At-Risk: What the Numbers Mean," *Conference Papers: Accelerating the Education of At-Risk Students* (Palo Alto, Calif.: Stanford University, November 17-18, 1988).

21. Michael W. Apple, "American Realities: Poverty, Economy, and Education," in Weis, Farrar, and Petrie (eds.), op. cit., 220.

22. Seymour B. Sarason, *The Predictable Failure of Educational Reform* (San Francisco: Jossey-Bass, 1990), 13.

23. Sarason, op. cit., 123.

24. See Donald Arnstine, "Freedom and Bureaucracy in the Schools," in Haubrich, op. cit.

25. Seymour B. Sarason, *The Culture of the School and the Problem of Change* (Boston: Allyn and Bacon, 1971).

26. Elting E. Morison, *Men, Machines, and Modern Times* (Cambridge, Mass.: The Massachusetts Institute of Technology Press, 1966).

27. Danner (ed.), "How Not to Fix the Schools," op. cit., 45.

28. National Commission on Excellence in Education, *A Nation at Risk: The Imperative for Educational Reform* (Washington, D.C.: United States Government Printing Office, April, 1983).

29. Ken Chavez, "Wilson Unveils Five-point Plan to Reform Public Education," Sacramento *Bee*, November 3, 1993.

30. Donald Arnstine and Judith A. McDowell, "Unfair Rewards: Merit Pay, Grades, and a Flawed System of Evaluation," *Teacher Education Quarterly* (20:2), Spring, 1993), 5-21.

31. See Douglas Sloan (ed.), *The Computer in Education: A Critical Perspective* (New York: Teachers Colege Press, 1985).

32. Here are two recent, widely read proposals for a new, improved curriculum: Mortimer Adler, *The Paideia Proposal: An Educational Manifesto* (New York: Macmillan, 1982), and E. D. Hirsch, Jr., *Cultural Literacy: What Every American Should Know* (Boston: Houghton Mifflin, 1987). If you pick one you can't have the other, and there are lots of other candidates when you're done with these two.

33. A discussion of the logical and practical impossibility of discovering the one best curriculum for all children can be found in Donald Arnstine, *Philosophy of Education: Learning and Schooling* (New York: Harper & Row, 1967), 341-346.

34. The proposals of Madeline Hunter for educational method suffer from both of these misunderstandings. See Hunter, op. cit.

35. John Dewey, "Education as Engineering," *The New Republic*, XXXII (September 20, 1922), 90.

36. Seymour Sarason (in *The Predictable Failure of Educational Reform* [op. cit], 27) clearly shows the need to deal systematically with problems that are embedded in a system:

> . . . One cannot ask that question [of how one decides where the change process should begin] if one's stance is: there is a problem A we have to do something about, there is a problem B, there is a problem C, and so on. When each problem is posed and attacked separately, when each of a number of important problems is considered equally important in terms of its system implications, the chances of failure are very high. This is not to suggest that all important problems be attacked at the same time. It is necessary but not sufficient to try to understand how these problems are interrelated and reflect the nature of the system. What is crucial is to decide which of these problems should be a starting point, because if one deals successfully, even in part, with that problem, changes elsewhere in the system are likely to occur over time.

Chapter 9

1. Thomas Toch, *In the Name of Excellence* (New York: Oxford, 1991), 232.

2. Ohmer Milton, Howard R. Pollio, and James A. Eison, *Making Sense of College Grades* (San Francisco: Jossey-Bass, 1986), 169.

3. Of the various subtests of the Scholastic Aptitude Test, the test of reading comprehension is probably the only one that depends less on memory than it does on other abilities—in this case the ability to understand a written passage from several different perspectives.

4. In the 1980s, a movement was undertaken to introduce the teaching of what was called "critical thinking" into school and university classrooms. The movement was initiated and given momentum by professors of philosophy and philosophy of education (e.g., Robert Ennis of Cornell and later the University of Illinois, Harvey Siegel of the University of Miami, Richard Paul of Sonoma State University, Perry Weddle of California State University, Sacramento). However much these scholars may have disagreed about the nature of critical thinking and how to teach it, they usually agreed that it was an activity involving regard for the rules of logic, respect for the role of reasons, and initiative and concern on the part of the critical thinker.

The critical thinking movement caught the attention of school administrators and state departments of education, who forthwith set about the construction of multiple-choice tests of critical thinking ability. Thus the conception of "thinking" implicit in the term "critical thinking" was considerably narrowed. Any "thinking" elicited in multiple-choice tests is virtually light years removed from the conception of "thinking" discussed in this book. For the latter involves the resolution of discrepancies—in what appeals to perception, or in the pursuit of curiosity or in dealing with problems—within a context of acting on one's own purposes.

5. When he was president of Educational Testing Service, Gregory R. Anrig acknowledged and deplored the way in which external testing could determine the curriculum of high schools. "There's no question," he said, "that if you want to have an American history achievement test or a biology achievement test, that you then shape your curriculum so that you will do well on that achievement test." See Thomas Toch (ed.), "An 'Outsider' on the Inside: New E.T.S. Chief Talks about Testing," *Education Week*, August 25, 1982, 13.

6. This mythology includes the following beliefs: because essay tests must be read by persons, judgments about them must be subjective; and because multiple-choice tests are scored by an impartial machine, judgments about them are objective. These beliefs fail to account for the fact that in multiple-choice tests, *persons* write the test items, *persons* decide which answers are supposed to be correct, *persons* decide that the test items faithfully reflect the content of a course or an academic discipline, and *persons* decide where to place the cutoff scores that indicate levels of competence or failure. So human judgment *always* operates when people's performances are at issue, whether it is sixth-grade reading or Olympic tumbling. It should be clear that just as much human judgment operates in the use of multiple-choice tests as operates in the use of essay tests.

7. James Crouse and Dale Trusheim write, "Admissions officers with whom we have spoken often acknowledge privately that the SAT [Scholastic Aptitude Test] provides only marginal academic benefits, and that they could get along quite well without it. But given the uncertain consequences of how high schools and the general public would view such a move, the officers are content to maintain the status quo, especially since the cost of the SAT is paid by applicants and not by them." See Crouse and Trusheim, *The Case Against the SAT* (Chicago: University of Chicago Press, 1988), 154.

8. Crouse and Trusheim (op. cit., p. 6) argue that "for the vast majority of colleges, an admissions policy that ignores the SAT admits almost the same freshman class as an admissions policy that includes the SAT." Thus, these authors agree with the conclusions reached here—although their reasons are entirely different. They would abandon or alter the SAT because, on statistical grounds, it adds little to what can be learned about students from their high school records. In contrast, I am arguing that the SAT, like other multiple-choice tests, interferes with education itself and tests for traits that are not associated with genuine scholarship.

9. Frederiksen notes that "multiple-choice tests tend not to measure the more complex cognitive abilities. The more economical multiple-choice

tests have nearly driven out other testing procedures that might be used in school evaluation." See N. Frederiksen, "The Real Test Bias: Influences of Testing on Teaching and Learning," *American Psychologist*, 39:3 (1984), 193.

10. Linda Darling-Hammond and Ann Lieberman, "The Shortcomings of Standardized Tests," *The Chronicle of Higher Education*, January 29, 1992, B1, B2. At the time this article was written, Ms. Lieberman was President of the American Educational Research Association; Ms. Darling-Hammond is a former member of the Association's Executive Council. Needless to say, even the enlightened officers of the AERA do not necessarily speak for the community of educational researchers—many of whose members have a vested interest in the continued use of multiple-choice and standardized tests.

11. Crouse and Trusheim's case against the SAT was not intended as a criticism of standardized testing. To the contrary, these authors urge that the SAT be replaced by standardized tests of subject matter achievement; they even offer some zany arguments to show that such tests would *not* shape the curriculum of high schools (see *The Case Against*, op. cit., 167, 170)! On the other hand, these same authors have no qualms about external agencies determining the high school curriculum: "using the Advanced Placement Model, the College Board might host various constituencies to work out principal objectives of the high school curriculum" (ibid., 169). And, "if colleges . . . were to require conventional achievement tests [for admission], and were able to convince students and the rest of the educational community that their scores were important, more secondary schools would feel obliged to offer courses explicitly tailored to the tests" (ibid., 166). Thus the authors never question whether high schools might have any other purposes than preparation for college.

12. See Robert Paul Wolff, *The Ideal of the University* (Boston: Beacon Press, 1970), 85-95, 139-144.

13. The language is Professor Thomas F. Green's, in a personal correspondence.

14. The possible (and impossible) roles of various educational change agents are discussed in Donald Arnstine, "The Use of Coercion in Changing the Schools," *Educational Theory*, 23:4 (Fall, 1973), 277-288.

15. See John I. Goodlad, *Teachers for Our Nation's Schools* (San Francisco: Jossey-Bass, 1990), especially 294-300; also see Seymour B. Sarason, *The Case for Change: Rethinking the Preparation of Educators* (San Francisco: Jossey-Bass, 1993), 192-193.

16. See Elisabetta Nigris, "Stereotypical Images of Schooling: Teacher Socialization and Teacher Education," *Teacher Education Quarterly*, 15:2 (Spring, 1988), 4-19.

17. When allowances are made for age and experience, people of all ages learn in much the same ways: the importance of purpose, of discrepancy, of thinking, and of aesthetic quality is not just for children and youth. Sarason argues correctly and forcibly that there are *not* two theories of learning—one for adults, another for children:

> Teaching teachers involves every psychological issue and principle involved in teaching children. The would-be educators, like the pupils they will later teach, are not unformed, empty vessels, devoid of knowledge, assets, interests, and experience in matters educational. To ignore what the would-be teacher knows and has experienced, what that teacher aspires to be and achieve, is to seal off a gold mine in the face of poverty. (*The Case for Change*, op. cit., 150)

18. Sarason makes a similar point when he argues cogently for the study of education as an integral part of the general education of all college undergraduates. See *The Case for Change* (op. cit.), 100-102. He omits, however, the philosophical study of schooling, without which studies are in danger of becoming dry surveys of the status quo, spiced with earnest protestations about the need for "reform." Sarason may not have noticed that his own significant and fundamental criticisms of the school system were possible only because he often took the trouble to write as a philosopher.

19. Teacher education programs in the larger, better-known, and better-funded universities have banded together and called themselves "The Holmes Group." These institutions aspire to be models of teacher education, and they have issued manifestos telling other institutions (like state colleges and smaller private colleges) how best to prepare teachers. Ironically, neither the deans nor the full-time faculty of the Holmes Group universities have much to do with teacher education. A person might wonder how they came to acquire their alleged expertise.

20. See Herbert M. Kliebard, "Bureaucracy and Curriculum Theory," in Vernon F. Haubrich (ed.), *Freedom, Bureaucracy, and Schooling* (Washington, D.C.: Association for Supervision and Curriculum Development, 1971), 74-93.

21. See, for example, A Report of the Holmes Group, *Tomorrow's Teachers* (East Lansing, Mich.: The Holmes Group, Inc., 1986). In less than one hundred pages, this document manages to recommend more emphasis on bureaucratic and hierarchical forms of teacher education and public school staffing, and it proposes what subjects to convey to the young ("because teaching is about the development and transmission of knowledge"). The report also urges a national standardized test for teachers. Also see The National Commission on Excellence in Education, *A Nation at Risk: The Imperative for Educational Reform* (Washington, D.C.: U.S. Government Printing Office, 1983); or the National Science Board Commission

on Precollege Education in Mathematics, Science, and Technology, *Educating Americans for the 21st Century* (2 vols., Washington, D.C.: National Science Foundation, 1983.

22. See, for example, Madelaine Hunter, op. cit.

23. See, for example, Lee S. Shulman, "Knowledge and Teaching: Foundations of the New Reform," *Harvard Educational Review*, 57:1 (February, 1987), 1-22.

24. Goodlad, op. cit., 265, 266.

25. See Goodlad, op. cit., 149.

26. Goodlad writes extensively of the support afforded to students who have been members of identifiable cohort groups. See Goodlad, *Teachers for Our Nations's Schools*, op. cit., 207-211, 288.

27. A classic commentary on the failure of educational change in response to inducements from outside the schools is Seymour Sarason, *The Culture of the School and the Problem of Change* (Boston: Allyn & Bacon, 1982).

28. See, for example, Ann Lieberman (ed.), *Building a Professional Culture in Schools* (New York: Teachers College Press, 1988). Of particular interest in connection with the collective role of teachers in initiating change, see the essay in this book by Judith Warren Little, "Assessing the Prospects for Teacher Leadership," 78-106.

29. See Dan Lortie, *Schoolteacher* (Chicago: University of Chicago Press, 1975).

30. The union movement in the United States, with a few notable exceptions, became focused on "bread and butter" issues like wages. That focus was exploited by management and the media to make working people appear greedy and selfish. Union leadership became bureaucratized and was easily and early coopted by management. With its leadership looking out for itself and with a bad public image, American unions have steadily dwindled in membership and power. Their history sets a poor example for the organization of teachers. For a history of unions from the point of view of workers (and an account of the wildcat strikes that stood up to the power of union leadership) see Jeremy Brecher, *Strike!* (San Francisco: Straight Arrow Books, 1972).

31. It may well be that only through organization and communication will teachers become intellectually and progressively effective in the manner sought by writers like Henry Giroux. See Giroux, "Educational Leadership and the Crisis of Democratic Government," *Educational Researcher*, 21:4 (May 1992), 4-11.

Chapter 10

1. The advantages of nongraded classrooms have been observed and documented for some time. See John Goodlad and Robert H. Anderson, *The Nongraded Elementary School* (rev. ed., New York: Harcourt, Brace, and World, 1963; or B. Frank Brown, *The Appropriate Placement School: A Sophisticated Nongraded Curriculum* (West Nyack, N.Y.: Parker Publishing, 1965). Among the earlier research studies, see Joseph W. Halliwell, "A Comparison of Pupil Achievement in Graded and Nongraded Primary Classrooms," *Journal of Experimental Education,* 32 (Fall, 1963), 59-64; or Maurie Hillson, et al., "A Controlled Experiment Evaluating the Effects of a Nongraded Organization on Pupil Achievement," *Journal of Educational Research,* 57 (July-August 1964), 548-550.

2. See Philip A. Cusick, "Adolescent Groups and the School Organization," *School Review,* 82:1 (November 1973), 116-126.

3. See Nel Noddings, *Caring: A Feminine Approach to Ethics and Moral Education* (Berkeley: University of California Press, 1984).

4. The research evidence supporting this point is overwhelming, but see Jeannie Oakes, *Keeping Track: How Schools Structure Inequality* (New Haven: Yale University Press, 1985); or Beth E. Vanfossen, James D. Jones, and Joan Z. Spade, "Curriculum tracking and status maintenance," *Sociology of Education,* 60 (1987), 104-122.

5. R. E. Slavin, "Achievement Effects of Ability Grouping in Secondary Schools: A Best-evidence Synthesis," *Review of Educational Research* (1990), 491.

6. United States Commission on Civil Rights, *Twenty Years after Brown: The Shadows of the Past* (Washington, D.C.: United States Commission on Civil Rights, 1974), 114.

7. The literature on the topic of what happened after the Court's order to desegregate is almost overwhelming. Here are a few of the best sources on that history: Richard Kluger, *Simple Justice: The History of Brown* v. *Board of Education and Black America's Struggle for Equality* (New York: Alfred A. Knopf, 1976); Meyer Weinberg, *A Chance to Learn: The History of Race and Education in the United States* (Cambridge, Mass.: Harvard University Press, 1977); Ray Rist, *Desegregated Schools: Appraisals of an American Experiment* (New York: Academic Press, 1979); Jennifer Hochschild, *Thirty Years After Brown* (Washington, D.C.: Joint Center for Policy Studies, 1985). In terms of the impact of the conflict over desegregation on individual lives, see J. Anthony Lukas, *Common Ground* (New York: Alfred A. Knopf, 1985).

8. Sacramento *Bee,* December 14, 1993.

9. Ibid.

10. See Nicolaus Mills (ed.), *Busing U.S.A.* (New York: Teachers College Press, 1979).

11. Sacramento *Bee,* December 19, 1993.

12. See Sara Lawrence Lightfoot, *The Good High School: Portraits of Character and Culture* (New York: Basic Books, 1983), and the writer's review of it in *Educational Studies,* 15:3 (Fall, 1984), 266-273.

13. Jonathon Kozol, *Savage Inequalities: Children in America's Schools* (New York: Crown, 1991).

14. "School officials [in the Sacramento area] say they also realize that poverty and discrimination limit many families' choices in housing, which often limits their choice of schools as well. Integration efforts largely exist for those people." See The Sacramento *Bee,* December 19, 1993.

15. "Lecture" may be too formal a term to describe the uninterrupted talking engaged in by most teachers. In their observations of more than 1,000 high school classrooms, John Goodlad and his associates found that "[t]eachers out-talked the entire class of students by a ratio of about three to one. If teachers in the talking mode and students in the listening mode is what we want, rest assured that we have it. These findings are so consistent in the findings of our sample that I have difficulty assuming that things are much different in schools elsewhere." See Goodlad, *A Place Called School* (New York: McGraw-Hill, 1984), 229.

16. Dewey wrote, "To find out what one is fitted to do and to secure an opportunity to do it is the key to happiness. Nothing is more tragic than failure to discover one's true business in life, or to find that one has drifted or been forced by circumstance into an uncongenial calling." See Dewey, *Democracy and Education* (op. cit.) 360.

17. See Harry F. Silberman, "Preface," in Silberman (ed.), *Education and Work* (Eighty-first Yearbook of the National Society for the Study of Education, Part II; Chicago: University of Chicago Press, 1982), xi. John Goodlad acknowledges the potential educative value of work experience without going so far as to incorporate it systematically in the public education of all youth; see Goodlad, *A Place Called School* (New York: McGraw-Hill, 1984), 343-349.

A strong case for the educational value of work was made in James S. Coleman et al., *Youth: Transition to Adulthood* (Chicago: University of Chicago Press, 1974); the authors argued that for many youth, work experience could substitute for school experience. They did not, however, entertain the idea that without some (perhaps school-initiated) critical analysis of that work experience, it might be more miseducative than educative. For a sharp criticism of what most workers learn at the workplace, see William H.

Behn, Martin Carnoy, Michael A. Carter, Joyce C. Crain, and Henry M. Levin, "School Is Bad; Work Is Worse," in Carnoy and Levin (eds.), *The Limits of Educational Reform* (New York: David McKay, 1976), 219-244.

18. For an example of commonly found violations of the law in the electronics industry, see Elizabeth Kadetsky, "Silicon Valley Sweatshops: High Tech's Dirty Little Secret," *The Nation*, 256:15 (April 19, 1993), 517-520. For a discussion of widespread crime in the banking industry, see Robert Sherrill's essay-review of five books, "The Looting Decade: S&Ls, Big Banks and Other Triumphs of Capitalism," *The Nation*, 251:17 (November 19, 1990), 589-623.

19. John Dewey, Chapter 23, "Vocational Aspects of Education," in *Democracy and Education* (op. cit.).

20. Dewey, op. cit., 242.

21. Dewey, op. cit., 321.

22. Dewey, op. cit., 372-373.

23. This is a more pedestrian way (than that proposed by Henry Giroux) of ascribing to teachers a leadership role in educational and social change. See Giroux, "Educational Leadership and the Crisis of Democratic Government," *Educational Researcher*, 21:4 (May 1992), 4-11.

24. Nike is the brand name of an athletic shoe. Along with other products of its kind, it has come to take the place of more idealistic goals associated with other times and other cultures.

25. For an account of the breathtaking gap between the lives of many schoolchildren and their teachers, see Stephen O'Connor, "Death in the Everyday Schoolroom," *The Nation* (May 24, 1993), 702-704.

26. "Demystify" is a term used by Illich, Riemer, and now by writers in the critical pedagogy movement. Broadly speaking, it refers to the fact that many of the practices and structures of schools have an impact on the young (and even on teachers) of which they are unaware. For example, it is part of the "hidden curriculum" when a teacher calls on *other* students after the one called on first fails to answer a question correctly. Eventually, students learn that the opportunity to show that *they* know the answer depends on the failure of others. In this way they learn to *hope* for the failure of others which, in turn, leads to mutual animosity. But these students *do not know why* they see their peers as rivals rather than colleagues, or by what process they have come to fear that their peers might get something right.

To demystify this situation is, essentially, to help learners understand how the hidden curriculum works. It is to reveal the manner in which the structures and procedures of the school have an impact on learners, so that they will see what is being done to them. Many people believe that demystification ought to be a central aim of schooling. For when the procedures of schools are demystified, the young are in a position to control their own learning instead of being controlled. Demystification, then, leads to empowerment. It would follow that to demystify the tracking system in a school would be the first step on the road to abolishing it. This is not to deny that there are powerful obstacles to its abolition that lurk in the wings. Since the tracking system, for example, seems to privilege some students educationally, and really does help some students and hinder others from climbing the school ladder, powerful voices will oppose its abolition.

27. Sources of stress much more difficult for teachers to reduce are the animosity and the violent dispositions of many students, particularly in schools in low-income neighborhoods. Teachers did not create these problems, and they are not in a good position to change the social conditions that have created them. See Stephen O'Connor, "Death in the Everyday Schoolroom" (op. cit.).

Index

D

E

G

H

I

J

K

L

T